AF361329

Power and Place

Power and Place

PRESERVATION, PROGRESS,
AND THE CULTURE WAR
OVER LAND

Melinda Bollar Wagner

UNIVERSITY PRESS OF KENTUCKY

Scholarly publisher for the Commonwealth,
serving Bellarmine University, Berea College, Centre
College of Kentucky, Eastern Kentucky University,
The Filson Historical Society, Georgetown College,
Kentucky Historical Society, Kentucky State University,
Morehead State University, Murray State University,
Northern Kentucky University, Spalding University,
Transylvania University, University of Kentucky,
University of Louisville, University of Pikeville, and
Western Kentucky University.

Editorial and Sales Offices: The University Press of Kentucky
663 South Limestone Street, Lexington, Kentucky 40508-4008
www.kentuckypress.com

Library of Congress Cataloging-in-Publication Data

Names: Wagner, Melinda Bollar, 1948- author.
Title: Power and place : preservation, progress, and the culture war over
    land / Melinda Bollar Wagner.
Description: [Lexington] : University Press of Kentucky, [2023] | Series:
    Place matters: new directions in Appalachian studies | Includes
    bibliographical references and index.
Identifiers: LCCN 2023030113 | ISBN 9780813197739 (hardcover) |
    ISBN 9780813198224 (paperback) | ISBN 9780813197753 (pdf) |
    ISBN 9780813197746 (epub)
Subjects: LCSH: Appalachian Region—Economic conditions | Appalachian
    Region—Social conditions | Energy development—Appalachian Region. |
    Culture—Appalachian Region.
Classification: LCC HC107.A127 W35 2023 | DDC 338.974—dc23/eng/20230706
LC record available at https://lccn.loc.gov/2023030113

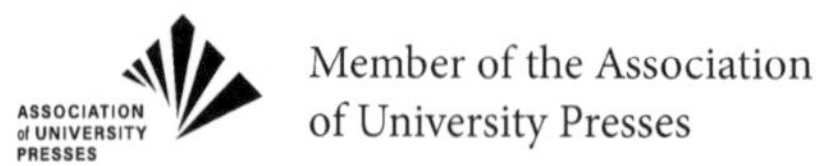

Member of the Association
of University Presses

To Stephen Everett Wagner, my Marty Ginsburg since 1966

Contents

1

The Place of Power

Seven homemade signs are set up Burma Shave style on a designated Scenic Byway rural road in Appalachian Virginia:

TAKE THE TIME
READ THE SIGN

POWER LINES
ARE NOT BENIGN

SHOULD YOU SACRIFICE
YOUR HEALTH

TO INCREASE THE
FAT CATS' WEALTH?

IF YOUR ANSWER
IS A NO

TAKE THE TIME
TO TELL APCO.

The last sign is a handmade drawing depicting a 765, as they call them, underneath the universal "no" red circle and slash. The 765s are the huge power towers that are eight stories high—132 feet—with 200-foot-wide rights-of-way. The literally looming 765,000-volt power line was seen as a threat to beauty and historic continuity—"seeing the same things the ancestors saw" would be no more. It would tear at the serenity residents praised, and thus be "just too costly in the human spirit." What we learned about people and their places will show why rural residents will nail their colors to the mast to defend their cultures and the land that supports them.

The backdrop for those signs began to be laid at least fifty-five years ago when Appalachian Power Company, now a part of Ohio-based American Electric Power (AEP), proposed a hydroelectric dam across the New River in North Carolina. Local protestors and national environmentalists eventually persuaded the US Congress to designate that part of the New River a National Wild and Scenic River. After that electric power project was defeated, an alternative dam was proposed in southwestern Virginia. Again, with much effort, local citizens together with national organizations defeated the proposal.[1] By-and-by AEP concentrated on moving power to population centers from coal-fired power plants insulated from current National Environmental Policy Act pollution standards by grandfather clauses. This meant beefing up the grid. In 1980, a 765,000-volt power line was built on parts of rural southwest Virginia, including across the Blue Ridge Parkway. Local residents protested the plan, to no avail, but their protests did lead to changes in procedures that allowed for more citizen input in future contests with utilities decision-makers. In 1992 AEP proposed another 765,000-volt power line, and protest signs began to appear along rural roads. The power line would cross rural mountainous counties of Appalachian West Virginia and Virginia, and some of the proposed routes would cross National Forest land.[2] The decision regarding whether to build the power line rests in the hands of state government bodies regulating utilities, labeled the Public Utilities Commission in West Virginia and the State Corporation Commission (SCC) in Virginia.

My students and I became observers on the power line frontlines in the spring of 1993, when Radford University's "Appalachian Studies Seminar" studied protest in the Appalachian region with the current power line controversy as an example. Activists from this and earlier environmental conflicts, power company executives, and academic experts on social movements and culture change visited the classroom and served as resource persons for students who interviewed them. The class created a twenty-five-page script for a simulated town meeting, with students taking on the various roles involved in the debate. They impersonated local land-owning protesters, company personnel, and representatives from the National Forest and the Appalachian Trail (Wagner, Scott, and Wolfe 1997).

Afterward citizens who had helped with the class asked us to do an ethnographic study of cultural attachment to land in their county. The study my students and I completed served as a supplement to the environmental impact assessment required because some of the proposed routes would cross federal public lands. By the time the citizens asked us to do a study, cultural attachment to land had already been designated a "significant issue" by the scoping procedures that began the environmental impact assessment process. As proposed routes changed, other counties asked us to study cultural attachment to land in their areas. We have continued studying cultural attachment to land for twenty-five years, in areas with and without external threats.

As soon as we were asked to learn about cultural attachment to land, we pivoted away from studying the power line protest. I did not attend any of the protest activities and caused my student researchers to do likewise. The difference was captured by a resident—the one who first asked us to take on the cultural attachment to land study—when we came to his house for an orientation to his county: "I know you have a culture to conserve, but we have a power line to stop." Our mission was indeed cultural conservation, focused on the question, "Is there cultural attachment to land here, and if so, on what is it based?"[3] We asked no questions about the power line. The journey described in this book, then, is not an analysis of a citizen-led social movement of protest against the power line. That is yet to be written. The resident protestors could well write it, but their time is taken up fighting the next and the next and the next threat against their beloved lands. We will be a megaphone for the voices of rural residents whose place at the table is far from assured when energy, environmental, and infrastructure decisions are being made.

The history of this controversy didn't really begin in the 1960s, or even in 1911, when American Electric Power, then American Gas and Electric, began its "interconnected power system," or even in 1831, when Michael Faraday figured out how to generate electric current. It began with competing proclivities that our founding foreparents brought with them. We have been playing them out, sometimes painfully, ever since.

Culture Wars: Preservation versus Progress

The power line protestors, the rescuers of places like New York City's Grand Central Terminal, and former farms and ranches whose names are enshrined on street signs leading to "Wilderness Woods," "Pine Meadows," and "Strawberry Fields" are all victims of America's culture wars.[4] We have heard this phrase before, with religious and political enmities deemed to be its core.[5] But there is another culture war simmering. It's the battle of greenbacks versus greensward: "Nowhere in the American national character, as it turns out, is there as deep a divide as that between our reverence for 'unspoiled' nature and our enduring devotion to 'progress'" (Garreau 1991:12).[6] The devotion to progress threatens "unspoiled nature," working land—farms and ranches—and beloved urban structures alike.[7] With the threat to rural land comes challenge to the way of life this land supports and requires.

A resident whose place would lie under the power line said, "They're going to peddle power over us."[8] The power line project joins a long list of Progress-cloaked land-based oppressions of residents of the Appalachian Mountains. Rodger Cunningham (1987) reminds us that these began against the Indigenous peoples. They continue against today's residents. They include strip and mountaintop-removal coal mining, pollution of water and air, deforestation, and fracked natural gas production and transmission pipelines.[9] All of the depredations have at their root economic gain for a distant population, and economic and cultural loss for the residents around and under the projects. The places that suffer have been analyzed as part of a satellite that serves the metropolis, as elements of an internal colony, a peripheral economy, and as sacrifice zones.[10] Outside ownership and control of land facilitated some of the inequities.[11] But the power of eminent domain eclipses "inside" ownership of land, whether ownership harks back eight or nine generations, or to yesterday.

Culture War Balancing Act: The Power of Eminent Domain

A battleground in the culture war of Preservation versus Progress is eminent domain. This power—use of due process by federal, state, and sometimes local governments to take or restrict the use of private land for the public good—is supported by the so-called "takings clause" of the US Constitution and has been interpreted as striking a balance between individual property rights and the interests of the community or the rights of neighbors. Eminent domain does generally serve the public good as it has been defined in the United States (i.e., progress) and sometimes works in the cause of conservation. But the power of eminent domain has driven some of the loss of farmlands and rural communities. Farmland and rural neighborhoods have given way to hydroelectric dams, highways, parks, transmission byways for fuel and electricity, industrial parks, military bases, etc. Eminent domain tends to lean more heavily on rural areas, where homes and property to buy out are less expensive and there are fewer residents (potential protestors) to deal with. And that's where the land—that's left—is.

These days, the power of eminent domain is being used more often, and for more purposes. Many governments now use eminent domain as an economic tool. Deregulation of utilities and the nation's infrastructure rebuild promise to add fuel to the eminent domain versus private landowner fire. Virginia's state government commission that regulates utilities predicted that "the real possibility exists that the same parcel of private property could be encumbered, against the will of the owner, by numerous easements of competing companies seeking routes for fiber optics lines, cables, power lines, etc." (Nixon 1999). We will return to the dominance of economics in decision-making in chapter 9.

Threats to the Pursuit of Happiness—Yours, Mine, and Rural Residents'

Wherever you live, this culture war has already passed over you, is at your doorstep, or is coming soon. The outcome of the culture war affects more than the rural residents who are its most obvious victims. Each individual's right to the pursuit of happiness enshrined in our Declaration of Independence—even if that happiness is tied to a rural area—is reason enough to care about the place-making in our story. But there are broader existential reasons to care. We'll show why rural life and culture are important to American society in both practical and symbolic ways. A key to the survival of our cherished values—and of ourselves as a species—is maintaining cultural diversity and the places that foster it—like rural America. Rural places may be the incubators for ways of thinking and doing and forging community life that an America with global in-reach as well as out-reach will require. They may be the places where America's headlong race toward greater and greater individualism is given a run for its money with the cultural alternatives of community and neighborliness. They may be the places that teach us to use land to make a living and to make a life, to forge and carry on identity, and to feel history. They may reap a harvest of policies for an environmental balancing act that will salvage resources for America's children's children. More practical still is the fact that, as the old song says, "The Farmer Is the Man Who Feeds Us All." Botanist and member of the Citizen Potawatomi

Nation Robin Kimmerer (2013:341), says: "Stories are among our most potent tools for restoring the land as well as our relationship to land. We need to unearth the old stories that live in a place and begin to create new ones, for we are storymakers, not just storytellers. All stories are connected, new ones woven from the threads of the old." And so, this book is a story, born, it is true, in a time of crisis, but harking back to relationships with land that predate the storytellers. Each chapter's stories will toll a potential loss if Progress overtakes all. The last chapter will suggest some strategies, negotiations, and even alliances that might begin to abate the culture war and strike a balance between Preservation and Progress.

2

The Loss

The Cultural Power of Place

For some people, what they are is not finished at the skin, but continues with the reach of the senses out into the land.

Barry Lopez, Arctic Dreams

Prologue

Picture in your mind this scene, and imagine where and when it is.

A husband and wife, their neighbor, and a guest are seated on benches at the table in the kitchen. Spread in front of them is a dinner ("lunch" to urbanites) of thin slices of fried venison, fried chicken, biscuits baked that morning on the wood cookstove, white clover honey made by the homeowner's bees, homemade cottage cheese, slaw, lime pickles, blackberry cobbler, and stewed apples. The host tells the names of each apple variety. He has grafted them over many years. In fact, all the ingredients have been raised on the land that surrounds the home, and turned into luncheon fare by the people who live here. At the end of the meal, the landowner offers toothpicks that he makes out of the quill feathers of Canada geese who stay near the pond that he built. On the wall above the doorway between the kitchen and the living room is a set of mounted deer antlers with a turkey beard hanging from each point—each feather beard bound with a gold-colored band. In the next room, a mounted bear's head rests on one wall.

Where are we? What is the time period? Is this the America of the 1800s? Perhaps we are watching a scene through a window of the Frontier Culture Museum, near Staunton, Virginia, or witnessing an interpretation of rural American history at Explore Park on the Blue Ridge Parkway near Roanoke, Virginia.

In truth, this is Greenly County, Virginia, June 6, 1994.

The leftover foodstuffs are stored in plastic containers in the refrigerator. After water is heated in the wood cookstove, it is piped into the electric water heater to bring it to temperatures that meet the standards of today. A microwave oven sits on the counter beside the wood stove. In the next room, over-the-counter patent medicines stay on the table. Along with a wood heating stove, there is a large television in this room, and a satellite dish in an unobtrusive spot in the yard. The long driveway leading up to the house is paved for its whole length.

This rural Appalachian region is not a place that time forgot; it is not a relic. It is a currently viable culture. It has strong ties to a past reaching back more than two hundred years in these same valleys, but has accommodated to life in a less agrarian-based society (a minority of the residents gain all of their livelihood from farming). Its culture bearers have plans, and have implemented policies, to try to assure that the essence of their way of life continues into the future.

America's Preservation versus Progress debate imperils rural America. The many issues concerning rural America's future are shadowed by a question—What is lost as it is diminished? Today, 15 percent of Americans live in rural areas; 1.3 percent are employed in farming. What does that part of our population preserve in the American cultural diversity storehouse that may be adaptive in the future? What do we know about the rural culture that a growing number of exurbanites are fleeing to? They see themselves as taking flight from the perceived problems of urban areas, but what are the relationships with the environment and with their neighbors that they will find in their new destinations? We will ponder these questions with data gleaned from ten rural communities in five counties in the Appalachian region. Appalachia is a place where cultural attachment to land has long been considered a mainstay but with few exceptions has not been studied in depth.[1]

The five counties are located in Virginia, which has a long agricultural history, "with almost 400 years of farming tradition, of raising tobacco and livestock, of harvesting abundant fisheries and forests" (Bearinger 1998). Today agriculture and forestry still comprise a considerable part of Virginia's economy, accounting for more than 442,000 jobs and 9.5 percent of the Gross State Product.

Of course an entire book could be written about the economic arena and the use of the physical landscape. It is well to remember that the rural families described in this book live and make their decisions "in a context in which land is expensive, capital scarcer than labor, and agribusiness powerful" (Chibnik 1987:281). But for us, as for our interviewees, this will be background. We are focused on what is in people's heads. What is their mental landscape, and how does it work in their lives? In Australia this is called "habitus"—"social space apprehended through mental structures; schemes of perception, thought and action in relation to one's environment, influenced by individual and collective histories and experiences" (Habitus 2000).[2]

Exploring Cultural Attachment to Land

To answer questions about rural life—and especially about the form and functions of the mental landscape in rural areas—interviews were conducted with residents. As different counties that lay in the path of various proposed routes for the 765,000-volt power line called on us, our study of cultural attachment to land expanded to include eleven semesters, more than one hundred undergraduate students, and 223 residents of ten communities in five counties. It resulted in more than four thousand pages of transcribed recorded interviews ranging from twenty minutes to six hours in length, and more than three thousand pages of computerized linguistic analyses of these data, along with some two thousand pages of thematic content analyses. More than three hundred slides and more than 150 photos of areas that residents pointed out to the researchers were taken (in some cases, the residents were handed the cameras and framed the pictures themselves). We also attended church services, subscribed to the local newspapers, and collected archival materials such as booklets of local history and the like that residents gave us. The eventual rapport gained between residents and university faculty and students who interviewed them yielded nearly a fictive kin relationship, and certainly a symbiotic one. A resident wrote:

> We're all proud of you and your students for helping us open our eyes and see that what we know, feel, and are can be of value and is not useless. . . . You know, Melinda, when we first started getting involved in this process . . . we were actually scared of our own colleges, as some of us thought they were looking down on us. But . . . we gained a lot from our involvement with you and your students and you all made us feel good about our station and way of life. So you, dear Melinda, learned from us and we learned from you, so in the end we're all winners.

Sense of place is "expressed through imagery and metaphor," and thus most authors who have pondered it recommend phenomenological approaches that value such representations (Hirsch 1995:16). The aim of the phenomenological method is to make a "return to the things themselves," without recourse to presuppositions. Alfred Schutz (1973) describes phenomenology as empirical—based on observation; systematic in its concern with the phenomena under study; and rigorous, because it subjects "its own procedures to critical appraisal" (Jackson and Smith 1984:28–29). These considerations "suggest that any attempt to capture the first-person meaning of significant human phenomena must involve procedures that interfere as little as possible with their ordinary mode of occurrence and description" (Williamson and Pollio 1999).[3]

This project utilized the insights of phenomenology but also counted and quantified things that could be quantified. (For example, it does substantiate a claim that residents have a detailed knowledge of their environment to know how they talk of their environment, how many different words for elements of their environment they use, and how often.) Postmodern science must "take as valid inside, subjective knowledge as well as objective 'outside' knowledge: Vico's *verum* as well as Descartes' *certum*" (Rappaport 1994:290).

It was a goal of this project to develop a method that combined phenomenologically captured nuances but that at the same time is practical for environmental impact assessment and community-based environmental protection efforts. It was hoped that the method could be anthropologically sophisticated, informed by symbolic and political economy theories and by scientific positivist and humanistic interpretive approaches—yielding a derivative that is nuanced yet practical, using ethnography.

Ethnography has been described as a "disciplined attempt to discover and describe the symbolic resources with which members of a society conceptualize and interpret their experience" (Basso and Selby 1976). Ethnography is a method that seeks to elicit from the people themselves the bases for the cultural significance of, in this case, their living place. Using ethnographic means, the anthropologist obtains the indigenous (insider's/native) perspective. (Anthropologists call this the *emic* point of view.) Ethnographic interviews are designed to elicit talk.

From this talk, anthropologists learn what is salient in a culture. In ethnographic interviews, the ethnographers are careful not to ask leading questions or make leading comments. (For example, questions and comments like, "Would you say you loved your land?" or "I'll bet you love your land" would never be used.) There were no answers implied in the questions that we asked; no multiple choice answers were supplied. The open-ended questions were used when necessary to elicit talk. Sometimes it was not even necessary to rely on them. For example, if a person shows you her home, pointing out the family photographs, and describing who all the people are and where they live, it isn't necessary to then ask, "How many members of your family live nearby? Where else do members of your family live?"

Long-standing anthropological theory contends that cultures contain themes that organize their rules for behavior and the meanings these behaviors have. To discover patterns or unifying themes, it is the ethnographer's task to analyze the data— the interview transcriptions and field notes. Anthropological methods have demonstrated that behavior and language provide clues to a culture's themes and values. For example, an often-stated motto would be evidence of one of a culture's overarching themes. Ortner's (1973:1339) method of discovering a culture's "key symbols" provides a stepping stone from Vico-inspired phenomenology to the analysis of data. She says that these key symbols (or cultural themes) "will be signaled by more than one of these indicators: 1) the natives tell us that X is culturally important; 2) the natives seem positively or negatively aroused about X, rather than indifferent; 3) X comes up in many different contexts. . . . X comes up in many different kinds of action situation or conversation, or X comes up in many different symbolic domains (myth, ritual, art, formal rhetoric, etc.); 4) there is greater cultural elaboration surrounding X, e.g., elaboration of vocabulary or elaboration of details of X's nature, compared with similar phenomena in the culture; 5) there are greater cultural restrictions surrounding X, either in sheer number of rules, or severity of sanctions regarding its misuse." Added to Ortner's list were: (6) the natives spend time on X, and (7) the natives spend money on X.

Analysis of the text of ethnographic interviews has as its goal, then, the discovery of the themes and patterns that mark what is salient to people in a particular culture. It proceeds by asking: (1) what do they talk about *first*?; (2) what do they talk about *often*?; (3) what *kinds* of things do they talk about?; (4) what things do they talk about with much *detail*?; (5) what kinds of things *could* they talk about but *don't*?; (6) how do they say they spend their *time* and *money*?; (7) what are the topics of the *stories* they tell?; and (8) what *metaphors* do they use?

The residents' talk captured in the interviews was subjected to a threefold examination utilizing thematic analysis of content, linguistic analysis of speech, and analysis of the stories told. A triangulation of the three analysis tools revealed overall patterns in the data gleaned from the interviews. For example, cultural knowledge of the environment—discerned in thematic analysis—was also discovered by noting an elaboration of vocabulary used in describing the environment, and by tabulating a large number of coded stories that utilized this knowledge. Anonymity was granted to our collaborators, so as we discuss the data, the names of people and places are pseudonyms.

Interviews with residents of Borden County, no longer under threat of a 765,000-volt power line, having acquired one in advance of the line protested by the other four counties, have continued to the present day. Interviews with 102 additional residents have been conducted through 2020. They teach about specific localities, migration in and out of the county, and the economy; they include farmers, World War II veterans, and the founders of alternative communities. All of these interviews were conducted as per the protocols of "basic research," but all were also in partnership with community or county organizations, including a conservation land trust, an economic development office, a community story center and museum, and a public school system. Of particular relevance with regard to rural farming life is a project partnering with a local government office, with Appalachian Regional Commission Appalachian Teaching Project funding, "Sustaining the Community Mind for Long-Term Community Resiliency: Appalachian Values Assessment." For this project we asked farmers some of the same questions as in the power line interviews, and received similar responses. This project will be discussed in chapter 11 to describe ongoing threats to place that are less crisis-like than the proposed power line.

"It's a Different World"

When I was told that we would find people who still carried the skills of subsistence farming, hunting, and gathering in the woods in Greenly County, the first area we studied, I was skeptical, to say the least. The student research team of interviewers spread out the maps of the county, and I said, "Look how close it is to —— City; don't expect it to be too rural."

After trips for field observations and interviewing in the county, the question changed from "Is it rural?" to "How rural is it?" When we recounted our field experiences, like the luncheon described in the prologue to this chapter, to spouses and friends, they said, "It sounds like a different world" (Field Notes 6/7.MBW). Just getting to and from our field sites was a lesson in how rural the counties are. For example, there are no billboards in the entire county of Greenly. Borden County has one fast-food restaurant and one stoplight. Though rarely slowed by traffic, we did find it necessary to stop for meandering cows, black vultures, collie dogs, and squirrels in the road. The deeper we went into the counties, the more likely we were to see a wave from the drivers of oncoming vehicles. Along the roads, we saw some stores, but they weren't fast-food restaurants or franchise convenience stores. A research assistant noted that inside the Greenly stores, there were "old cash registers, not computers or even digital read-outs. They had a friendly atmosphere, with dogs on the porch. They weren't formal inside; employees sat around a table in their everyday clothes, not behind the counter in a uniform. They had the old bottled drinks that you have to have a bottle opener for—haven't seen those since . . ." (Field Notes.SS).

Not everyone makes their own cottage cheese like our luncheon providers described in the prologue, but many know how to. The cooks of that household go to —— City for groceries. Yet people pride themselves on sustaining as much self-sufficiency as they can muster. Virtually all of our interviewees in Greenly who had access to land kept gardens. "We canned ourselves to death," they said. They used wood—often from their own land and felled by their own efforts—for heating and cooking (in the winter).

Most of the research team members were from suburban areas in northern Virginia. They were astonished by the small size of the school classes, and by the fact that a man in his fifties graduated from the same size class as the current class. They were surprised to learn that when hunting season begins, "first day they close school so the kids can go hunt" (Interview 9/16.JH). They noted that nearly everyone in Greenly had a wood stove—a rare sight for them. "New houses stand out," they reported, because so many of the homes, as well as the churches, are old. They were surprised that the denizens of these houses don't lock their doors—some even leave their keys in their cars—because, as they see it, "we don't have any problems" (Interview 9/21. MG). They had never seen aerial photographs of farms and home places like most residents displayed on their walls. They were surprised to learn that a referendum for liquor-by-the-drink was voted on by Greenly County residents in March 1995, and lost, 544 to 67. On the other side of the ledger, recently the largest moonshine still ever found in Virginia was destroyed by federal Alcohol, Tobacco, and Firearms agents here.

Demographic characteristics substantiated the counties' rural nature. The populations in the counties ranged from about five thousand people to more than twenty-five thousand, with low population densities ranging from fifteen to fifty-five people per square mile. Greenly, Farlane, Woodrow, and Cranston Counties are contiguous, with Borden County nearby. All five counties are in the Ridge and Valley topographical province of Virginia, but the highest mountains and narrowest valleys are in Farlane, Woodrow, and Cranston. More than half of Greenly County is owned by the National Forest Service. The area owned by the National Forest Service partially accounts for the low population densities in the counties. Greenly is the most agrarian. The average size of farms in Greenly is 260 acres; it's less in the others, down to a low of 168 in Borden. Principal crops in all of the counties are beef cattle, hay, and corn. Rolling hills and valleys between high ridges provide the pasturelands. Greenly has had a livestock and grain agrarian base since first settled in the 1700s. But today the largest share of employment is in manufacturing and wholesale and retail trade. Yet the county residents' earnings come mostly from jobs in state and local government, as is the case in Woodrow County. Cranston and Borden Counties' residents are also mostly employed in manufacturing and trade but bring in the most earnings from service industries. Agriculture employs from 3 to 5 percent of the people and accounts for 2.5 to 19 percent of the earnings in all five counties.

The Indigenous peoples of this area, probably Tutelo/Tutero and Monacan groups, had gone by the time the ancestors of the current families arrived, likely beset by conflict and disease (Egloff and Woodward 1994). Most Greenly families have long roots to European settlers on this land. As in all of the counties, residents say their ancestors were Scots-Irish, Irish, English, and German. That fits the historians' view that this part of Virginia was settled largely by "Germans and Scots-Irish coming down the great valley" (Yancey 2022:2; see also J. A. Williams 2002). There were few newcomers until recently, but the county grew 16.5 percent in the last decade.

In Farlane County a smaller proportion of the county is owned by the National Forest Service. A large manufacturing industry now dominates the county's economy, but the communities we studied have had an agrarian base since first being settled somewhat later than Greenly County, by people walking from Greenly to Farlane through mountain passes. Most families in the two rural communities we learned about are descended from the original settlers. To date, most newcomers have been assimilated into the local community, although they are still referred to as "brought-ins."

Farmers in Cranston and Woodrow Counties add tobacco to the cattle, hay, and corn crops common to all the counties. Both counties have National Forest land; more than three-quarters of Woodrow County is wooded. The counties' planning commissions have designated 51 percent of the land in Cranston and 77 percent of the land in Woodrow as areas of conservation and/or recreation. Both counties list future use of the land for tourism, recreation, and wildlife conservation as desirable goals.

High altitude along with the Ridge and Valley topography have, in the last three decades, rendered Borden County home to nurseries and Christmas tree growers (at this latitude high-altitude climates are necessary for growing specialty trees such as firs). There are up to ten times as many nurseries here than in the other four counties. These coexist with the more traditional livestock pasturing, dairy farming, and raising grain for livestock. The county has no federally held land, unlike the other four, but does have a few small industries. The population is more mixed between natives and newcomers than the others. Back-to-the-landers have settled here (some in communes) since the 1970s. In the late 1990s survivalist escapees from potential Y2K problems migrated into the county. Hispanic families who came originally as migrant workers on the tree farms and retired professionals from urban Virginia add to the population mix. These groups all bring reactions to urban industrialized society's values with them. The retirees have just finished their work lives within it. They bring desires for wide-open spaces, and also for the conveniences of urban life (e.g., weekly trash pickup at the end of the driveway/lane). They bring the wherewithal to buy land at high prices and to build large houses with large landscaped lawns/yards. The communal groups see themselves as escaping industrialized values. The most committed live "off the grid," shunning electricity carried through the power grid and striving for self-sufficiency. Past crises of major import, such as the threat of a high-voltage power line (now built) brought the various groups together. Current issues have sparked heated controversy among residents who desire/do not desire change of various kinds and have been markers for cracks in the communities.

In each of these counties, residents feel that their rural way of life is threatened. The most tangible threats discussed are a proposed high-voltage power line in all of the counties except Borden, which already has one; clear-cutting timber; subdivision of farmland for housing; and, especially in Borden County, cultural clash from population mix. Residents lament that the rural life that they enjoy does not provide sufficiently for young people, who leave to seek jobs.

Analyses of the 159 interviews with 223 residents revealed that functions of the cultural landscape include: (1) using place to establish identity; (2) using land to make a living and make a life; (3) using place to create and maintain historical continuity; (4) using place to build and maintain living community; (5) using place to teach culture's ways; and (6) using place to confront threats to the environment and culture. A chapter is devoted to each of these functions.

The presentation of data in these chapters is meant to do three things. It will show you what we will lose if we fail to protect rural areas. It will let you see why the residents fight so hard against environmental threats. Combined with the final chapters, it may make you aware of how fragile your own hold on your place may be if current trends continue.

3

Using Place to Establish Identity

That tree is on John.

Appalachian surveyor

If you heard the sentence "It's on John," what would you make of it? It might be a sweater that John is wearing, or maybe an insect that has lighted on John. Actually it's a phrase that means, for example, "This tree is on John's property." But the shorthand, "It's on John," is a clue to the identification that occurs between person and land in these cultures. Perhaps, though, the land does more than surround them; perhaps it is "in" them. In Jesse Stuart's novel *The Good Spirit of Laurel Ridge* (1953:245), the protagonist "had often thought of the Sandy River as a big vein in his body."

> This land is mine, for I am part of it.
> I am the land, for it is part of me—
> We are akin and thus our kinship be!
> It would make me a brother to the tree! (Stuart 1963:245)[1]

A local farmer explains what she'll be doing for the next few days. She doesn't say, "I'll be mowing my hayfield." Instead, "I'll be in the hay." Asked on a radio talk show to explain her relationship to the environment, a Native American woman says, "I am the environment."

Identity derives in part from the cultural knowledge and attachments that a person carries. By engaging residents in these ten communities in talk about their lives, we heard about a strong cultural attachment to land and to rural life that was manifested in many ways. What is an attachment to "place"? "Place" is space made into "an organized world of meaning"—"space made culturally meaningful." Anthropologists and folklorists, as well as psychologists, observe that "place" is "an extremely meaningful component of individual identity."[2] "These places have an impact on our sense of self, our sense of safety" (Tuan 1977:179; Low 1994:66; Ryden 1993:252; Tuan 1974:282; Hiss 1990:xi).[3] Fritz Steele (1981:204) allows that there are nine "major characteristics of place that account for much of the richness in our relations with our settings." He lists these as: identity, history, joy, security, vitality, memory, fantasy, mystery, and surprise. Certainly the first six in this list were obvious in our interviews. According to Erik Cohen (1976) attachments to land that turn space into place might be based on "orientations to the environment" that are instrumental (based on economic benefit), symbolic (based on aesthetic enjoyment and moral-religious meaning), or sentimental.[4] For the residents whom we interviewed, economic attachments are not missing. But in their talk, these footings take a backseat to genealogical, historical, aesthetic, and even spiritual foundations.

Thus, the farmer who raised the fare feasted upon in the lunch described in chapter 2's prologue earns his living from his land. But he is literally "rooted" in his place in many other ways. He is rooted by his genealogical tie to the land that was owned by his ancestors. He is rooted by the work that he himself has done to maintain the buildings these ancestors built. He is rooted by the cemetery at the top of the hill that contains his relatives' bones and where he knows his own and his wife's will one day be. He is rooted by the sight of the huge "sugar trees" that he planted as saplings when he and his wife first moved back here, and by the taste of the apples from the trees that he began grafting fifty years ago (Field Notes 6/7.MBW). He is rooted by the past, present, and future on the land.

Analyses that showed how place can function as a component of a rural person's identity and life satisfaction included investigating the content of their talk, discerning the length of time residents spent talking about nature, and measuring the degree of detail they used in their talk about nature.

Nature and Culture

I feel like the land is not mine; I'm just takin' care of it.

Interview 6/17.MBW

The dichotomy anthropologists label "culture-nature" is the contrast between the "ordered world of human culture and the untamed world of animals and nature." Culture implies an "order" laid upon nature by humans. In this dichotomy of tamed-untamed, "all that is social is conceived of as domesticated, cultivated, and controlled, and all that is identified with nature is thought of as wild and unrestrained" (Barrett 2004:144, 146). Often societies have rituals that attempt to "go back" to a state of nature—for a while—and then culture and its rules are ceremoniously laid back on.

A perceived dichotomy between "culture" and "nature" is thus a long-standing one. One of the criteria for judging the location of a society in classifications of subsistence modes is the relative degree of freedom from environmental constraints. So, for example, a society that had not invented fire would fall into a certain classification because cold weather and darkness would constrain its activities. Societies that have furnaces and light bulbs, on the other hand, would be in a different classification, because they are able to do things like hold university classes in the dead of winter and at ten o'clock in the evening. The farmers who are able to produce crops year after year on the same piece of land would be would be in a different classification than the hunters and gatherers, because they are "freed" from being nomadic. This is, of course, a technology-based criterion and was created, to no one's surprise, by Western anthropologists (Sahlins and Service 1960). It does, however, let us see that in some societies, nature would not have been as "conquered" by culture's technology.

Pondering culture-nature links prompted anthropologist Tom Plaut (1979) to develop a continuum of human-land relationships. On one end are societies who view land as sacred space and who see themselves as part of nature. Plaut uses North American Indian people as an example. Black Elk, Oglala Sioux holy man, tells of the two-leggeds, the four-leggeds, the wings of the air, and all green things living in peace and harmony on the earth (Neihardt 1961).[5] This is common in nonindustrialized societies. It includes identification with place—seeing the land as a place of belonging.

On the other side of the continuum is seeing land as property, a relatively recent phenomenon. In fact, in the history of humankind, the idea of ownership of land did not exist until the onset of agriculture, which allowed for production year after year on the same piece of land. Here land is to be bought and sold for gain, or used. It is useful for what it can produce, as infrastructure for development, as investment, or, it is "overburden" (as in strip mining). "Land as property" harmonizes with the Judeo-Christian ideal that humans should take dominion over the land.[6]

Another anthropologist, Gisli Palsson (1996:68), labels Plaut's "land as property" as "environmental orientalism" and says that the separation of nature and society came about during the Renaissance and the Enlightenment, spurred by the early positivist science of Descartes and Francis Bacon. The relationship with the land became land "management"—"a technical enterprise, the rational application of Baconian science and mathematic equations to the natural world." Christopher Toumey (1996:15) says that abroad in the American land in its early days were a few leaders who "embraced a different vision[,] . . . which subordinated useful knowledge to a larger plan of intellectual enrichment." Their view of "progress" itself was different: "Material increase was good, but moral progress was better, and the former was expected to serve the latter by illustrating the benefits of human reason." But this view "was all but gone" by the 1840s, "eclipsed by the simple view that progress consisted of material increase generated from technology and uncomplicated by philosophical baggage."[7]

The view of land in these counties seems to fit neither end of Plaut's continuum—neither land as sacred space nor land as property. True the Navajo Indian person, thought to dwell in sacred space—though Basso (1996) and Callicott (1989) remind us to take care when imputing sacredness—and the county native sound alike when they decry activities they see as harmful, like mining that turns their homelands into dust and then mud. The Navajo person may speak of the sacredness of the land, the countian of his family's ties to the land. But here people do *own* the land and treasure it as theirs and pass it down. Its meaning "combines the diverse concepts of utility and stewardship." So Plaut makes a place for the Appalachian view of land in the middle of the continuum. Here land is social space; it is a crucible for the social world, a carrier of social history (Eller 1979:105; Hicks 1976:50–62). Here, the land is identified with the people who have lived here; the land is given meaning by the human activities that have happened, and are happening, upon it.

Gisli Palsson (1996:68, 72) labels Plaut's social space "communalism" and says that it rejects "any radical distinction between nature and society." This perspective is "often metaphorically represented in terms of intimate, personal relationships" and is characterized by contingency, participation, and dialogue. The tenet the resident quotes in the epigraph above—"the land is not mine"—denying ownership—certainly is not consistent with the "land as property" concept, nor with land as an element in Progress-making. It expresses an attitude that Relph (1976:39) has described as being "sparing" of the land, which means "letting things, in this context of place, be the way they are; it is a tolerance for them in their own essence: it is taking care of them through building or cultivating without trying to subordinate them to human will. Sparing is a willingness to leave places alone and not to change them casually or arbitrarily, and not to exploit them."

The dichotomy between "culture" and "nature" is even reflected in environmental impact research that separates "social impact assessment" from "natural impact assessment." But in-depth ethnographic study reaches the conclusion that in these rural Appalachian valleys, the cultures and the natural environments are inextricably bound together.[8]

Taming the Valleys, Revering the Mountains

Taming the valleys: "To keep it clean and habitable, it takes some work."

Interview 6/14A.LC

Revering the mountains: "I can see that God's hand sort of shaped that mountain."

Interview 9/14.SH

It is possible to take photographs in these counties that show no trees that human hands have purposely planted, no fences, no cleared pastures. But to do that, the photographer must make an effort to move the camera's eye up near the horizon. A more honest photo shows nature *and* the signs of culture—a culture that has been in these valleys since the 1700s.

When the ancestors of the current residents came to the valleys of Stanley, Heath Creek, Elton's Creek, and the rest, the land was verdant, as it is now, but there were no cleared pastures and fields. "Climax forests" of white oak and lesser quantities of hickory, tulip tree, black oak, and white pine with an understory of blueberry, flame azalea, rhododendron, bush-clover, and tick-trefoil covered "the Ridge and Valley Province of western Virginia during prehistoric and historic periods" (Diamond and Giles 1987; Klatka 1991:12).

The "old people" who are the ancestors of the current residents carved cultures out of this wilderness, and their descendants are still maintaining the carvings.[9] The valleys hold the cultural carvings; the ridges are natural wilderness. All the talk of the flora, the fauna, the weather, the water, the woods, and the natural formations provide ample evidence that the residents care about and know about nature. But in the valleys there is also a culture laid onto this nature. Fields and pastures have been cleared, wood has been cut for firewood, ponds have been built, streams have been stocked with fish, yards have been mowed, lanes have been paved, Japanese gardens have been built, deer and bear have lent their heads to hang on walls. This culture knows and admires nature, but in the valleys there can be a tension between the two: "It's hard to build fields, when you don't want to get rid of no trees. And trees is one of my favorite things, too. I like big trees" (Interview T331 11/30.DCM). But residents will cut down trees in the tamed valleys to get a better view of the wild mountains: "I cut down a bunch of trees so I could look at [the] Mountain. And you know, I can stand there and I can see that God's hand sort of shaped that mountain" (Interview 9/14. SH). The rural cultures of these counties value both keeping the wilderness wild and maintaining the rural domesticity of the valleys.

In the valleys, culture keeps nature at bay. Carolyn Adkins, a native of Greenly County in her fifties, who is a cattle farmer, bookkeeper for the family construction business, part-time secretary at a college, and the local historian, says, "When you have another job, you just can't keep the brush cut and the weeds cut, you just do the best you can, and you hit the high points, hope it won't grow over like some of them around here" (Interview 6/17.MBW).

Fences have to be rebuilt when "it rains hard" and "little flash floods" "take them out": "Poor Daniel, it keeps him busy building fence" (Interview 6/7.MBW). The deer, lovely as they are to see, threaten the crops and the gardens. Residents devise ways of trying to keep them out. David Evans, who lives in the wildest of the tame areas, showed us a small area beside his house, fenced with a split rail fence, where an almond bush and some other domesticated plants grow—where he tries to keep the deer out. He has built small wire fences around wild plants—berry bushes and ginseng—that he wants to preserve and use.

Brush is a symbol of nature's attempt to come back where it should not be. Paul Carter, a thirty-four-year-old engineering technician who has lived in Clearview in Woodrow County all of his life, said: "Well, basically around here, I cut brush. . . . I spend my time just cuttin' brush. Just this, that and the other, just maintaining stuff. Bushhogging some of the old fields. . . . After hunting season goes out, then I'll basically spend my winter months cutting brush. When I'm not working on the job, or in the shop. I'll go up and cut brush, or I'll bushhog, or I'll cut wood" (Interview T304 11/05.JD). "There were briers up to here," Frank Dudley says to describe his place before he moved in and started mowing (Interview 6/24.MBW). "You used to be able to see over here, but the people who bought that have just let the trees grow up," says David Evans of his new neighbors (Interview 6/7.MBW). "So it's sad to see it keep growing up," says Carolyn Adkins about another place (Interview 6/17.MBW). The coming of snakes is a metaphor for what happens when land that has been tamed is allowed to "grow up" or "grow over." Residents explain that snakes will come and live in the briers.

Grace Fraley, an eighty-year-old retired teacher born in Borden County who has lived in Greenly County for twenty years, observed the cultural trait of wanting things to "look nice" and described it this way: "Everybody takes pride in their farms and keeps them looking nice. You very rarely see a grown-up thing unless somebody has just died and they haven't settled up their estate, something like that, but most of them are just as clear as you keep your yard" (Interview 9/21.MG).

Richard Goens, a thirty-one-year-old from the Walnut Cove community of Cranston County who does grading work to help make a living, says: "All the time [I spend caring for my land]. All the time. Every chance I get. I try to make the perfect place. I think that's what I'm trying to make anyway. It's hard work" (Interview T331 11/30.DCM).

The link between the residents' identities and the nature that surrounds them is manifested in multiple, complex ways. The bonding together of culture and nature is signaled by the content and detail of "nature talk" that residents do. This talk shows the part nature plays in the history, folklore, and stories of the culture; the cultural knowledge of nature that people carry; the residents' orienting by the geological markers in their environment; and the residents' emphasis on perceptions of the environment's beauty. These elements—together with the long genealogical history on the same land that many of the culture bearers possess—help create the residents' identities.

Culturalizing Nature

The undivided character of nature and culture—the way the one surrounds, penetrates, and finally becomes the other—can be appreciated by examining the major role nature plays in the culture. Nature is a part of the history, folklore, and stories. Knowledge of nature is passed down from generation to generation. Nature is used, nurtured, admired, feared, and kept at bay. The length of time residents spend talking about nature, and the detail they use in their talk, symbolize its significance in their lives. The number of words people have for things is an important clue to the salience of items in their culture. Linguistic analysis that takes this into account is part of the triangulation of analyses we described earlier (Ortner 1973; Wartmann and Purves 2018; L. M. Johnson 2000).

A computer-aided analysis of all the words in each interview showed the words that had both depth (being used frequently) and breadth (being used in many interviews). These words met two tests for each county: they were the most frequently occurring words in many interviews (at least 16 percent), *and* they occurred at least once in most of the interviews (at least 51 percent). (Often used words like *a, and, be,* and *from* were eliminated from the analysis.) The words that met these two criteria display the many-sided mix of culture and nature. *Home, house, farm, garden, cow, road, school, county, place, live, drive*—signs of human habitation—take their turn with natural labels such as *mountain* and *creek,* and with nature bent to human use— *land, property, acres, hunt.* The importance of work is denoted by the presence of *work(ed)(ing)* and *farming* on the list. People are in the mental landscape: *family, parent, dad, husband, child, couple, friend.* The importance of what is seen is shown by the presence in the most-used words list of *see(n)/saw, beautiful,* and *pretty.* Prepositions that denote directions were used frequently: *around, at, back, out, over, up, down,* and *behind.* Words show the importance of history—*old, year(s), always, remember, generation*—and concern for *where* and *time(s) when* events occurred. Analyzing the words that did *not* appear on this most frequently used list is instructive as well. *Beautiful* is on the list; *ugly* is not. *Old* is on the list; *new* is not. *Good* is on the list; *bad* is not. *More* is on the list; *less* is not. Both *big* and *little* are on the list. Words that use an economically based idiom—*money, cash, dollars, pay*—are not on the list of frequently used words.

Embedding Nature in History, Folklore, and Stories

In any culture, the content of the stories that people tell is a clear signal of what is important in that culture. Telling stories is common practice in these communities. Many things that people told us could be labeled stories. But what we counted as stories were the replies people made when we asked, "Do you have any favorite stories that you like to tell?" and things that people volunteered, usually following an opening like, "The story on that is . . ." or "I could tell you a story about . . ."

Of the more than 1,200 stories that our interviewers heard, more than one-third concerned nature. They included stories about animals, sinkholes and other geological formations, the weather, and plants. Telling stories about nature requires a good deal of knowledge of nature's attributes, and is one way of passing this knowledge on to the younger generation.

Knowing and Nurturing Nature

> In rural cultures group and self-definitions are inexorably interlocked with their knowledge of their local environment.
>
> Downing 1996:36

As the inhabitants of these counties told us about their lives, much of their talk demonstrated the cultural knowledge of nature that the residents carried. We did not ask a question that said, "tell us about the animals and plants of the area." Nevertheless, we heard, in detail, about the behavior and characteristics of, for example, purebred cattle, mixed-breed cattle, sheep, mules, pike, trout, beavers, bears, copperheads, blacksnakes, rattlesnakes, deer, coyotes, foxes, minks, 'coons, groundhogs, squirrels, rabbits, dogs, bats, turkeys, wood ducks, hawks, owls, cardinals, bluebirds, hummingbirds, purple finches, swallows, grosbeaks, Baltimore orioles, brown thrashers, yellow finches, rufous-sided towhees, Canada geese, and martins.[10]

There were usually sightings of deer or turkey when residents took us on trips to see their places. The residents always saw the animals long before the interviewers did. We observed the birds at their bird feeders—a show that was described this way by

Karla Dudley, who was born in Europe and retired to Greenly County with her husband, Frank, who has historic family ties there: "Oh, gosh, I tell you, it's really something. They're flying in and out—all kinds of different colors, different shapes. And it's just—you could just sit there. It's like watching a movie" (Interview 6/24.MBW).

Likewise, the residents discussed the flora of the area in detail. When neighbors visit each other's places, they mention, by name, the flowers and flowering bushes. Plants are an important topic of conversation, even in church; for example, there was much discussion of each of the plants noted in a Sunday school lesson on Exodus (Field Notes 7/3.MBW). Analysis of every word in each interview showed that a resident would use as many as fifty-five different names for plants (including varieties) and fifty-two different names for animals. For example, residents volunteered the names of the different kinds of apples that they were growing: Soft Delicious, Strawberry Apple, Cinnamon Striped, Green Thaliwates, Black Wigs, Boston Golden, Golden Delicious, Northern Spy, Transparent, Yellow Delicious, Early Blades, Thomas, Krause, Thompson's County King, Stamen, Paris, Winter Apple, Summer Apple, Golden Spy, Early Transparents (Interview 6/7.MBW; 6/24.MBW; Field Notes 7/3.MBW).

Another sign of the intricate linking of nature and culture is that people carry a knowledge of the *derivation* of natural items. Just like genealogies for people, residents trace the human links to long-living plants. For example, Angela Griggs notes a reticence to cut down an aging tree because "it's nowhere near the house. It's a good shade tree. And John Taylor, the fellow that [lived here before] planted that tree. He planted it for apples" (Interview 6/21.MBW). Names for *places* are often derived from the families who created the history of the place. But even the names for *plants* can hark back to history. Ruth Haley, born in nearby Andrews County seventy years ago and who has lived in Greenly County for thirty-eight years, says: "Now you get a look at those apples there. They're just red. I asked Leo what they were. He said they call them the Krause apple. They just came from down the creek where the Krauses live. And I grafted it to begin with. And that's all I call it" (Interview 6/15.MS&SS).

Residents not only know nature; they also nurture nature. This is shown by, for one thing, the bird feeders and birdhouses we saw at nearly every home we visited in Greenly, and comments such as, "I try not to put anything out that will harm them" (Interview 6/17.MBW). David Evans (and his neighbors) noted that he had put out eight hundred pounds of birdseed last winter (Field Notes 6/7.MBW). He collects all the "American chestnut" wood that he can find. He points out living chestnut trees and tells how large they will probably become before the disease that consumed their forebears kills them (Field Notes 7/3.MBW).

The relationship between humans and animals in rural areas is generally more pragmatic than suburban and urban pet pampering. It is reminiscent of other cultures whose livelihood depends on animals, such as the !Kung San of the Kalahari Desert in Namibia and Botswana, who divide animals into those that are useful and those that are useless (because they aren't hunted). Yet the relationship between farm people and animals can be a close one, and it can be ambiguous, as with the deer. On the one hand, Alice Lockhart, a forty-five-year-old mother with grown children, told us that her family, who live in Woodrow County,

> had the experience of raising a baby deer back when my kids were little. . . . It came to my house, and stayed. And I remember people goin' and drivin' down the road and we'd be walkin', and instead of a dog following you, there was a deer. And they'd stop and they'd look and I've had people stop and ask, "Is that a deer in the sandbox with your kids?" I've got pictures of it standing in the middle of my living room drinking a bottle with my kids in diapers on standing there feeding it. But, just that type of thing, you wouldn't get to do that anyplace else. (Interview T338 02/13.RUCart)

More typical is the farmer who described to us how beautiful the deer were standing in the fields, and how he took visitors on drives to see them—it pleased him to see them, no matter how often; then showed us with despair areas of forest that had been ruined by deer overbrowsing (since there are no natural predators left); then he showed us how he and his neighbor feed the deer corn if it has been a dry year—at the same time hoping the deer won't jump over their garden fences; and he showed us the deer antlers he had had mounted over the years, each with a small bronze plaque that bore the name he had bestowed on the deer and the date of its demise; and finally he took us to the building where he dressed and butchered the hunt so that his family and neighbors could eat the meat provided.

The same is true for domesticated animals. They are raised for livelihood, but attachments between people and domesticated animals were the theme of some of the stories people told us. One farmer described going to —— City to get the end-of-the-day leftovers from a Krispy Kreme franchise to feed to his cows. The cows developed individualized tastes for certain doughnut flavors—one preferred chocolate-coated; another was partial to raspberry-filled, etc. Bottle-feeding became a symbol for human intervention that led to human-animal bonds. Carolyn Adkins, wearing her cattle farmer hat, says:

> Sometimes the mother won't claim [calves]. And I have to raise them with a bottle. They get to be very attached, and I get to be very attached. I've got one that I raised—it's out on the farm—and all I have to do—the calf is nearly blind, it was born that way—but all I have to do is go out there and stop my car and yell "Lulu." Don't have to say another word and he comes at a gallop, if he's three fields away. That's how spoiled he is; he thinks I've got a bottle. . . . [The ones that I don't bottle feed], I know most of them, too. Well, they come up to the fence when I feed them and water them. Some of them drink out of the hose. (Interview 6/17.MBW)

Nancy Kelso, who has lived in Greenly County for twenty-four of her sixty years and was born in Cranston County, says:

We used to have sheep when the kids were home, and we had lambs. Pet lambs, you know, that you had to feed on the bottle. And we had as much as ten at a time. That's quite a job when you got to mix up milk for ten lambs. And of course they're really little tiny things—just growin'—and you got to feed them all through the night—about two or three times in the night. . . . We have had them in the house. After they're born, they get chills and you're afraid they're gonna die. And you bring them in so they can get warm. Our neighbor, Rose Mundy, said to give them a little bit of whisky in their milk and it'd just perk them right up. And sometimes they'll get pneumonia, you know, and that [little bit of whisky] will help them. (Interview 6/14.MBW)

For John Lewis, a thirty-year-old native of Greenly County, taking care of the animals is linked with his memories of his place and of his grandfather: "I enjoyed [living here] because I got memories of cows having calves and going out and carrying them in. They would just get out in the middle of the snow or whatever. We had to go find them because we knew they were going to have a calf at any time. I've heard my grandfather tell of taking his overcoat and taking them in the barn" (Interview 7/21B.MS&SS).

Thus, the commanding link between nature and culture is given voice by the residents' knowledge of nature, the tracing of the relationships between humans and animals and plants, and their accounts of nurturing nature. In fact, knowledge of the land is so important that, when it fails (or is said to have failed), it's worthy of comment—worthy of a story, like this one told by Alan Littleton, a sixty-four-year-old retired floor supervisor at a plant in —— City who has lived in Greenly County all of his life:

About twenty years ago—more than that now—I was just a young fellow, in my 20s, and we belonged to a little club. I guess you call it a hunt club—forty members—and we went over here in Madison and came up on what was to be Granite Gap. Five of us. [It was] foggy, oh my goodness, and we were going to hunt toward Beaverton. And to make a long story short, three of us stayed together and the other two went around the other way and we were going to meet them. We didn't meet them and we came out, finally, with a church in sight, a steeple, and a farm house. And I asked the lady where we were and she said, "Silverton," and I says, "Ma'am?" She says, "Silverton," I said, "Whose house is that over there?" She says "That's Mr. Goods.'" Well, I know Mr. Goods as good as I know myself. The other boy looked at me and I looked at him and, well, "Which church is that over there?" Said "Silverton Christian." I says, "You mean Beaverton." She says, "No sir, Silverton." Okay, lady, you don't know what you're talking about. So we walked on over to the road and waded the creek about fifty foot below where the bridge was, because we didn't know there's a bridge up there. It was in November, pretty cold. We came out and a friend who lives up the road here about a quarter mile, still lives up there, came by in a truck and stopped and picked us up, said, "Where ya going?" Said, "We're going home. What you doing over here?" He said, "What am I doing over here? I'm going home." Says, "You want a ride up to the house? It's around the road." Says, "Yeah," so he brought us up. Stopped right up here at the end of our drive and this house was on the wrong side of the road. And I came down the lane. I could see where I was and all, but things were backwards. The barn was on the wrong side. I came in the house, went in the kitchen and the stove was on the wrong side of the room and the sink was on the wrong side of the room. My wife says, "What's wrong with you." Says "Nothing." Says "I been lost, we got lost back there on Granite Gap." And I say, "To tell you the truth, things are backwards right now," and they were all afternoon. I went to bed and when I woke up the next morning, I was all right. But that's a fact. And a good friend of mine up here, Clyde, he's dead now, he came out behind us and he had the same conversation with the lady that I had just had with her and he tried to convince her that wasn't Silverton, but Beaverton, and he caught a ride home—lived up the road here a couple of miles—and he didn't know where he was either, so I don't feel so bad. He was a few years older than I was. But when you're lost, you're lost. It's a bad feeling. Everything is out of perspective. (Interview 9/14.HZ)

Knowing Weather

We have annual rain records. We keep track of what comes every day and totals for the month and then I draw a chart every year, to see what kind of rainfall we're getting.

Interview 6/21.MBW

Anthropologists who have observed hunting and gathering groups say that the evening air is filled with talk of animals and where they have been sighted, and plants and whether they are sufficiently moisture-filled to gather. As we listened to rural residents talk to each other, and as they showed us around their farms, it was clear that for them the weather is a major topic of conversation, and that knowledge of weather is prized. An analysis of every word of each interview showed that a resident would use as many as forty-one different words referring to weather. When we returned to the neighbor's house after a trip to see David Evan's cabin, the first thing he said was, "How much did it rain?" Without hesitation (for they had already checked), the neighbors called out the amount (Field Notes 6/7.MBW). Frank Dudley walked into his house after seeing to the family dog; the first thing he said to his wife was, "Karla, we need rain" (Field Notes 6/24.MBW). Precipitation is talked about in exact detail.

And everywhere else around kind of gets beat up with a thunder shower. You know, it gets like an inch, half-inch of rain in thirty minutes—which is not much use—but darn, I sure would like to get it. And we haven't had any rain. My neighbor on the other side of Arch's Valley, here—last week, I was balin' hay for him, and I got washed off the tractor. He had seven-tenths of an inch in half an hour (Interview 6/23.SLV).

How to predict weather is part of the lore that people carry in their heads: "When it's warmer at my house than it is in —— City, then I know it's going to rain" (Field Notes 6/7.MBW). "[Storms] usually go down Stephenson's Mountain or down the other side. Sometimes they'll come crashing through" (Interview 6/7.MBW).

There was much talk of storms that had caused damage to trees and buildings, most notably Hurricane Hugo's wind and rain. The weather even came into the discussion of a Sunday school lesson. To explicate the lesson on Exodus, the Sunday school teacher said, "That's about like our cattle out there now—dry—eating down to the roots, aren't they?" (Field Notes 7/3.MBW).

Knowing Water

This is the big spring down at the fish hatchery which flows down into the creek; this is the creek coming down; this is the spring coming out of that hollow over here where that farm's growin' up; back over here there's an old house and there's a spring coming out of the mountain there.

Interview 6/17.MBW

If we consider the land to be a separate branch of the family tree then the water that flows through it is its blood.

Perdue 1994

Greenly County is known for its many "bold" springs. These springs provide the water for the residents and their domesticated animals, as well as water for the wild fauna and flora. Residents offered us water to drink to show off their spring water and its taste. They know the locations and flow rates of the springs on their property. They know, and showed us, where springs come up out of the ground, where the water flows, goes back underground, and comes back up again. Many residents directed us to see the sign that marks the location of a Continental Divide, and several took us to see it and explained it in detail.

Knowing Natural Formations

This is an elevated valley.

Interview 6/21.MBW

We have different types of land here. We have some that is shale and wouldn't grow an umbrella if you turned it upside down, and there is some that is very fertile and productive land.

Interview 9/27.LK

The residents' knowledge of nature extends to the geological formations and soil types in the county. Angela Griggs, a young newcomer to the area, transplanted from northern Virginia eleven years ago, shows her knowledge and explains where she got it: "Actually, this is really kind of a unique spot because on a topographic map—this I was told by the mailman—this is an elevated valley, and they suspect that it was just tall mountains and the top just wore out. So, this is an elevated valley and we are at the mouth of the valley" (Interview 6/21.MBW).

As residents show us the views that have meaning to them, they reel off the name of each mountain in sight; they also tell you the names of any mountains that are not in sight on this particular day. They know the derivation of the names, as well. These quotations are typical of residents' talk as they gazed out at the familiar views from their home places:

> Well they call it Little Mountain. And the small one is Stephenson's. When it really clears out, you can start seeing clear over to Kent Knob. And you can see down the holler to Talbot and see the mountains across. . . . You can see the mountains clear to Talbot at times. Clear over to Madison County.
>
> This is Creek Mountain, or Stanley Mountain. And you get down close in the mountain called McDougall Gap; they've got three or four names for it. Some call it Big Mountain, Stanley Mountain, McDougall Gap Mountain. (Interview 6/7.MBW)

In this talk, sometimes a "possession" of the mountains is heard. Showing the interviewer a photograph that she had taken, Carolyn Adkins explained, "And there's *my* mountain in the ice" (Interview 6/17.MBW).

In Greenly, where karst topography containing limestone caves is common, sinkholes and caves are a frequent topic of conversation. The analysis of stories told to the interviewers showed that 5 percent concerned sinkholes. They told of pets and cattle who had fallen victim to sinkholes, and the rescue efforts mounted to save them.

Orienting by the Geological Markers

> The mountains are our bearings.
>
> Interview 6/21.MBW

A local journalist wrote, "For me there's something unsettling about not seeing a mountain on the horizon, as if I've lost a compass and can't find my life's direction" (Fries 1997:NRV2). Indeed, the configuration of the place provides "bearings" for identity (Relph 1976). So much so that for some residents, being away has its effects: "When my husband and I go visiting you really miss the mountains. I mean, even though they are around all the time, it's like bearings or something. And when we finally get off 34 onto 61, you almost sigh because you recognize the mountains and you say, 'Oh, I'm almost home. I'm almost there.' [That is our] bearing" (Interview 6/21.MBW).

Another resident reported that when she was at the ocean, she would "see" imaginary mountains, "like a mirage," in the background for three or four days (Interview 6/7.MBW). Residents orient themselves by geological markers. In answer to our request for directions to his house, a resident sent (via a fax machine) these directions: "I think the easiest route to this west end of Greenly County is via Route 230 past Jonesville over Mason Mt. 8 mi to Whitesville. Go 12 miles to our house on left in the valley" (Field Notes 6/7.MBW).

The "over Mason Mountain" is superfluous; if a vehicle is traveling from Jonesville to Whitesville via Route 230, it will inevitably go "over Mason Mountain." Yet this is so much a part of how he organizes his world that he includes it in instructions. Likewise, his house is "in the valley." Interviewers in Woodrow County heard directions like this: "Well, go up West Creek until you get over Brushwood Ridge, then go down into Deays River Valley and around the west end of the ridge. Then you'll be at Jack's place."

Rather than asking me, "Do you want to come over to my house?" or "Do you want to come over to my place?" a resident asked, "Do you want to go up on The Mountain [where his house sits]?" (Interview 6/7.MBW). Other residents use language like "up Stanley," to describe where their neighbors live (Field Notes 6/14. MBW). An analysis of every word of each interview showed that a resident would use as many as fifty-eight different words for geological formations. Words that denote direction—*up, back, over, out, around, down, at, behind*—were among the most frequently used words.

Sensing Beauty in Nature

People here place great value on the beauty of their farms, their community.

Interview 2/13.DW

The "view," the scenic beauty, is important to residents, as measured by their interest in it, and knowledge of it. They talked about it often, at length, and in detail. *Beautiful, pretty,* and *see/seen/saw* are among the often-used words in the interview transcriptions.

During many interviews, it wasn't necessary for residents to describe the beauty of the land that provided the medium for their lives. They would, instead, take the interviewer for a walk or a drive, and say, "Look." "He wants to take you up on The Mountain," a resident explained to me as we headed for the truck. "That's the most beautiful place up there you've ever seen. You're going up on The Mountain. That's the top of the world" (Interview 6/7.MBW).

But when interviews took place after dark, residents needed to describe the panorama, and they waxed poetic about the scenes they loved. Carolyn Adkins, the local historian for Greenly County who has lived there all her life, has named the fogs that she sees from her patio: peach fog, bronze fog, lake fog, witches' brew, silver, gold, and melon:

[To show you] my favorite spot . . . I would have to have you at all hours of the day because the scene is different every time you look. I marvel every time I look because I see something I've never seen before, and I have lived here [in this house] for thirty years. . . . Sometimes it looks like the whole mountain's ablaze. . . . And back during the ice storms, the snow—I can't describe what those mountains looked like—and when the sun came out it was millions of diamonds. So I . . . take hundreds of pictures of that scene, every season. (Interview 6/17.MBW)

When describing the beauty of the land, people most often depicted what could be *seen,* but sometimes they described enjoying the land with the sense of hearing, smell, and touch, as well: "A lot of times we go over that mountain to Greenly's Creek just for the scenery and just for the peace and quiet" (Interview 6/25.LC). "I laid in bed the other night—we have no screens—well, we have screens—we don't have them in place—and I lay there thinking, 'My goodness, the air smells wonderful. Just good to breathe'" (Interview 6/9.SLV).

As many as eleven different adjectives describing the physical surroundings were used in a single interview, including *beautiful, pretty, wonderful, clean, neat, peaceful,* and *quiet.* Researchers have demonstrated the worth of scenic areas in reducing stress and promoting pleasurable sensations and good mental health. A survey citing "the emotional appeal of a beautiful countryside setting" showed scenic beauty to be the most important criterion Americans use in choosing parks and recreation areas (President's Commission on Americans Outdoors 1987:40). These findings of researchers are echoed in the voices of residents: "Farmland, you know, [there's] just the serenity of the place and nice well-kept property" (Interview.KG). *Comforting* was a word used to describe the setting. Angela Griggs, the young owner of a fish hatchery, says: "I guess it's good for the soul. It's just peaceful. Just very peaceful. There's something very comforting, I guess, about the gentle roll in the hill and the green in the grass and cattle lazily munching along—grazing, tails swagging" (Interview 6/21.MBW). Another youthful resident, Alvin Underwood from Clearview, agrees: "I would have you sit on the porch for a while, have a cup of coffee, watch the deer come out in the fields. . . . It is the most beautiful, comforting scene [I've] ever witnessed" (Interview T308 12/20.JD). Researchers agree that scenes like the residents showed us are good for mental health and well-being and that threats to these environments have consequences (Eyles and Williams 2008; Ellis and Albrecht 2017; Lengen and Kistemann 2012; Sangaramoorthy et al. 2016).

4

Using Land to Make a Living and a Life

That's cookstove wood, all that. This here wood like that will be for the heater. . . .
We already got it cut, all we got to do is haul it. . . . That wood holds fire longer,
that there burns up too quick; that makes a fast fire, that makes a slow fire.

Interview 8/22.MBW

It is somewhat arbitrary to separate "using land to form identity" from "using land to make a living." Landscape architects tell us that exercising control over meaningful spaces "helps people define who they are." They can manipulate space by "construction, subtle changes, decoration, modification, and the re-creation of previous settings" (Downing 1996:6).

The rural residents did manipulate space, and their relationships with land did incorporate an economic orientation, as well as preeminent symbolic and sentimental attachments. A typology of Illinois farmers devised by anthropologist Sonya Salamon (1992:94–113) made a distinction reminiscent of Plaut's continuum of place as sacred or place as property. "Yeoman" farmers are attached to a particular piece of family land, to heirlooms, and to heritage. They carry a rich oral tradition concerning the past; their speech treats money as irrelevant; instead worth is measured by continuity of land ownership, by keeping the "sacred family trust." The yeomen's identity is tied to the land. Farming is a "way of life," not primarily a business. For the "entrepreneur" farmers, on the other hand, land is viewed as a commodity—its symbolic value is seated in its financial worth (and thus, ties to any *particular* pieces of land are tenuous). The entrepreneurs are oriented toward the present more than the past; few family mementos or artifacts are displayed in their homes; old buildings are torn down. The entrepreneurs' compensations are found in "the search for autonomy and financial reward rather than [family] farm reproduction." The rural people we interviewed in Appalachia are overwhelmingly of the "yeoman" variety. This is not surprising even from a purely economic point of view, since flat fertile land on which entrepreneurial farming can best grow is found in greater abundance in other parts of the country. The yeoman farmer's identity is more likely to be bound up with the land.

Using Nature

The locust posts that we got off the north are the best [for fence posts].

Interview 6/29.LC

Whenever our questions touched on how time was spent, we heard about construction, decoration, and modification of space, and attempts to preserve previous modifications and construction. The rural culture of these communities *uses* aspects of nature to maintain itself. For example, wood is used for building, for fence posts, and for heating homes, for cooking and for heating water. Spring water is used to serve the needs of people, and for raising cattle and fish. Soil is used for producing crops and fodder; grass and hay are fed to cattle. Rocks are used for fences, and for chimneys and buildings. Clay has been used for bricks. Native plants are gathered and animals are hunted. Each of these activities that turns nature's substances into culture's products requires a good deal of knowledge of nature's attributes and a good deal of time in nature's storehouse.

Spending Time on the Land

There's always something to do on a farm.

Field Notes 8/22.MBW

Anthropologists note that the way people spend their *time* reveals what is important in their cultures. One of the measures of a "core value" is the large amount of time devoted to it. In these communities, then, we listened for how residents spend their time and what activities are important to them. We learned, in the words of one interviewer, "the land is their place of work, their history book, and their place of fun and enjoyment." The work on the land means that it "becomes a part of their everyday thoughts" (Burk 1994). When a resident drove me from a neighbor's place to his own, we stopped at other neighbors' along the way, and I could eavesdrop on neighbors' talk. They talk about cattle (and the problems of keeping them fenced and off the roads), cutting hay (and the problem of having enough rain to make it grow and a dry time to mow and bale it), refurbishing and maintaining old houses and outbuildings, and hunting. They talk of the damage deer can do to crops and fruit trees, and of how noisy dogs can be (and the possible need for a noise ordinance) (Field Notes 6/21.MBW; 6/7.MBW).

Appalachian studies scholar Ronald Eller (1979) notes that in agrarian times, Appalachia "was a region where most living took place out-of-doors." According to residents' accounts of how they spend their time, this is still true in these modern-day communities. Even those who commute to jobs spend much of the rest of their time outdoors. As in most farming cultures (and other nonindustrial cultures), residents do not split time into clearly defined segments of "work" and "leisure" as is common in industrialized life. Like the languages of hunters and gatherers, the farm residents' talk made little distinction between work and play, constantly stymieing researchers' efforts to pigeonhole time spent in one or the other category. Instead, they reported that the work on the land was a part of them and that it was enjoyable. We have, however, made the work/play analytic distinction here, in order to clarify how residents spend their time.

Working on the Land

You have to be a certain kind of person to make a living from the land, you
really do.

Interview 6/29.LC

I told Leo, there will be work here when we're dead.

Interview 6/7.MBW

Most analyses would surely put the activities attendant on farming operations under
the category of an *economic* tie to the land. Yet the residents always bring in other
reasons—based on sentiment, or emotion, or job satisfaction—for doing the farmwork. And many claim that economic benefits are illusory. Even the most commercial of the farmers say, "By the time you build fences, and lime and fertilize and all
that, and pay for your cattle and everything, about all you're getting out of it is the
taxes." "Taking care of the taxes" and "it goes back into the farm" were the refrains we
heard. "So whatever you earn on the farm, it helps to put it back into the farm to make
it more special." Some residents lease their land for pasture, in order to maintain a
rural lifestyle, but note: "We're not operating a commercial farm. We're enjoying it
just for our own pleasure. . . . It's not a money-making operation" (Interview 6/28A.
LC; also Interview 6/14B.LC; Interview T325 11/28.RM; Interview 6/14A.LC).
Indeed, net cash returns from agricultural sales, average per farm, in 2017 amounted
to less than $5,300 in three of the counties, about $10,600 in the fourth county, and
minus $1,700 in the fifth. A farm wife told us:

> There is a joke that my husband had heard that I think really illustrates
> farming. And the joke is that a farmer won a million dollars in the lottery,
> and he was asked what he was going to do with his money. And he said well,
> he was going to keep farming 'til the money ran dry. And that's basically
> farming. You know it takes a lot of time and a lot of money, but it's a good
> life. I kind of enjoy it. It says a lot, kind of set your own hours and . . . even
> it out when the working is done. (Interview 6/21.MBW)

There is a pride in farming, and in the farmer's contribution to feeding the United
States and the world. Curtis Lewis, a thirty-five-year-old native of Greenly County,
says: "People don't realize—even a small farmer like me—I read in the paper the
other night—one of the farm magazines—how many people a small farmer like me
feeds. . . . It was a pretty big number. Even a small operation like me makes a difference in feeding the United States, or, you know, feeding the public, period. And that
makes me feel good" (Interview 9/20.BD).

Peggy Barlett's (1993:6–7, 79, 80) study of farmers in Georgia found dimensions
of life satisfaction that differed from those found in urban life and in other occupa-
tions. She found an "alternative vision of work, family, and community" that "values

property ownership and independent production" and is centered around certain satisfactions. A shorthand list includes: independence, personal empowerment, "freedom from supervision and flexibility of work pace"; association between work, family, and community; sense of attachment to land, connection to nature and to "deeper spiritual realities embodied in the work process"; and "the sense that work and play, effort and leisure, flow into each other." As Barlett says, "farming becomes more than an occupational identity; the work creates a compelling emotional attachment." The rural residents we interviewed expressed why they like farming with words that echo Barlett's list of life satisfactions, including "freedom from supervision and flexibility of work pace." Curtis Lewis, who also works for a government agency but talks only of his farming, advises:

> Stay out of the cattle business right now, the way the market is. But, it's a fun thing to do, and I think if you ever do it any amount of time, it'll get in your blood and you'll want to do it all the time. You know, out here in the wintertime, me and my boys, or my daughter, or my wife, either one'll get out here and it might be six or eight inches of snow on the ground, you're out there feeding them cows, got a newborn calf just come or something. Makes you feel pretty good. (Interview 9/20.BD)

Lawrence Miles, a twenty-seven-year-old former military man who is a full-time farmer, volunteer fireman, and active in local Greenly County politics, says:

> I like to make hay. I like foolin' with them aggravatin' cattle. There's really no limit of what you can do farming. And, it's not dull because you don't do it eight hours a day. You know, you weld for a few hours and you kind of fix what you need to fix, and move on to something else, and most of the time, it's always fresh, and new. That's what I love about farming. I mean, yeah, I can go and work for a welding shop, and just sit there and burn welding rods for eight or ten hours a day, and you would become a fantastic welder, but your mind would go numb. And this—this keeps you fresh. (Interview 6/23.SLV)

Ralph Metcalf, a seventy-four-year-old retired government worker who transplanted from the Midwest to Walnut Cove in Cranston County fifteen years ago, says:

> I mow almost an acre of ground. And I mow it with a self-propelled push mower and I enjoy doing it. People tell me I should have a riding mower, but I enjoy it. And I love, I like the sight of fresh mowed grass. And I like the smell of it. And I like going out in the garden and working in the garden. And you put something in the earth and you don't know if it's going to come up or not, and in just a few days or week or so, you see that popping up. I'm a city fellow—I was—but I'm countrified now and I enjoy that. That's

something that I've done and grown with the help of God. (Interview T333 01/05/00.DCM)

There are, of course, downsides to the risky business of farming. Lawrence Miles from Greenly reported this talk from another:

Sheep—a buddy that I was baling there for the other day—he used to have sheep, and he finally just got out of it. He said that you're lambin' the darn things and it's just like handling a light bulb. They might make it, they might not. And a sheep—he says you can just go out there, and they'd be *dead*. And he said dogs get in them. And then the price of wool and mutton—it's just, real fickle, but it's never good. And he said by the time you shear them, cram it in the bag and take it over there, and they throw out a little money for you, it's just not worth the bother. (Interview 6/23.SLV)

(In fact, sheep farming is on the decline in the county. The number of beef cattle, hogs, and horses has increased, and the number of dairy cows is stable. Beef cattle, hay, and corn are what's farmed most in all five counties, along with tobacco in Woodrow and Cranston Counties.)

The land-based activities reported to us (and again, not clearly delineated as either work or play) that we'll list here under *working* on the land, included planting, fertilizing, liming, and baling hay; planting and picking corn; farming alfalfa; caring for cattle; raising chickens and selling eggs; raising fish; raising sheep and selling wool and lambs; growing gardens, orchards, grape arbors, and berry canes; freezing and canning garden and orchard produce; planting and maintaining herb gardens and flower gardens; making wreaths from dried herbs and flowers; planting trees; making maple syrup; keeping bees and "taking the honey off"; fishing and selling the catch to the grocery store; carrying rocks; "going to the top of the mountain to get these rocks to build the patio with"; pruning, trimming, cutting brush, bushhogging, and mowing; building and repairing stone, wooden, and wire fences; building, repairing, and maintaining outbuildings; cutting, splitting, hauling, and stacking wood for firewood; and renovating, repairing, and maintaining homes and outbuildings.[1]

Caring for the land, that's the total farming picture. When you're farming, you not only have to care for land but the livestock that runs on that land. I guess that includes the health and welfare of the sheep and the cattle, the liming and fertilizing to preserve the pasture fields and fields that grow the hay, mowing the pastures, clipping or spraying the weeds or brush, keeping the farm in good shape, keeping the fences repaired or built. The farm isn't beautiful without work. That's what we do. We try to maintain it. (Interview T339 12/22.BM)

The prominence of work in the lives of residents is demonstrated by the variety and frequency of words associated with it in interviews. *Work, worked,* and *farming* appeared on the list of words occurring most frequently. There were twenty-seven different words for work in a single interview. Those included *digging, growing, cutting, grading, hauling, mining, canning, burying, washing, picking, carrying,* and *boiling.*

In gardens, residents grew beans, October beans, lima beans, green beans, green snaps, corn, white corn, potatoes, sweet potatoes, onions, radishes, peas, cucumbers, pickle cucumbers, tomatoes, cantaloupes, watermelons, green peppers, lettuce, zucchini, pumpkins, gourds, cabbage, broccoli, Brussels sprouts, celery, carrots, beets, squash, yellow squash, winter squash, rutabagas, turnips, and herbs. They grew strawberries, black raspberries, red raspberries, grape vines, apples, peaches, apricots, pears, plums ("damsons"), "prune trees," walnuts, chestnuts, and pecans.[2] Eighty-two-year-old Henry Meyers, a resident of the mostly African American community of Clearview in Woodrow County who lives with and cares for his sisters, said: "I have three [gardens] and one down there at the church. I used to have seven some . . . on my nephew's place, but when age comes up on you, . . . but I still have more to eat . . . I got food in there now stacked from floor to the top. In there, you can see right now" (Interview T302 11/29.JD).

Paul Carter, a much younger man in his thirties from the same community, is following in the older man's footsteps:

> We can a lot of what we grow. We canned forty quarts of green beans, about fifty quarts of tomatoes, and about forty pints of tomato juice. And the rest we put up through the winter months. The meat that we kill when we're hunting, we eat. We process all our deer into steak and roast and hamburger. With the turkeys and stuff, we buy very little meat. If we buy beef, or if we kill beef, we'll usually split it with someone. . . . Just this household, we probably eat about seven deer a year. (Interview T304 11/05.JD)

We wanted to know the *amount* of time residents spent working on the land. The answers we received from the farmers were like this: "[How much time do we work on our land?] All the time" (Field Notes 6/14.MBW). "[How much time does my father spend caring for the land?] One hundred percent. Probably 150 percent. . . . As long as there are daylight hours, he thinks he is supposed to be working" (Interview 6/29.LC). One incredulous interviewer tried to elicit a more precise answer by asking again, "So how much time do you think you spend working on your land approximately every day—besides twenty-four hours?" "Forty-four hours," came the reply (Interview 7/18.SS&MS).

When residents talk of kin and neighbors, they show that they admire hard work on the land: "Well, see, my dad will be 81 and he . . . never stops. He still is working. Not full-time but he's still working" (Interview 6/7.MBW). Of an elderly man in ill health, they said: "But he still cuts hay. He works so hard" (Field Notes 7/3.MBW). Another man who had recently been in the hospital with heart and other problems was "out cutting thistles; he can't stand to let 'em go." (Some do look askance at those who work on Sunday [Field Notes 7/3.MBW].)

Some people spend their vacation time from salaried jobs working on the land—"I took a vacation this week to build a fence." "[My husband] was off all last week to help my father put up hay. . . . That was part of his vacation" (Interview 7/18. SS&MS; Interview 6/29.LC). Some people don't take vacations, because of the need to care for their animals: "What we have found is that—and it's probably true across the board—when you're keeping something live, nobody takes care of your animals like you do. Nobody understands their idiosyncrasies like you do. We are around them all the time. We know what their behavior is, we know what their activity means" (Interview 6/21.MBW).

Farmer Donna Morrow, who has lived in Forsythe in Woodrow County all of her forty-one years, sums it up: "I'm on the farm year-round. I haven't had a vacation in twenty years. . . . I try to take care of my fences. I try to keep the brush down" (Interview T315 12/30.JB).

Playing on the Land

I love these woods. I used to take Bernard's dog, and cover this whole place.
                    Field Notes 7/3.MBW; see also Field Notes 6/7.MBW

Languages used by hunting and gathering cultures make no distinction between *work* and *play* (words distinguish between active and passive, but not work and play). While this degree of unity would not be true of our residents, they did make very little distinction between working and playing on the land. Barlett (1993:6–7) notes "the sense that work and play, effort and leisure, flow into each other" was one of the satisfactions for farmers in Georgia. Our residents concur: "It keeps me busy all the time, keeping this place up. I guess you call the farm and the house my hobby. It relaxes you" (Interview 9/14.HZ).

Residents spend their "leisure" time on their land, or nearby in the county. One of our questions asked: "If you had a day when you could do anything you wanted to—nothing needed to get done—where would you go? How would you describe this place to someone who couldn't go there?" In the interviews where this question was clearly asked, 2 percent of the interviewees could not answer the question because they could not imagine having a day with nothing to do; 30 percent would not go anywhere off their own place; 40 percent would go to other particular spots in the counties in which they lived; 11 percent would travel somewhere outside the county. Some people gave two answers to the question: 12 percent said they would either stay home or go elsewhere in the county; 4 percent would stay on their own place or go outside the county; and 1 percent would leave their home place and go to somewhere either within or outside the county.

This quote from sixty-seven-year-old retiree Darrel Murdock from Farlane County is typical of what people would do on a mythical "day off": "Myself, I'd like to just sit and view nature and enjoy the surroundings around me. I'd go up to my home place and just relax up on my porch. Or just walk around and maybe if I need a little board or hinge fixed on my barn, or maybe a place to fence, to look about to see what I was able to do. Why it's just something to relax at. Or just walk around; you always see something" (Interview 9/19.KG).

It's said that farming requires vigilance—which is attained by "walking the land." Indeed, the most frequently discussed activity was walking the land. They liked to "walk in the woods. Just listen to nature" (Interview 7/20C.MS&SS). "I'd be up in my mountain. Up on my land. Roam around" (Interview T331 11/30.DCM).

> I walk the farm every morning. I walk, me and my wife walk two miles at least, sometimes I walk anywhere from three to five every morning. I have me a mowed trail around the creek. (Interview 9/14.HZ)
>
> I like to hike, and I like the outdoors. I love digging in the dirt. I've always said that. I love flowers and gardens, and I love just getting out on this farm and walking. (Interview 6/25.LC)
>
> I would take a walk over the farm, because no matter how hard and how tired you are, or how hard the day has been . . . it's so restful and relaxing just to get out and smell the fresh air and feel the earth under your feet when you're walking. It's just nice . . . to walk. I love to get out and walk, and breathe the fresh air, and just see all the beauty that surrounds this area. It's just breathtaking. (Interview T325 11/28.RM)

The residents characterized themselves as "outdoor person[s]" and one resident said, "Most all of the time [I'm] just knocking around one thing and the other and fooling with my flowers, and I keep bees, and I grow apples and peaches and pears and all kinds of fruits and grapes and things thata way" (Interview 9/27.LK). Activities the residents reported that we will list here as "leisure" activities nearly all took place on the land and included: walking in the woods; deer hunting; turkey hunting; bear hunting; hunting for rabbits, squirrels, turtles, grouse, doves, and quail; fishing for trout, bass, and pike; mountain biking; hiking; gardening; raising flowers and drying them; climbing; picking blackberries; carving; identifying wildflowers; having a family picnic; going to a church picnic "outside in old Chestnut Grove"; showing horses; taking the boat out on the pond; giving the grandchildren a tractor ride; and sitting in the neighbors' porch swing. "We entertain ourselves here" (Interview 6/28B.LC).[3]

There were as many as twenty-one different words or phrases for recreation in a single interview, which included *hunt, climb, maypole wrap, race,* and *play jack rocks.* Recreation words that appeared throughout interviews included *picnic, walk, explore,* and *roam.* The only exception to leisure activities being land-based came from one resident who said that if this imaginary day off were a Saturday, she "would go to a University football game" (Interview 9/21.MG). Another resident reported taking part in indoor recreation, but he tempered his statement, too: "We will take off on Sundays, you know and watch a football game at our house perhaps, but then we still have to keep count on our cattle to see if the coyotes are getting any" (Interview 9/16.JH).

Some residents reported using the land as sanctuary: "[I would] sit under a tree by myself, here in Stanley" (Interview 9/12.JD). "On the other side of the mountain I . . . just go back in there and kind of hide. I don't have much time for hidin'" (Interview 6/23.SLV). "I have a couple of places I just go, when life gets tough here. I go down to the overlook on the mountain which is two miles away, nobody can get to me on the phone, and you can just see forever down there, and I know the names of the mountains" (Interview 6/17.MBW).

Another activity that residents report is sitting in the neighbors' porch swing and talking. What are the topics of conversation?

> We just really enjoy these people's company. We just sit and talk about nothing or anything . . . the deer population and what it's doing to the crops, what it's doing to the fruits and the vegetables. . . . We talk about politics, you know. Rural problems, county problems . . . personal health. Some of our neighbors are elderly. Farming operations, what equipment is working, what isn't. And, you know, how the herd is, what kind of problems you're having and what successes that you have. What's going on with the neighbors, who has had babies and who has been in the hospital, who has been on vacation. . . . Some of our neighbors that are elderly do talk about what they've done and how things are different and how things have changed. . . . And . . . when it comes to work, particularly the hay season, getting the hay up off the field. (Interview 6/21.MBW)

Sharing the Land with Visitors

My mother . . . she just thinks that this little county is just a slice of heaven.
Interview 6/21.MBW

We asked the residents to tell us: "If I were new in the county, and I had seen your place, and I wanted to see some of the rest of the whole of the county, where would you take me?" Residents told us that when visitors actually do come, they stay close to home: "Most of the friends and family that come and visit really just enjoy sitting on the porch" (Interview 6/21.MBW). Angela Griggs, the young eleven-year newcomer to Greenly who owns a business with her husband, has visitors from her native northern Virginia:

> When people come to visit—they come for the quiet. They come for the cool. They love to hear the running water. And a lot of times, what we'll do is—and a lot of times it's even requested—we'll just get in the car and go back on the back roads, and it just thrills people to death to see deer standing in the field. But you know, it even just still thrills my husband and I although we've seen so many of them. We'll just be driving coming along 34 and the few fields we've been by enough times to know that that's where the

deer congregate, and we'll say, "Wow! Look at that! Look at that!" So, it's the wildlife, the beauty that's here. To be able to go for such a long time and just see one farm. One farm. It's not just—house, house, house, house, house, you know, the way things are spread out. When people come to visit, that's what they see. Just run the back roads. Look at the farms. (Interview 6/21.MBW)

Rose Mundy, a seventy-year-old native of Greenly, also has visitors from elsewhere: "We got a lot of relatives and they live in Richmond and around and when they come here they don't want to go anywhere else. They just like it right here. They just stroll all over the place, pick up rocks and take 'em back home with them. Yeah, they like to roam around. They just like the mountains" (Interview 8/22.MBW).

Strategies to Stay on the Land

I carry the mail to make a living. Farming's what I want to do.

Interview 9/20.JPC

Val Farmer (2000:A6), a rural mental health specialist, says that "a strong percentage of farm families who are forced out of farming stay in their local communities. Why? Because they are place-bound people. To move to an unknown place and not know the history and the people is a drastic uprooting and immersion into another way of being. They don't know how to act in a place where 'place' is not important."

Several residents reported working at jobs to which they commuted and caring for cattle after they came home from work, like the resident who told us, "I work a job to support the farm is what it boils down to" (Interview T314 12/28.JB). In the five counties, 57 to 63 percent of the farmers work off the farm some, and at least 40 percent work off the farm more than two hundred days a year. In fact, more than half of the farm operators in each of the five counties have another occupation as their principal one.[4] For those residents, care for land and animals (on their own place or another owned by relatives) takes place before and after their full-time jobs: fifteen to thirty-five hours a week, or "every bit of time that we're not working [at our jobs]" (Interview 9/24.TC; 9/17.KW; 6/28/A.LC). Barry Patrick reverse commutes, living near his day job, and commuting back and forth to work on the family land in Greenly County:

I was over there this morning, I'll be back over there tomorrow. We're doing some work over on the farm now. They're fine people and I'm happy that I grew up over there. I want to keep the association with these people. You won't find farm people that are more interested in farming and preserving the history of that area. They take great pride in the area and in the farming. And when someone dies they're always anxious to find out what's going to happen to this farm. Is it going to be sold, or is some member of the family going to come in and take over? So they want to try to preserve the history that has come down through generations and generations of farm people. They hate to see a farm sold or subdivided. (Interview 9/15.BF)

Long commutes are a sacrifice made to live in these counties. In Greenly County half of the workforce commutes to work. The average commute is a little more than a one-hour roundtrip to —— City, Williams County, Carthage, Madison County, Farlane County, and Ringel County. In each of the five counties, at least 5 percent of the workers commute at least an hour one way; in Borden and Greenly Counties, 10 and 13 percent do. In Woodrow County, 44 percent of the workers commute to at least eight other Virginia counties and two other states. One resident, when asked, "How far would you be willing to commute to stay in the county?" answered, "as far as it would take." She modified this by saying that when she was younger that would have been true, but now, "an hour would be as much as I could take" (Interview 7/20D.MS&SS). One of our interviewees had commuted two hours to work (Interview 7/21.MS&SS). Nick Nixon, a twenty-five-year-old man who commuted fifty minutes to work as an engineer in —— City said that during bad weather "it was tough to get to work, the commute to work was. I missed two or three days because of the bad weather—because of ice. But other than that I'm used to it. It's inconvenient, it's tough on the animals, but that's part of farming, part of living out here, too. We're a thousand feet higher right here than surrounding valleys and that makes the winters up here a little bit colder" (Interview 7/19.MS&SS).

Some residents opted to lease their land when they could no longer maintain adequate care of their farms themselves: "A lot of the people, you know, they've just gotten older . . . want somebody to look after the place. You know, run livestock and plant corn, and put up the hay" (Interview 9/20.JPC). When residents lease their land, they expect it to stay well maintained. A fifty-seven-year-old returnee to the family place who lives alone and leases, explains the relationship between the landowner and the renter: "One of the terms of his lease is that he's got to . . . keep the . . .stick weeds [*Helenium*] and this kind of stuff under control" (Interview 9/18.DNS).

It was in the mostly African American community of Clearview in Woodrow County that we most clearly saw other strategies common in Appalachia since World War II—movement back and forth between the homeplace and a place of industry, or out-migration during working years and return migration after retiring.

Sacrificing to Live on the Land

It's a lot of inconveniences we have here, a lot of 'em.

Interview 6/24.MBW

There are elements of rural life that are seen by economists as problematic; for example, low farm income, lack of employment opportunities, lack of public transportation, lack of access to more affordable water and sewage systems, and, of more recent note, lack of fast internet service. When these were mentioned by the interviewees, they were rarely framed as problems. More likely was a discussion of sacrifices people have purposely made to live a rural life. They are willingly inconvenienced to live in an area with low population density, few roads, little pollution and crime, no noise, etc. Their perceptions of low crime rates are borne out by, for example, an average of twenty-nine crimes per year in Cranston County. They see the sacrifices as trade-offs for the desirable situation of living in an area of great beauty that holds cultural and historical significance. They decry the attitudes of some newcomers who want convenient services and shopping, which would change the character of the place, and ask, rhetorically, "Why did they come here?" As newcomers adjust (to varying degrees) to their new surroundings, certain businesses boom—like Lehman's Hardware ("For a Simpler Life," as its catalog says) and Blue Ridge Wildlife Management, which locates and removes the bats, squirrels, skunks, and snakes that some of the exurbanites fear (Macy 2000). Some of the differences in urban and rural life satisfactions were brought home to me while driving with my family to a farm in one of the counties we're describing here. My mother-in-law, who had for all of her eighty-plus years lived in a city, asked, with her failing eyesight, "What are those? Are those houses? Do people live out here?" As we continued down (and up) the curvy road, the distance from the nearest town lengthened, and a few more houses appeared. She asked, "Who would want to live here? Where would you shop? Where would you go? What would you do?"

Although the earliest urban sociologists at the University of Chicago noted that "Stadtluft macht frei"—city air makes you free—because the city offers more anonymity and an accompanying "freedom to be," rural residents often don't see it that way. They see freedom in being "free to roam," saying, "People live in the country because they enjoy the scenery, they enjoy nature and they enjoy the privacy and being able to yell if they want to yell, without someone calling the law" (Interview T335 11/28.DL).

Residents do make sacrifices to live here. Those sacrifices come in the form of, for example, less income than they might have elsewhere. Per capita income for all but one of the counties ranks in the lowest third of the state's 134 counties and independent cities. Residents note that when carving out a place to live in a rural area, it's necessary to provide your own water source and septic system rather than simply hooking onto services provided by a municipality. In some cases the flow of water is not as reliable as it could be. Building materials have to be transported farther from their point of origin, thus increasing the cost of building a home or outbuilding. They note, too, that to live the rural life requires procuring the tools to maintain the land: "There are all these tools and all these expenses that you have." "I've got a truck, a car and a tractor, a riding mower, three push mowers, two weed eaters, two chainsaws, and a tiller. That's twelve" (Interview 6/24.MBW). Residents report other sources of financial sacrifices. For example, some report paying higher taxes than at other places they have lived. Residents don't want to see the land subdivided but note that it does cost more to buy the large lots required. And, they say, insurance is higher in an area far from a fire department.

Twenty-year resident of Woodrow County Robert Nichols observes the difficulty of balancing limited career options with a desire to remain in the area. He acknowledges sacrifices residents make: "I mean, everyone that lives in the county gives up economic opportunity. Constantly giving up something . . . as far as that goes. And people work—golly. . . . I mean the work of these people . . . always doing something. . . . It's just unbelievable how much people work for not a tremendous amount of material gain . . . as far as . . . money. . . . Probably the satisfaction is just greater in other ways" (Interview T338 02/13/00.RUCart).

A newcomer to Greenly, Laura Dell, describes her trade-offs.

> We're mostly trying to approach a sustainable farm just for our house. And well, we really don't make enough money to buy Christmas gifts like little old crappy plastic things that break and people throw away. The kind of Christmas gift that *I* like to receive is homemade jams and jellies, and breads. And so, that's what we make and give out for Christmas—and we can afford to do that. That may be one of the downsides of living here, but I don't really see it as a downside of living in Greenly County. We don't market our stuff, really. We also don't make a whole lot of money. But we sure do enjoy our lives. I don't know how some people live. I couldn't live in a city. I would die. I would wither and die. In town is marginal. Out here I thrive. I just sort of feel like this is the right place for me. I know that. (Interview 6/9.SLV)

Residents do decry slower access to the internet, but for the most part, residents make light of lagging somewhat behind in technology, as this family story from Bonnie Glovern, a lifelong resident of Harwood in Farlane County, shows:

> One of the stories I thought about—it's from my husband's family. His uncle Vernon went to the New York World's Fair in 1933, or '39, whenever it was in New York. And he saw one of the first television sets that had ever been invented. And so he came home and said he saw this box that you turned the knob, and you could see a moving picture on it. And of course everybody was astounded. It was unbelievable back then, you know. There wasn't even electricity here in this area. And so when he was telling it to his sister she said, "It ain't nothin' but a damn lie." (Interview 9/20.TLP)

Even those who don't commute to work have to travel to buy groceries: "I have a cooler and I can keep my milk and cold food with me. I have ice packs in the cooler. It only takes thirty or thirty-five minutes" (Interview 7/20.SS&MS). "We don't have that luxury [of eating out] here. If I'm too tired to cook, I'm too tired to go all the way to get some food" (Interview 6/29.LC).

Travel is necessary if children want to take part in school extracurricular activities: "The only drawback to raising a family here is that you have a lot of extra driving to do, to keep [the children] involved in the community, but it's worth it" (Interview

6/20.MS&SS). Indeed, one set of siblings from Greenly County reported missing a "straight month" of school due to snowstorms when they were growing up (Interview 7/21B.MS&SS). Greenly County has one part-time doctor now, and sometimes has had no doctor. To go to doctors, residents report traveling to Carthage, —— City, and Jonesville, forty minutes to more than an hour away. For parents who work in —— City, a call from Greenly school reporting a sick child means driving back to Greenly to pick up the child, then returning to —— City to the doctor.

The farmwork—caring for the animals and crops—presents daily sacrifices in time and relatively little monetary reward. Young Lawrence Miles says:

> I have [considered leaving], but not for more than about ten or fifteen minutes. After my original anger or whatever had annoyed me passes. You fight with some old cow, and she still dies. Or they get out in the road through the night. Continuously. Or you fight, fight, fight, to get hay put up and you can't get it put up. Or the weather turns really dry forever, and the hay kind of burns up. Or it doesn't quit snowin' or freezin'. You kind of say, "You know, the people at Taco Bell do not have any of these problems." (Interview 6/23.SLV)

Another sacrifice that residents make is the potential wealth they would realize from subdividing and developing their land for residences or other nonfarm purposes. When the ancestors of the current residents of these communities came from Ulster, Scotland, Ireland, England, Germany, and France more than two hundred years ago, they were granted or bought huge tracts of land. These tracts were generally divided among the children (some were handed down to the eldest son), and so became smaller and smaller over time. In this generation, several residents told us of buying and *combining* farms, either to join small family parcels, or simply to connect contiguous pieces of land in order to make a larger piece (Interviews 6/7.MBW, 6/17. MBW, 6/21.MBW, 6/29.LC, 9/14.SH, 9/15.BF).

Indeed, we heard more stories about combining tracts of land, and "buying back" tracts that had gone out of the family, than about farmers subdividing. (And, of course, residents tell in detail the history of the land's ownership, whether it has abided in their own families or not.) Residents do not have good things to say about subdividing the land.

> And it seems now, over the years, it has been sold. . . . some people just died off, you know. The kids didn't want to keep it up. . . . And a lot of it's probably greed! You know, they're after the money! (Interview 2/28.KLH)
>
> And I'm like my wife, I hate to see these farms split up and busted up and sold off five acres here or ten, or fifteen, and the people that come in and buy 'em don't want you having cows next to them, or chickens, or nothing else because they say they're noisy or stink or something. You know, they don't realize what we produce out here farming, they eat every dang day on their tables. (Interview 9/20.BD)

It's strange, every now and then a big farm will come up for sale and some of the local real estate agents will buy it and then subdivide, and you'll see all the signs along the roadside for ten acres and so forth. And a lot of times what happens, someone will come by who maybe didn't want a two hundred acre farm, but wanted fifty acres, will buy five of them, five of the ten acre lots to make fifty. [And for one example], oh I forget how many tracts they were going to have in there. And two people bought it all up, and it ended up only one little house was placed on the whole farm. And it basically looks like it did. So you know, I'm just delighted when this happens. (Interview 6/17.MBW)

Some residents are taking steps to ensure that their children and their children's children can stay on the land, or to assure that their land stays in one piece—that it is "not subdivided." Some of these steps use new means to keep the land in the undivided form that provides continuity between the past and the present. The residents talk of "family corporations," "conservation easements," and "fixing it where it can't be subdivided." Even residents without children are taking these steps, because they "just hated thinking about it going on in new hands and cutting out and putting trailers and subdivisions all over it" (Interview 6/7.MBW; see also Interview 6/17.MBW; 9/16.LU). We will return to these strategies in chapter 12. Others think about planting things that will eventually provide small amounts of income for future generations, such as sugar maple trees. A resident's great-grandfather piled rocks in his spare time as a legacy to the great-grandson, who now sells them to contractors in need of rock for building (Interview 6/9.SLV).

Another sacrifice, made at the county level, is less tax money because four of the five counties house National Forest land, which is not taxable. However, 25 percent of gross revenues collected by the Forest Service from timber sales, grazing fees, recreation, and mining is returned to the state, and then to the counties. In 2019, the counties received from $11,000 to $325,000 in payments, depending on the number of acres the Forest Service owns. But these payments aren't equivalent to what property taxes on private lands would be.

Residents make sacrifices to live in these rural areas, with their natural beauty, watering springs, and cultural and historical worth. Of the more than 1,200 stories that residents told us, 8 percent bore the theme of sacrifices people had made to live here. In a cynical light, these stories in praise of rural life could be viewed as a rationale for the "choice of the necessary," "an attempt to present one's way of life, about which one may have few choices, as a conscious preference" (Creed and Ching 1997:18, following Bourdieu 1984:372), but these sacrifices, or "inconveniences" as the residents call them, are spoken about as if they are genuinely gladly made. A more realistic question is whether the *children* of these residents are willing to make the same sacrifices. In Virginia as a whole, only 15 percent of the population is over sixty-five. In these rural counties, 22 to 23 percent are.

5

Using Place to Create and Maintain Historical Continuity

It's more than just the land; it's our legacy. It's our heritage. It really is.

Interview 6/29.LC

On the Progress side of the culture war, concern for things historical takes a backseat to providing the convenience of parking lots and new buildings. But in the rural cultures we learned about, the care for preserving history was palpable; it was a major "theme" or "core value." It is glossed by the residents as concern for "heritage" and attention to what the "old people" (early settlers and ancestors) did. There is a documented cultural history dating back 250 years in these valleys, and a partially documented prehistory of North American Indian cultures dating back ten thousand years. For many of the residents, maintaining the land as they described in the previous chapter maintains their family's legacy. The places where ancestors' and descendants' lives meet are a bridge spanning ties to the past and hopes for the future. In the words of Kent Ryden (1993:252), familiar places "provide a reassuring sense of the world's continuity and stability." Cross-cultural research shows that this relationship holds up in other cultures. For example, for the Kwaio people of the Solomon Islands, land is "structured by history." In central Australia and in northwest Greenland, the land embodies both present experience and the ancestral past (Klatka 1991; Keesing 1982:76; Morphy 1995; Munn 1970; Nuttall 1991).

Living in the Genealogical Landscape

[From my house] when I look out one way, I see where [my ancestors lived], and when I look out the other way, I see where my husband's lived.

Field Notes 6/7.MBW

He goes back to the Eastmans who settled here right at 1800, and I go back to the Grahams who were here in 1754. So the two families, his family and my family, lived side by side. So they owned five hundred acres—his did—right in here, and mine started in this direction and went on up the road.

Interview 6/17.MBW

Time and again, as residents swept their hands across a landscape, they would say a variation of, "From here to here, this has been in the family for generations"

(Interview 6/29.LC). The number of generations that can be accounted for goes back to twelve for the young people of some families.

"You know when you look around that you're seeing the same things they saw." This is how folklorist Lynwood Montell explains the importance of living in "the genealogical landscape" where the land is a carrier of social history—a "historical anchor that reaches several generations into the past." This "history is a representation that provides a matrix of meaning for the present." A community interviewing partner in Borden County explained the land-history connection: "What you see is the generations of your family life—not just land. Looking over the land is—for those whose long-term heritage is tied to this particular piece of land—looking not just at the land itself. The vantage point may overlook the path your grandmother's funeral procession took and the place where she was laid to rest in the family cemetery. It may overlook the place your mother and father came back to when they were first married." As a resident put it, "it means something to put down roots and to know your family—your people—have been here all this time." Another labels himself "deep-rooted" (Allen 1990:161; Hicks 1976:50; Foster 1988:36; Interview 9/24.RRE; 9/19.HCK).[1]

Rural mental health professional Val Farmer (2000:A6) says for "place-bound people," "the fascination with life involves teasing out historical connections, understanding the context of events and connecting people with people like a pedigree chart where everybody fits." Detailed and long-ranging knowledge of county history and family genealogies illustrates the inseparable link between land and culture here. Indeed, residents' knowledge of their own genealogies, and exactly where their ancestors had settled and lived on this land, is vast. Anthropologist Stephen Foster (1988:67), who studied in Ashe County, North Carolina, labeled the family history "an indigenous literary genre." For the sake of brevity, I'll use an example that goes only three generations back, rather than the seven, eight, nine, ten, or twelve generations that some residents recount. Sometimes the details can be confusing to the outsider, but they are clear as a bell to the native. Lois Osborne, a sixty-eight-year-old retired teacher who left her native Forsythe in Woodrow County and returned ten years ago, says:

> Well, my grandfather's family was originally from Allen County, and he was born in the house up the road about three miles, roughly three miles, Oak Grove, what was last known as the Tom Brown property. My grandfather was born in that house and the family, the Stones, had moved from Allen County prior to his birth. After he was married, he and my grandmother bought the farm that was where I was born, and it was bought from the Luths, and the land that we're on right now was my uncle's father and mother-in-law's farm, which they inherited, and they sold us this land. I heard when we came to Woodrow County, "People in Woodrow County buy land—they don't sell it." But because we were relatives we got this wonderful piece of land. (Interview T312 12/27.JB)

But residents also know the genealogies of families *other than their own* who lived in the county. Even residents who did not grow up in the county, and who have no relatives there, know the "genealogies" of their *houses,* and of their neighbors. They know them by heart and reel them off easily, with no prompting, as a natural adjunct to telling how they acquired their homes.[2]

The longevity in one place tends to make the tie to the land a family-like attachment: "Every tree, every creek, every building is not just a structure or a piece of nature, but a part of their family history. . . . When land has been owned by a family for so many generations, it ceases to be simply property: it moves from commodity to family member" (Usack 1994). A resident explained to us: "It's like another member of their family. It's almost as important to them as one of their children. To keep it, keep it in the family [is important]" (Interview 9/16.LU). The importance of keeping the land in the family is substantiated by this resident who sees the land as part of her living heritage and as a way to connect with her family. Lucy Palmer, a fifty-two-year-old life resident of Linwood Fork in Woodrow County who inherited the family's long-held farmland, says: "I feel that the land we own is a gift from God, for as long as we live. And even though it's ours for such a short time, I would not want to share it with anyone, so it would just be family that I would be willing to have on the land" (Interview T325 11/28.RM).

Dennis Patrick, a fifty-one-year-old lifelong resident of Farlane County who is heir to his family farm, says: "Well I guess it's kind of a heritage you have that your father instilled. This is your land . . . if you take care of your land, it will take care of you. It's just something I knew I was going to do when I was ten years old. That's why I want to stay here, keep my farm, and keep the Patrick farm going" (Interview 9/20.JPC).

For many residents, the genealogical landscape is both historical and contemporary in nature: their ancestors lived there; their relatives live there: "Everybody that I own in the world except my nephew is in Greenly County." "All of [the members of the family] live nearby; they live within two miles of us." "Everybody around I'm related to unless they just moved in" (Interview 7/20D.MS&SS; 6/28A.LC; 7/21B. MS&SS.).[3]

In each home we visited, with absolutely no prompting from interviewers, residents showed us artifacts and told us who had owned them previously. These treasured heirlooms included "documents," "parchment paper deeds," "liens against things," letters, logbooks and diaries, carpenter's tools and shoemaking tools, "a lot of tools from my grandfather," railroad lanterns, a cotton gin, a spinning wheel, a loom, a hundred-year-old plow, a bicycle wheel, horse collars, and "things horses pulled," rakes, tobacco cutters, "old razors and old dishes," quilts, butter churns, clocks, an old piece of chestnut with initials on it, a chest that once belonged to a slave, bricks made in Greenly County, "an old banjo in the family that's got a groundhog top," guns, and fishing poles.[4]

Deeds, especially—signifying long family ties to particular pieces of land—were objects of veneration. Eugene Puzey, a fifty-two-year-old resident who has been back in Linwood Fork for twenty-seven years, told the interviewer:

The first deeds to the farm were back in the 1700s. As far as we can tell, probably around 1781 was one of them. . . . In fact one of the deeds is the second deed recorded in Woodrow County in book 1, page 2 when the county was formed in 1861. And the farm has numerous deeds to it. It has been deeded back and forth to the family. Heirs have bought and sold. There are approximately twenty handwritten deeds here that we still have that were from most of the heirs that describe the transactions and the history. When my father died in 1981, we did a platting of the farm and took all the deeds in order to determine that the real estate was here before we bought the farm from my mother and my sisters. And we put it back together as far as the plat of 1,200 acres to verify what we had. This was all original land that was owned by the family somewhere. We're the sixth generation that lived here. (Interview T339 12/22.BM)

Each resident we visited in his or her home showed us family pictures, some dating back to the earliest photographs made. The photographs showed family members and other significant people, of course, but also automobiles, farm buildings, homes, and churches. We interviewed a few residents at their places of business, and were surprised to find family pictures there; these were not the pictures of immediate family that most of us keep in our work space, but heirloom photographs of family members from many generations past. (I recently attended a wedding in the area where the photographer took dozens of pictures of various family groupings, and no pictures of the wedding party per se.) As one resident listed items that belonged to his grandfather and great-grandfather, he assessed the cultural worth of the heirlooms and of the land itself: These are "things that help tie the family together, and are maybe not as important as the land, but are important in the same kind of way. Sentimental value. But the land has so many values—sentimental and practical both— that it's definitely the biggest tie" (Interview 9/16.LU).

Twenty-nine percent of the stories told to the interviewers by the residents concerned history. They told of the history of the family, or of the county, or they chronicled heirlooms. Another 14 percent of the stories concerned the doings of contemporary people in the county. When old-timers and newcomers alike talk about other residents, they show that they especially admire those who carry knowledge of the history of the land and the genealogies of its inhabitants. Those who know these old ways—the purposeful students-of-history and the relatively naive culture-bearers alike—are esteemed and discussed. Describing a person known for her mastery of local history, eleven-year resident Angela Griggs says: "Boy, is she interesting to sit and talk to! She can tell you, from the Civil War era on, who married whom, who was the daughter, who the daughter married, what kids they had, and where they lived, and where they went. And it's just fascinating!" (Interview 6/21. MBW).

Situated squarely on the Preservation side of the culture war, individuals, families, and organizations expend time, money, and effort to preserve history, including researching genealogies and deeds, recording local folktales, and protecting historic artifacts.[5] For example, a Greenly resident had typed and bound 206 pages of journal entries his grandfather wrote about the Greenly County of his day (Field Notes 6/24. MBW). Each county houses active historical societies, museums in renovated historic structures, and painstakingly compiled books of local history, cultural landmarks, church histories, and cemetery catalogs. Extensive oral history and photo preservation projects supported by the local museums and schools and partially funded by state and national grants have been underway for several years in Woodrow and Borden Counties. In Greenly and Farlane Counties, local historians have extensively mapped their communities. A Farlane County local historian has mapped the land ownership from the time of the first white settlers including each subsequent change in land ownership up to today. Twenty-seven farms in the five counties have applied for and received recognition as "Virginia Century Farms"—currently working farms that have been owned by the same family for at least one hundred years. Localities in Greenly and Farlane Counties undertook the onerous task of applying for recognition as historic districts. Ongoing traditions like family reunions, church homecomings, agricultural fairs, and fall festivals link the past with the present.

Newcomers soon catch the history bug. A husband and wife who have no ancestry in Greenly but have lived there for twenty-four years tell about the cemetery close to their house. From memory, they recite the detail that is written on the stones. "One of the graves is marked 1817?" asks the wife. "1816," her husband corrects her (Interview 6/14.MBW). The same couple have photos in their home of the family who built the home—to whom they are not related. They have decorated with local artifacts, and know the origins of each one. Even though she is not a native, the current owner of a fish hatchery knows when it was built and its entire history since (Field Notes 6/21.MBW). She says: "I understand that this place has more history—on its own— than I have with it. I mean there's a lot of people that will come by because their mother or father brought them here when they were kids and they've got a lot of fond memories" (Interview 6/21.MBW). Like her, other newcomers see the longevity of the community and the concern for history as unique and count them among the elements that attracted them and that attach them to this place. Oscar Payne, an Ohio native who has been in Farlane County for five years, says:

> And we really fell into it . . . the richness of the community. And the people have really quite fascinating family histories. . . . Their families have ancestors up here for 200 years. . . . They have a strong sense of that history. (Interview 9/19.MED)
>
> And I think we happened upon a very unique place. We looked over in Dennison Valley and so on. My sense is it wouldn't be anything, maybe almost as beautiful, but it wouldn't be anything like . . . that sense of community, like the people, like that really very long history. (Interview 9/19. MED)

Taking Pride in the Old People

They just didn't waste any motion, those old people didn't.

Interview 6/7.MBW

The sheer amount of talk about life in the counties' pasts demonstrates the salience of history. But it is not just an object of interest. The "old people" are virtually revered. The "old people" is the residents' label for ancestors, especially in Greenly. But it doesn't necessarily refer to one's own ancestors; it refers to the people who settled and lived in this land in earlier days. When speaking of their *own* ancestors, residents are more likely to use specific kin terms, for example, "my great-great-great grandfather." The residents who have spent a lifetime in the county, as well as some newcomers, told the interviewers, in great detail, how the "old people" (and sometimes they themselves) used to build houses and barns; farm grain; care for farm animals; butcher hogs and cattle; smoke meat; preserve vegetables and fruit; start and build churches; and get themselves to market, to church, and to school (or the impossibility of getting to school). They told how the ground was plowed, how grain was threshed and flour and corn meal ground, how cotton cloth was woven, how butter was churned, how cottage cheese and ice cream were made, how homing pigeons were kept. They told how the old people sold produce to get cash for taxes, even though they would have liked to have eaten it themselves. They told about the artifacts the old people used (many of which they still had), and the techniques for using them.[6]

Residents report musing about what the counties' settlers did. One says "[when we were a] group of kids, we used to take great pleasure in whatever our ancestors had done just to see what it was like. To mimic it just to see what it was like" (Interview T301 11/27.JD).

> I go down to the overlook on the mountain. . . . And I wonder what kind of hardships they had to go through to get to this place, and try to imagine Silverton as a possible fort that George Washington visited. So I get up here and I picture what life would have been in 1753 and 1801 and 1865. (Interview 6/17.MBW)
>
> I often wonder what those first people that came in here felt about the land and where they cleared that first piece of land . . . Just how they . . . knew which land, which pieces were going to be productive. Why they didn't ever clear anything here on this ridge that doesn't have good land on it. (Interview 9/18.DNS)

Activities that took more effort and time without modern technology are one source of marveling about the inhabitants of an earlier day: "To go to —— City, they used to use a team of horses. . . . Two days it would take them to cross the mountain [with] four horses and a wagon." "Used to cut hay with a hand scythe . . . and a pitchfork . . . and it'd take a week to cut it and stack it and put it away, and nowadays you can run over it with a tractor in one day and bale it the next." "They just didn't waste any motion," a resident says of the "old people," as she and another resident exchange stories of the way the earlier settlers conserved water and effort and yet accomplished amazing feats with little technology, such as building stone walls and fences and hauling a steam threshing machine up a narrow road to a steep farm (Interviews 7/18.SS&MS; 6/21.MBW; Field Notes 6/7.MBW). The same farm was the object of conversation in another interview, when Ted Rohrer, a resident of ten years who farms and sells real estate, said: "At that farm, at some places it's only thirty feet wide and it straddles a mountain and it illustrates what incredible lengths the [old people would] go to maintaining a farm. It's just a farm where no farm should be, but there it is. Incredible—and you can see the hard work just sticking out of it everywhere" (Interview 7/04.AM). Feats of know-how are known, commented about, and respected. Pointing to a rock in a stone retaining wall built by one of the "old people," a resident tells a neighbor: "I bet that rock will weigh 600 or 800 pounds or maybe 1,000 pounds. . . . They slid it in from above . . . You wonder how. I guess it's the leverage and knowing how." "They just knew how to do it," the neighbor agrees. Another of the "old people" is admired because "she knew all the herbs and plants that was good for your health and sickness." And "those old people could cook" (Interviews 6/7.MBW; 6/14.MBW).

Another source of awe about the old people are the "horror stories about the early settlers and the things that went on around here" (Interview 6/17.MBW). The "old people" are admired for their fortitude in the face of hardship. For example, the members of a family "are all buried down there under that tree. . . . He died during the war and his widow lived over here with I think nine children, and six of them got sick, and six died in six months, and three of them in one week" (Interview 6/17.MBW).

Besides hard work, technical know-how, and fortitude, the current residents admire their forebears' attention to learning. They told how the "old people" created poetry in beautiful handwriting; kept track of the weather, finances, and county business in logbooks; and of the efforts they made to go to school. An often-told story was about a Greenly County resident who was "the first student that registered at the college. And he walked from over here [a distance of more than twenty-five miles]; they lived in that big house on this ridge out here" (Interviews 6/14.MBW; 6/24. MBW; 6/7.MBW).

An additional clue to the importance of history here are the efforts spent on maintaining and refurbishing old homes and buildings.

Maintaining and Restoring Material Culture

See those things are all bored and keyed in with pins. They wasn't *nailed* up, see there.

Interview 6/7.MBW

A farmer is showing me a barn that he has refurbished. He carefully used the same carpentry methods that the "old people" (in this case, his own ancestors) who built it used: "I tell you, it's a lot of boring and hollowing and chiseling out" (Interview 6/7. MBW). Ronald Patrick, a sixty-three-year-old farmer, tells of a house that was born, not only of the old people's sweat, as many are, but also literally of the dirt of Greenly County. In fact, the farmer speaks of the house as being "born," like his grandfather, rather than "built":

> The main nice story to tell about the farm that my brother owns . . . is that the bricks for that farm—for that brick house there—were made right there. . . . They were made when our grandfather was six. He hauled them in a wagon, you know. He rode the wagon and they baked them down at the house. Must have been four or five hundred yards from where they made them to the house. He rode them in the wagon. He was born in 1866, the house in 1872. (Interview 9/16.JH)

In Greenly, the local historian says that if you scratch most of these old houses, you'll find a log cabin underneath that has been framed over. At least 250 homes and 100 barns and outbuildings in Greenly County are more than seventy-five years old. In the five counties, from 17 to 24 percent of the houses date from prior to 1939, compared to just 5 percent of the houses in nearby Daley County, which surrounds (but does not include) the nearest city.

Burial in the Genealogical Landscape

You see, the funny thing is, that even though we enjoy living in this county, it's welcoming to be buried here.

Interview 6/9.SLV

The residents express their concerns and hopes for the future by talking about their own mortality, their children and their children's children, and the future of the counties themselves. In each case, the land looms large in their talk. Being buried in the genealogical landscape is important. Residents sometimes took us on tours that included the cemetery where they knew their bones would one day rest. For some, these cemeteries already hold the remains of generations of their family members. But newcomers, too, had chosen their burial grounds, and these were planned as resting places for future generations of their families (Interview 6/7.MBW; 6/9.SLV; 6/24.MBW). Ruth Haley, who was a newcomer thirty-eight years ago, reports: "Now I'm like all the rest of them. I wouldn't leave anyway since we purchased our cemetery down there. A little lot we purchased and when I leave this house that's where I'm going" (Interview 6/15.MS&SS). Lawrence Miles, a veteran of the Persian Gulf War, has the same visceral need to be buried in the unchanged land of Greenly County. He points to a place on his family's land:

I wrote home during the war and told my little brother if something happened to me, I wanted them to bury me right here. And that rock pile—[that my great-granddaddy piled up when he was clearing this land]—is going to be my tombstone. . . . I want to be *here*. . . . That was one of the things that really worried me during the war, and I went and talked to the chaplain about it. I could tell by how he was answerin' my questions—he was worried—he was thinkin' I was worried about dyin'. I says, "Sir, I don't want to die, but that's not one of my concerns. I'm going to do my job and if that's what happens, it happens. It *is* my concern whether I end up rottin' here." I says, "I don't want my soul's container to be left here. I want to get *home*." I said, "Now, that's what matters to *me*." He said, "Well, there's no guarantee, but there is every effort made." So that's all I can ask. And so that was what worried me was being *left* there. Because, I mean, the desert, even at its least, is a unique place, and I think that it is a beautiful place, but it's also an inhospitable place. And it's not my *home*. (Interview 6/23.SLV)

Land Is Freedom in an African American Community

Discussing using place to establish identity in chapter 3 separately from maintaining historical continuity in this chapter has been a convenience for the writer and the reader, but the two glide into each other. One of the most poignant connections between past history of the land and its current meaning is in the community of Clearview, where, in the words of a local historian, "land equals freedom." Clearview is a predominantly African American community in Woodrow County. The details of its founding are well-known to all residents. In the words of Ella Carter, a sixty-year-old native of Clearview who went to the Midwest to work and has retired to the home place:

My grandfather. Now, one of my brothers says that he was a slave. . . . He was turned loose as a slave and he had a horse—a horse or a sack of flour or something that they gave him when they turned him loose. . . . He came to Cranston County and then I guess he . . . heard about this property and came in here. . . . His property here is two hundred forty-seven and three-quarters acres here. He also owned a piece of property down the road that once was called Crandall Place. (Interview T303 10/31.JD)

The local historian told us:

This community was founded by freed slaves. . . . Land was the guarantor of freedom. . . . The main families, are still there. . . . The Carters, the Woods, the Settles, and the Yates. The families are still there . . . many of them lived on this original 220-some-acre tract. They have not divided it [legally]. It's still one piece. Because it's very important that his original tract that

William Yates got, remain in one piece. . . . They're not dividing it. . . . And to me that relationship is extremely powerful. And these people . . . many of them had to leave [to work in industry], and they've come back. But many of them are still there. (Interview T338 02/13/00.RUCart)

To make a living and be able to keep the land, families farmed, gathered, hunted, and worked as laborers on neighboring white-owned farms. Men worked in the coal fields and on railroads and returned home on weekends. During the Depression working for moonshiners was profitable. Women worked as domestics for white professionals in a nearby city. In order to maintain the land intact, it has been passed back and forth among different family members who could afford to keep it at different points in time. George Settle, a seventy-nine-year-old man who has also returned from work in the Midwest, explains:

Well, from a kid up, old enough to remember, my grandfather come in here and . . . bought over 200 acres in here in slavery . . . and so it was handed down, some of them was able to pay for it, some wasn't, so what they did, the ones that couldn't pay for it, they would take it back and let the other one have it. . . . So my grandfather bought fifty acres, and he let his sister have it. She couldn't pay for it, so then he took it back and let my daddy have it, so my daddy bought another fifty acres joining it. It made him a hundred acres down at this other place. . . . That's our home place, that's where I was born at and raised on the other property down there. . . . I claim two farms. I claim my granddaddy's farm, and I claim my daddy's farm because we're all one and the same. . . . They bought it separate. . . . I inherited two pieces of property. . . . Then my grandmother died, and then they divided it up, and so my other uncles and aunts got part of it, and my daddy got this part. He bought his brother out and got this part, and this is the part that he gave me. I asked him for it, and he gave it to me. (Interview T309 11/14.JD)

The meaning of this land—"247.7" or "247 and ¾" acres—is rendered poetic in the words of Oscar Sheldon, a forty-seven-year-old man who served a stint in the military and returned to the home place, making his living as a government worker. He is speaking of the original boundary "line" between land owned by white residents and land bought by Black settlers:

In our original I'll call it "land grant" or our original settlement, it starts at the Fred Settle line. From there, I don't know, there is a feeling that comes over you. I can't convey to you, coming in when you hit that line, there is a feeling, "I am at home." And the peace, the serenity, the pride, is something that just wells up within me. The casual viewer might not even see it. The mountains, when I look and see the head of the mountains I know I am coming home. In the winter sometimes I look and they're snowcapped, and the rest of the mountains coming down, just looking at the beauty of it, it brings me a peace. And the snow cap on the top of the mountains is like someone with wisdom, like I am looking at an old friend, like a mentor. This is the way that I see. To take you in and show you—the average citizen that doesn't live there—probably wouldn't see too much, they wouldn't see the same things I see: the history, the memories. It speaks to me. (Interview T301 11/27.JD)

6

Using Place to Build and Maintain Living Community

America's Alter Ego

These little family farms are really the core of America. This is where it all started.

Interview 6/21.MBW

Rural Appalachia is consistently seen as a "world apart," the "other America," even as archaeologists, historians and demographers compile data that suggest that it never was as isolated as it was thought to be.[1] Farms, fields, mountains, meadows, woods, and the cultures that reside there provide urban and suburban America with its symbolic alter ego. Cottagecore/Farmcore/Countrycore, a visual and lifestyle movement that idolizes the softer parts of pastoral life, has 151 million mostly young followers on the TikTok social media platform (Wylde 2020). Discussing the impact of the decline in ranching, Patricia Nelson Limerick, a University of Colorado historian, says, "It's a big piece of what Americans would like to think that they once were and still retain some part of" (Tomsho 1998). This is even more true for the Appalachian farmer, whose agrarian life combine(s)(ed) hunting and gathering in the forest with domestication and cultivation. The Appalachian farmer's way of life—domesticating animals and cultivating the soil, hunting and gathering, timbering for firewood, sometimes timber-cutting for income—combines the woodsman with the yeoman farmer in symbolism. (The popular vision, however, sees Appalachia as "wilder" than it is—both naturally and culturally [Wagner et al. 1986].)

But lest anyone think that with this discussion we are merely raising a sometimes romanticized vision to an academic level, Barlett (1993:253) notes: "Writers who dismiss the national homage to the family farm as romantic nostalgia for a simpler, pre-industrial past fail to acknowledge its roots in frustrations with the industrial life.... Family farms represent a kind of human cooperation and commitment to neighborly principles." As the US economy changes, "Americans can expect to see new orienting values arise and find acceptance."[2] The rural experience may be the incubator for these values.[3]

And while the otherness may be exaggerated to make a better fit for the alter ego, there are certainly differences between rural and urban and suburban lifestyles.

Community versus Communitas

A model that may be instructive in analyzing why urban America looks to rural America and rural Appalachia, and what it expects to find here, is anthropologist Victor Turner's delineation of *community* and *communitas*. *Community* is Turner's label for a society's social structure. It is a norm-governed, institutionalized, and abstract structure that delineates how people behave toward one another according to the roles they play. *Communitas,* on the other hand, represents spontaneous, immediate, and concrete relationships among human beings as human beings rather than as role bearers. Communitas suggests not what is (that is social structure), but what could be; it is the crucible that holds human potentialities and universal human values. It is existential and speculative. Turner (1969:203) sets forth the idea that society "needs" both: "Society seems to be a process rather than a thing—a dialectical process with successive phases of structure and communitas. There would seem to be—if one can use such a controversial term—a human 'need' to participate in both modalities."

This could be said to be akin to "culture" seeking after "nature" (or "absence of culture"), with the caveat that *communitas* is opposed both to acting only in terms of the rights and obligations conveyed by virtue of a role in the social structure and to "following one's psychobiological urges at the expense of one's fellows" (Turner 1969:105).

Some societies seek communitas in rituals, where, for the moment, the rules of social structure are loosened, abandoned, or made to stand on their heads. In ritual, the structural underdog becomes the symbolically superior. The structural "boss man" undergoes penance to achieve an experience of communitas. The states reached in rituals imply "that the high could not be high unless the low existed, and he who is high must experience what it is like to be low" (Turner 1969:97).

Urban America seeks communitas in rural America. Rather than experiencing communitas through rituals that pass through a "liminal" state (a state of transition, or marginality, or being on the threshold), urban America looks to rural America, and by looking, experiences a sort of vicarious liminality.

But why is America's alter ego to be found particularly in rural Appalachia? Appalachia is on the American mind.[4] Some clues to why can be found in the characteristics that Turner finds are common to representatives of communitas. Turner's examples of bearers of communitas include court jesters, holy mendicants, Good Samaritans, seekers belonging to millenarian movements, beatniks and hippies, and matrilateral kin in patrilineal systems. The roles these persons play represent the "soft," the personal, the morally and ritually (as opposed to structurally) true. I don't know why Turner didn't think to include Appalachian farm cultures in his list of examples, because they seem to fit on many counts. If we look at the traits that Turner finds are characteristic of carriers of communitas, we'll see that many actually apply to Appalachia, and all have been attributed to Appalachia.

The millenarians and hippies Turner uses as examples show that it is persons who occupy a weak position in the society's social structure who represent communitas. The structural underdog is morally and ritually superior. Secular weakness is sacred power. Thus, Appalachia's economic and political position in the society—its place as an internal colony (Lewis 1970, 1978) or as a satellite for the metropolis (Jorgensen 1971) or as part of a peripheral economy (Walls 1978) or as a national sacrifice zone (Fox 1999; Kuletz 1998; Scott 2010)—helps to make it a repository of communitas. The family farmer's precarious place in the economy stands him in good stead to play the communitas role.

Turner implies that the way individuals relate to one another differs in community and communitas. The community here—urban America—is known for its individualism, for the expression of "self," and for relationships that are largely "secondary," partial, and segmented, governed by the rules of roles.[5] We Americans are quite familiar with this individualism that characterizes modern Western societies, but it is said to be exceptional among the world's cultures.[6] What is the alternative? At the risk of oversimplifying the world's diversity, let me describe a dichotomy between individualism and an alternative we might call *communalism,* or a collective orientation. For examples, we can look to some of the North American Indian groups, peoples of the Pacific, and people closer to home, such as the Hutterites, the Amish, and subcultures within Appalachia where "familism" or a "person orientation" are thought to abide.[7] Let us look at various aspects of these two ways of being in order to clarify the dichotomy.

In individualistic societies, there is a "task orientation" as opposed to the "person orientation" that is common in collective societies where there is an overriding concern with making things go smoothly within the group. What this means is, if you are confronted with the choice between accomplishing a task *and* hurting someone's feelings, versus *not* accomplishing a task *and not* hurting someone, you will tend to choose the former if you are a member of an individualistic society. The latter choice is exemplified by anecdotes from the Appalachian Mountain region. For example, a Presbyterian minister tells of wanting to fix the road to his newly assigned church. With the elders of the church, he discusses getting slag, a by-product of coal mining, from the coal companies free of charge. Subsequently he has the slag laid onto the road, and on the first rainy day, it turns to a slimy, slippery mess that eventually has to be bulldozed away. He asks the elders, "Why didn't you tell me this would happen?" They reply, "Well, Reverend Weller, you seemed to want to do it, and we didn't want to hurt your feelings" (Weller 1965).[8]

The modes of identity associated with these two orientations differ, as well. American culture, especially in recent years, has been noted for its expressions of "selfhood." In collective societies, on the other hand, a person's identity is ultimately bound up with the community; the self is a product of the collectivity. Kai Erikson (1976:86) discusses the embeddedness of the self in the collectivity in Appalachia this way: "One's stature in the community as well as one's inner sense of well-being is derived largely from the position one occupies in a family network [and in peer groups] and to step out of that embracing surround would be like separating from one's own flesh." People invest much of themselves in the commonality and become "absorbed by it." "The larger collectivity around you becomes an extension of your own personality, an extension of your own flesh."

Dorothy Lee (1986:12) would label this the "open self": "In such societies, though the self and the other are differentiated, they are not mutually exclusive. The self contains some of the other, participates in the other, and is in part contained within the other." The difference between individualistic and collective identities has been likened to the difference between eggs hard-boiled together in a pan, and eggs fried sunny-side up. The (egg white) identity stays separate in the first case, and becomes one in the second. (Although, just as the egg yolks remain separate in both pans, so in both kinds of societies individuals have their own egos.)

Thus, social structure and communitas represent two sides of a coin reflecting ways people perceive and play out relationships among themselves. Our research revealed a communitas-like set of relationships among the rural people we learned from.

Living Community

On our farm, that [place is] where I go to count the cattle, check the neighbors, check out the weather, stare around, communicate with nature, right there.

Interview 9/16.JH

These rural areas are home for "communities of residence." The relationship between community and place is a powerful one—each reinforces the identity of the other. "Feelings of commitment and identity are most likely to occur among people sharing the same piece of ground." Cross-cultural research supports the idea that the land can function to create and cement relationships among people. For the Piro of Amazonian Peru, "the land is an aspect of kinship," and "they use the land in their relations with other people." For Australian "aboriginal people, land is humanized, it's social, it's read in social terms" (Relph 1976:33; Gow 1995:47–48; C. Anderson 1992:82; Birckhead 1996).

But to our suburban-born student researchers, the relationships people in these rural areas had with one another—relationships that had the land as their reason for being—were extraordinary. Most of them had grown up in a world where friendships are made, not from common *residence* or care for a particular piece of ground, but by virtue of meeting at an *institution*—the workplace, or the school, or perhaps the church. Neighbors, for them, were rarely linked in the way that they heard about here. Yet again, we do not wish to portray the residents we interviewed as insular and isolated. Three-fifths of the farmers in these counties have jobs that put them into contact with people other than neighbors and kin some of the time. Lichter and Brown (2011:567) argue that "drawing sharp rural-urban distinctions" is problematic due to a set of drivers that have blurred the boundaries, including "information technology, globalization, and governmental devolution," as well as "past technological innovations" (e.g., railroads, interstate highways, and air transportation). Tilly

(1973:236), in an attack on the limitations of the social science community/society dichotomy, notes that while "local ties have diminished little or not at all, extralocal ties have increased." "The *balance* between 'relations of presence' [local ties, communities of residence] and 'relations of absence' [extralocal ties, communities of interest] has moved in the direction of the latter. But this has not led to the demise of place" (Agnew 1989:24).

Robert N. Bellah, a chronicler of American individualism, notes with his coauthors (Bellah et al. 1985) that we even lack a language of community: our many words, phrases, and mottoes that express individualism overwhelm the few that convey a communal bent. But in these rural counties, there is a "language of the land" through which rural residents express their relationships with each other via their relationships to the land.[9] For example, the work on the land, primarily cattle farming, forges connections between people. (When my husband and I sought to buy land in a rural county, sellers instructed us to somehow get connected with cattle—even if it was having only one cow—so that we would be able to talk to the neighbors.) Thus, there is a "shared language and understanding of farming" (Delicate 1994). Even though the land no longer provides the sole livelihood for most of these residents, it continues to function in this symbolic and relational sense.

Mobility, of course, fosters the general trend away from communities of residence. The difference between the genealogical landscape and the annually relocated life that nearly 20 percent of Americans lead is captured every December 15 or so, when one or another of my colleagues who grew up in this area asks me if I've done my Christmas shopping yet. I reply, "Oh yes, I had to mail presents to my family in Maine, New York, Rhode Island, Illinois, Colorado, and California earlier this month to make sure they got there on time." My colleague says, "Really? I've never mailed a Christmas present in my life. My family's all here." In the United States, 53 percent of the people over five years old lived in the same house in 1990 that they did in 1985. In Cranston, Farlane, Greenly, Woodrow, and Borden Counties, 75 to 81 percent did. Morse and Mudgett (2018) researched the experience of staying in one place. Just as with our residents, contented stayers valued landscape and community, and exercised a variety of forms of mobility to ultimately stay put. Place-based factors and family ties were the main reasons for staying. The land itself plays a part in establishing and maintaining rural communities.

Land as Social Space

> It's a very close-knit community. And most of the farms in this immediate area have been in the families for generations.
>
> Interview 6/29.LC

As we have noted, ties to the land that are economically based are not missing in these counties. Although the exact boundaries of some large mountainous tracts may not be clear, most residents know how much land they own, some down to very specific detail, like a resident who reported owning "9 and 53/100s of an acre here" (Wingfield 1994). (The specificity of knowledge of place ownership is familiar to me. I knew that we farmed "113 acres of Indiana sandy loam" before I could spell my name.)

But, more than an economic matrix, the land in these counties functions for its inhabitants as "social space." The land binds people by virtue of the links in the chain of title to ownership; or the group work needed to maintain it; or the produce distributed from it. Daily cultural activities that take place in the enduring environment connect the revered past to the quotidian present and help to tie the people of this place to one another. These activities include orienting by the social matrix, using the place-names, and participating in reciprocal work and exchanges.

Orienting by the Social Matrix

Unless someone's moved in, I can drive down the road and tell you who lives in almost every house.

Interview 7/21B.MS&SS

The genealogical landscape extends beyond knowing the link between one's own ancestry and the chain of title to one's own land. As Barbara Allen (1990) notes, when mountain natives are talking to one another, route numbers and intersections never come up (Field Notes 6/7.MBW). They navigate by, and identify with, geological features and historical circumstances that have marked the land with cultural meaning. The human connection to the land is the orienting force to be reckoned with. Of course, when a native is giving directions to a stranger, he may use route numbers—if he can recall them to mind, since he doesn't use them himself. He is more likely to use a part of the social matrix like "the old red barn": "This old barn down here was kind of a landmark. They call it the old red barn; it's not red anymore because the paint is off of it, but anybody's asking directions they'd say, 'Go to the old red barn'" (Interview 7/20C.MS&SS). Even when giving directions to a stranger, residents fall back on the social matrix. David Evans drove me around a section of Greenly County, knowing that I did not know the roads and needed to be oriented. But when we came back onto a certain road, he said, "Now we're on Leo's road again." He didn't say, "Now we're back on Route ——" (Field Notes 6/7.MBW). One of our interviewers reported becoming lost on his way to an interview: "I pulled into a gas station to make sure I was headed in the right direction. At first, when I asked the lady working there if she knew where the road was, she did not know. But once she asked me the name of who I was looking for, she gladly helped me out" (Wingfield 1994). A poem by Appalachian poet Jeff Daniel Marion highlights the land/people connection by describing the way directions are likely to be given.

It's just
over the knob
there—

you know the place,
the one
up there next to
Beulah Justice,
your mother's second cousin
on her daddy's side.
Or
if you go in by
the back road
it's the farm across the way
from Jesse's old barn
that burned down
last June
with them 2 fine mules
of his.
Why hell, son,
you can't miss it. (Marion 1976)

Using the Place-Names

Local landmarks have been indelibly marked with the names of the families who first came to, and continue to live in the county, and what they have done there.

Delicate 1994

Place-names symbolize both the genealogical and the geological landscape. "Place names, linked with landscape features, encode the shared past, distinguishing members of one group from another. . . . Places and their names are sources of identity and security" (Hufford 1987:21–22).[10] Familiarity with local landscape features emerged throughout the interviews. As many as thirty different words for particular place names could be used in a single interview. As people identify themselves as from "Heath Creek," and their neighbors as from "up Stanley Creek," and gaze upon "Arch's Knob," they daily make a connection between the present and the past. Settlements and landforms are named for people who were a part of the county's history, a history familiar to the residents. Frank Dudley, sixty-six, who was born in another county and has returned to the area of Greenly most of his family called home, says: "My great-great-great-grandfather received a grant from the king of England just before the Revolutionary War started. His name was Elton Bradford and Elton's Creek is named for him" (Interview 6/24.MBW).

Until recently the county roads were officially designated by numbers. With the advent of 911 emergency identification, it was necessary to erect signs with the *names* of the roads. When the official name conflicted with the natives' traditional one, residents presented petitions to county governments to have the road names changed (usually successfully).

Forging Links by the Chain of Ownership

If I had a day when I could do anything I wanted to, nothing needed to get done,
where would I go? I would ride around on the farm and look over the property
and probably spend the day with my daddy.

Interview 6/29.LC

The link between the generations of kin is forged by blood and by land—the older
generation has worked to acquire or maintain it—the younger generation has grown
up on it. Many interviewees carry in their heads memories of long chains of title for
land that has been in their families for generations. Kin connections were often
described in past, present, and future contexts. Some residents received their land
from ancestors, lived on the land with kin, and preserved the land for future generations. As many as thirty-seven different kin terms were used in a single interview.
These included terms like *mother, mama, granny, grandpa, dad, nephew, aunt, uncle,
daughter, baby sister, oldest brother,* and *sister-in-law* and specific names like Aunt Ida
and Uncle John.

> Every house that I have been into in Woodrow County, family is a big thing.
> I mean there are family pictures everywhere . . . pictures for every occasion.
> Not just special pictures of weddings. . . . I've got a picture in my living room
> of my little boy. He's sitting in a wash tub out under the tree. . . . There are
> just pictures for everything and they don't put their pictures in an album
> and put them up someplace. They're displayed. Family means a lot to people
> in Woodrow County. They're proud of it. (Interview T338 02/13.RUCart)

Family reunions—on the family land—serve to preserve the memories of the links in
the chain of title. Residents of Swanson in Farlane County told us:

> Well, we have a reunion every three years. This summer there were three
> Howard reunions . . . Too big for one reunion. . . . close to a hundred people
> at each one of them. My mother was one of seventy-two first cousins. . . .
> One of the people . . . well I guess he's my generation, has figured out how
> many fourth cousins and on down we are. . . . I'm working on some geneal-
> ogy trying to update what's already been done. (Interview 9/18.DNS)
>
> Yeah, we have a family reunion here every three years sometimes. My
> great-grandfather's descendants. Of course this is where he built this house,
> so we have the reunion here. (Interview 9/17.JAE)

Kin obligations sometimes call back to the farm family members who have left to
find better jobs. Daisy Simmons, a farmer and retired teacher who has been back on
the farm for sixty-six of her eighty-seven years, remembers: "We had to come back to
take care of Grandmother and the farm when he [Grandfather] passed away. . . . They

called Frank to come. . . . Granddaddy lived about a month after that. And of course there's nobody on the farm to look after anything. We had to come right in the middle of the school year. We didn't go back after Christmas, the children and I. Frank went and packed our things in the truck and moved us back [here to the farm] in January" (Interview T326 12/24.BM).

The tie between successive owners of the same piece of land extends even to those who are *not* also linked by kinship. When showing us their homes, the "newcomers" would display pictures of their houses before they began renovating or building anew, and pictures of the people who had owned this home before. They would discuss this family—whose only connection to them was the land they had owned in common—in detail, as if it were their own family.

Sometimes the attachments weaving together the land and the people who live on it develop into the practice that anthropologists call "fictive kinship." In this extension of the genealogical landscape, fictive kinship is constructed for those who take on the needs and obligations of a kinship role, but who are not actually kinspersons. For example, some outsiders who moved into Greenly County bought the house of an elderly woman and let her remain there after they moved in. Originally and actually, their only tie was the house and land itself. The two families in the household cared for each other, physically and emotionally, as if they were kin, and came to see each other as kin. Since the older woman has passed away, her blood kin and her fictive kin have remained close. Residents reported calling older neighbors "aunt" and "uncle." While that practice is not as much in evidence today, diminutives—symbolizing bonds of familiarity—are: Iola is Olie, Lida is Lidie, Charles is Charlie (Interview 6/28B.LC); (Field Notes 6/14.MBW).

Working Together on the Land

I wouldn't hesitate to call a soul around here, because I know they would say, "Yeah, I'll be there as soon as I can."

Interview 6/17.MBW

Student researchers noted that work done collectively on the family's land brought *kinspeople* together. They contrasted this to work done individually in urban areas, which served to keep family members apart for as long as they are in the workplace (and nepotism rules that prohibit kin in the workplace). But there are also things that need to be done on a farm that one farmer or one family can't do, especially when the season and the weather necessary for getting them done are short and unpredictable. This work brings *neighbors* together. The work that neighbors do on each other's land functions as an adhesive. Diana Sled, a Greenly native in her thirties, tells what she recalls from her youth:

The thing that I always remember is when I was a little girl and Daddy was out working in the hayfields. We could start home, and it could take us two hours to get home. Because we'd drive by one place where they might have cattle that they were trying to get in, and Daddy would stop and help. And then we might drive on down the road to maybe Jones' or Patrick's, and then they would have to stand and talk and visit, and then say, "Would you like for me to help you with that?" And that's what this community is like as a whole, everyone working together helping one another. It's a very close-knit community. And most of the farms in this immediate area have been in the families for generations. (Interview 6/29.LC)

Others gave more specific examples of neighbors helping neighbors live and work on the land:

The fence that went down the side of our property . . . [was 225 feet]. A board fence down through there. [The neighbors] took that up in a day. All the neighbors came and helped, and had a fencing. And one year, the first summer that we were there, they put it up across the back. And the next year they put it down the side. And they did all the way down the side in one day. I thought that was amazing. (Interview 6/29.LC)

So we learned some [about making money stretch over longer periods of time in a business with no regular paychecks] from the neighbors because most of the neighbors are doing agriculture and farming. (Interview 6/21. MBW)

The activities that residents reported giving and receiving help with included mowing hay, baling hay, getting advice on when to mow and bale hay, spreading lime, loading sheep's wool into rail cars, feeding cattle, castrating pigs, grafting trees, learning about apple tree varieties, removing fence, building fence, plowing snow from lanes, learning to handle finances without a regular salary, finding and corralling cattle that had gotten out, kicking storm-downed corn back into the rows so that it could be picked, building a stove and learning to use one, repairing damage from storms, moving vehicles, getting water, keeping pets, cutting hair, and "everybody watches out for everybody's cattle."[11]

Keeping an eye out for neighbors—"We look out for each other"—is a habit. Farmers have places on their land where they "go to count the cattle, check the neighbors" (Interview 9/16.JH). "[I would like to] just get away from everything. So I go over there and maybe talk to the cows. That sounds strange, but I enjoy checking them out, the ones I'm going to sell or the ones I recently bought. Just walk around over the farm or maybe just go over and talk to the neighbors. See if they're having problems or how they're getting along with the farm. Maybe visit the country store" (Interview 9/15.BF).

The residents most often discuss their neighbors' willingness to help in terms of problematic situations, times of trouble, and times of tragedy. I attended a gathering recently in Borden where the gravel road to the hostess's house was filled with some twenty-five cars. An hour into the party, two neighbors appeared at the door to inquire whether everything was all right—was someone ill? A few minutes later another neighbor called to ask the same thing. A Greenly County resident says: "We have really good neighbors. In the last big snow a neighbor came with a big four-wheel-drive tractor and cleared our road" (Interview 6/28B.LC). Woodrow County residents have snow problems, too:

> We've had . . . big blizzards in Woodrow County and all of the VDOT trucks . . . they're concentrating on the Interstate. So, that left our community to fend for itself. . . . Our community was kind of cut off for about a week there. Tom Long has bulldozers . . . and broke the road for the whole community. Every road—scraped the driveway, did everything, so that people could get out, because we had been in about a week and we were without electricity at the time. And I know that when some of the neighbors—who had four wheel drives—could get out and go to the store, they called all their other neighbors around to see if you needed anything. If you did, they picked it up for you when they went out. (Interview T338 02/13.RUCart)

In Borden County several farmers took turns milking an injured farmer's cows for several months until he recovered. Another Borden County dairy farmer told us about the morning his barn caught fire.

> We had all the cattle in a big barn there. Had to go out there and try to get them out . . . Turned them all out, turned them all out together—that was the problem. . . . I chased them around in the barn; they just kept going around in circles; they wouldn't go out the daggone gate. . . . Smoke was getting in there. You couldn't hardly see where you was going, but I finally got them to go out.
>
> The unique thing about all that was that night, didn't nary a cow miss milking. Because all the neighbors around here came in with their trucks and trailers and loaded up [the cows] and took them to their farms. And we had a milk hauler from down there in Carolina—our milk used to go to Winston-Salem—and he came up and called some places down there and they said bring so many head, they could handle so many, and before that night was over we had every one of them cattle moved out and they took them in and milked them down there that night. We had people all inside [the house] taking numbers, writing down who had what so we could keep up with it, you know. Neighbors all the way around here showed up and people were just in there, really just on top of each other, helping us sort them out. And I happened to look out there at the barn and there was trailers sitting from right up at the barn all the way down to the road and back around there, people come in to haul for us. It really touched me, you know that people would show up for something like that. . . . We [neighbors] talk to each other all the time and aggravate each other. They're great people, all of them. (Interview 10/14.HS)

Residents from Greenly and Woodrow agree that neighbors help:

> Ted went to sleep on the sofa and he heard the timer go off and the timer sounds very much like a church bell in the distance and he's hard of hearing anyway and he thought it was a church bell. And the church bell tradition-ally in Appalachian society means fire. So he rushed over to Clara's house and pounded on the door and when she didn't come to the door, he opened it and walked in and awoke her from a sound nap. And then apologized for there being no fire. (Interview 7/07.ABM)

> Whenever somebody in the county, whether you know them or not—and this has happened quite a few times. No matter what you think of the person or their family, if some tragedy happens—their house burns down, a family member dies suddenly—bank accounts are opened at the local bank to help them rebuild their lives, rebuild their homes. Newspaper articles are written. I think, in my mind, that typifies the people of this community. They really overlook their differences when it comes to somebody needing something. (Interview 6/21.MBW)

> The farmer next door isn't going to bother you. Sometimes the bull gets out or the cow gets out, but you got to get them back in. I tell you all the people in Greenly get along good. If you have any problems they are right there. They do things together. They are very compatible peaceful people, very, very. (Interview 9/21.MG)

> I consider a good neighbor as a person that treats me with respect just like I try to treat them. In other words, treat people just as I would like them to treat me. A good neighbor is if your cows get out on them, they come and say, "Your cows are out. Come on, let's get these cows back." And you get along, you work together. That's the thing, work together, and you can go to their home and feel like they're a part of your family even though they might not be. (Interview T315 12/30.JB)

What makes a good neighbor was made clear in these quotations from residents, which tell, in the first case, what makes a good neighbor ("[we] need help, they help us"), and in the second, what *doesn't* make a good neighbor ("[they] don't want to be bothered"):

> We've got some good neighbors down here, they bought that property right down there; they're good neighbors. And the Bradfords up here, they're good neighbors. Need help, they help us. . . . Leo Bradford is a good neigh-bor; him and Dave helps us too. (Interview 8/22.MBW)

> That is one thing about this community, all the people are very close. And if you need anything, that's all you've got to say. Not for everybody—there's some neighbors that are not that way—that don't want to be both-ered. Some of them are that way. (Interview 6/20.MS&SS)

Practicing Reciprocity

You do things for each other. If I've got something that I can do that you can't, I'd be glad to do it for you.

Interview 6/21.MBW

Interviewees discussed neighborliness by describing classic cases of reciprocity. Reciprocity is the back-and-forth movement of goods and services under stimulus of obligation, in anthropological parlance, or "you scratch my back, I'll scratch yours," in the vernacular. Ever since anthropologist Marcel Mauss published his famous work *The Gift* in the early part of the twentieth century, anthropologists have known that the giving of gifts is not merely an economic enterprise; giving gifts creates and maintains relationships between people. Coleman (1988) labels this "social capital" that "generates strong networks, social support and reciprocal trust among community members." These "networks are instrumental as well as socially supportive" (Salamon 1992:227, 180; Wilkinson 1990).[12]

Anthropologists recognize three kinds of reciprocity: generalized reciprocity, balanced reciprocity, and negative reciprocity. The examples we cited above of neighbors coming to the aid of others when they are in need would be examples of generalized reciprocity. Goods or services are given to those in need, by those who have the wherewithal, with no thought of return. Generally, this kind of reciprocity is practiced only with close kin, or people who have forged a fictive kinship-like relationship.

More frequently, the examples of reciprocity told to us by rural residents were of the balanced variety. This is the giving of goods and services with the unspoken understanding that the givers can expect to be recipients themselves in due course. This is usually practiced with less-close kin and with friends. Capturing the essence of balanced reciprocity, an eighty-four-year-old resident who keeps two large gardens says: "Sometimes the neighbors help me. That helps them, too. They get corn and beans." Neighbors reported trading work in the hayfields for permission to hunt and "getting together" on prices for hay and calves (Interview 6/21.LC). The owner of a fish hatchery paints the connection between friendship and the act of gift-giving, as she first describes the gifts, then the relationship between the gift-givers:

> This one fellow—I look forward to it—I look forward to it every year; but for Christmas, he'll give me a ten pound sack of flour, which is great because I do a lot of baking. It was a huge sack of flour! He gave me sugar, and, let's see, white sugar and brown sugar and he gave me a bag of chocolate chips. And I made him some chocolate chip cookies. And another neighbor gave us eggs. So, we take them fish, you know.... So we do a lot of trading. Yeah, they're just good friends. They're just good friends. (Interview 6/21.MBW)

A resident reports that the same activity might be carried out as generalized reciprocity or as balanced reciprocity, depending on the recipient's particular needs at the time. This example illustrates that neighbors' *knowledge* of each other's circumstances provides the basis for the judgment about which form of reciprocity to use.

> My husband goes and helps a lot of neighbors [with baling hay], you know. He used to be the one that would throw the bales up on the truck, but now they want him to be the one that drives the truck, because so few of the farmers trust anybody driving their truck. You know, most of the farmers' trucks are old, and they need them to last. So they need somebody that knows how to go about doing it slowly. Somebody who won't grind the gears or run the truck into a fence post or what-not.
>
> They try to [pay him]. In fact, you know, there's kind of a ritual, I guess would be the best word. You know, you really would like doing things for other people here. It's a network. It's a community. You do things for each other. If I've got something that I can do that you can't, I'd be glad to do it for you. They try to pay us when we do something for them and we try to pay them when they do something for us. I guess it might be crazy.
>
> But in some instances, you know, some people won't argue too much because they need it. And you know they need it, so. . . . It's like I say, you want to do these things because of how you feel about the person. But in a lot of instances they'll pay my husband with checks as a way of keeping track of what it costs to put up hay. You know, what is the realistic expense? What is it costing me per bale? . . . But for people that we know that are living on fixed incomes or we know that it is costing them a lot of money to pay their help, then my husband will do it free. (Interview 6/21.MBW)

A common example of balanced reciprocity is neighbors giving their garden produce to each other: "Now they are all sharing the bounty of the gardens with us; you know, they just give us a lot of stuff" (Interview 6/21.MBW). Nearly everyone has a garden (and grows more than they need), so actual need for produce is not at issue. As in the South American villages of the Yanomamo Indians, where arrows might be exchanged for arrows, in these counties the gift of one kind of tomato might be returned with another kind of tomato. In both cases, the relationship that the exchange creates, maintains, and symbolizes is more important than the exchange itself. For the Yanomamo, these trading partners become allies in times of raiding (Asch and Chagnon 1970). For Greenly County residents, the gift givers provide advice and aid when needed, and are partners in both work and play on the land. Trading arrows for arrows or tomatoes for tomatoes serves cohesion-building and obligation-setting functions.

These reciprocal helping relationships can turn into fictive kinship relationships. David Evans describes the relationship he has with an older couple in whose home he now virtually lives.

> I met Leo and Alice at church. . . . And after my last child left home, I got to helping Leo farm and we just started pitching in together.
>
> [Interviewer: I bet you're a big help to them.]

> Well, they were a big help to me [after my wife died]. We're just like family now. It's been twenty years. (Interview 6/7.MBW)

(No instances of negative reciprocity, which consists of each party trying to gain as much as he can for as little as he can, were reported by the interviewees. This kind of "reciprocity" is usually practiced with strangers and in business relationships.)

The neighborliness and turn-taking betokened by the practice of reciprocity can even be seen in driving habits. At big events like the Fourth of July celebration, the Borden County High School parking lots fill to capacity and then some. Everyone stays until the last fireworks are shot off in a blaze of glory, and everyone goes to their cars all at the same time. When leaving, the thousand-odd cars arrive at several intersections. At each one, the cars take turns going onto the next leg of travel to the main road. This is an area of two-lane roads. One car from the crossroads goes forward, then one from the main drag, and so on. Where two main streets cross, cars coming both ways stop and allow one driver to make a left-hand turn, then one car crosses on the main drag, and so on. This all occurs with no intervention from traffic police or other personnel. Compare this to Interstate 75 (Florida to Michigan), where it can take one hour and ten minutes to travel fourteen miles in two northbound lanes because, at the end of the fourteen miles, the two lanes narrow to one due to construction work. Lane jockeying and one-upmanship prevent cars from taking turns to form the one lane and then proceeding at a good clip (Field Notes 1977–2021).

Land as Commons

> Our farm has always been one that is not posted. My father said he was just the caretaker for God. And people had the privilege of hunting and so forth.
>
> Interview T051 9/19.CLC

We have said that in the history of humankind, preagricultural societies had no concept of ownership of land. This is not, of course, true of Appalachia. And yet many authors allude to a more open view of ownership than is found in fenced suburbia. Galax, fallen trees, and wild fruits belong to the gatherer, not necessarily to the owner of the property: "Apples are plenty and neighbors few, and there is little objection to your climbing anybody's rail-fence and eating your fill."[13] When old uses of the land and the freedom to roam on it are threatened, feelings become raw. Summer people who post their land are a bone of contention: "Land that was used for hunting and shortcuts isn't ours anymore, and there are so many signs you need a plat to tell where you can go" (Hicks 1976:52; Miles 1905:82; Parlow 1978:189).

Perhaps this "different" sense of ownership can be explored by harking to another anthropological continuum—this one describing types of land use. The earliest relationship with the land is kin-based and is centered on the land's produce, rather than the land itself. If I am a hunter and gatherer, my right to hunt or gather on this land is based on the fact that I was born here, or that I have kin here. The !Kung San of the

Kalahari Desert of southern Africa call the right to use the land "melon rights"; moisture-laden melons are crucial to survival in this arid land. They do not have a constitution that lays down the "melon rights"; if they did, it would read like this: "If a person is born in a certain area he or she has a right to eat the melons that grow there and all the veld food. . . . A man may eat the melons wherever his wife can and wherever his father and mother could" (E. M. Thomas 1958:84). When anthropologist Elizabeth Marshall Thomas went to study among the !Kung, she had to be reborn as a !Kung woman's sister so that she could eat. No one has the right to *own* a particular piece of land. Who would want to? It's not the land itself that is useful, but the game and plants upon it. Who would want a plot of land where a herd of kudu antelope might graze every other year?

When societies practice horticulture (generally slash-and-burn cultivation for subsistence) or pasture animals, each family has the right to cultivate some of the village's garden or use the pasture. Called "usufruct," this is the right to use; there is no right to sell or buy or pass on a particular piece of land. Who would want to? The gardens and pastures are continually moving toward land which is more fertile, so who would want to hang on to a particular worn-out piece?

In "chiefdom" societies, which stand between the least and most complex societies, anthropologists were puzzled when they asked who owned the land and were told, "It's my land, it's the head of the lineage's land, it's the chief's land." They came to realize that this was an "inclusive" ownership of land where all have rights to what the land produces, but none have the right to dispose of the land itself (no buying, selling, or investing) (Sahlins 1972).

With agriculture that used the same piece of land continuously, developed about ten thousand years ago, came the notion of private ownership. In this "exclusive" ownership of land, which we in modern-day America are familiar with, if I own it, you cannot—unless your name is also on the deed. I own it to the exclusion of all of you. And I can do whatever I want with it, inside the boundaries of zoning regulations and suburban restrictive covenants. You, on the other hand, can't do anything with it. I can sell it or will it or dispose of it any way I want to. I am the only one who has rights to the products of my land.

In Appalachia, there is exclusive "ownership" with paper to prove it, but traditionally there is an almost inclusive right to the wild products of the land. For some, it seems that the "inclusive" right to the land extends to sharing it with a Supreme Being: "I want the children to remember that in addition to us owning this, it's God's" (Coles 1967:219). In the areas we learned about, the Commons concept has been attenuated because of National Forest land and National Park Service rights-of-way that abut some residents' land. When surveyors began surveying for the Mountain Valley [gas] Pipeline, residents posted No Trespassing signs on their land for the first time. The welcome of the Commons does not extend to strangers, especially those who may portend an environmental threat. Residents mourned the loss of the Commons: "And if I'm going out hunting on the other side, I don't know where I may end up. I might go over on [Dennis]. I might go up over on [Jim Brown]. I'm going anywhere, but if I see all these posted signs, it kind of restricts my movement" (Bengston and Austin 2016:45).

7

Using Place to Teach Culture's Ways

Granddaddy taught me how to mow the yards. And dad taught me how to play catch on that land. I killed my first deer on that land. Just many firsts on that land.

Interview 9/18.CMH

A Way of Seeing, a Way of Knowing

An understanding that people who live in the midst of nature learn—probably by observation more than by being told—is the interconnection among things. Aldo Leopold's *Sand County Almanac,* a compendium of observations of nature he made on his piece of land in Wisconsin, is a treasure trove of examples of the truism that everything in nature is connected, yet he rarely says so outright. Another function of rural place-making, then, may be that the place-makers emerge with a clearer "systems" view of the world. This is a valuable addition to our cultural storehouse of diverse epistemologies.

Just as the intense American cultural bent toward individualism affects relationships among people, it affects our relationship with the environment: "The common sense of conscious reason which has its loci in individual organisms, proposes a sense of separation. Consciousness separates men from each other, each man in solitude behind his own eyes, each one imprisoned by his own skin, each enclosed alone between the dates of his birth and of his death. The common sense of separation endorses the common sense of self-sufficiency and autonomy, notions that are sanctified virtually to the point of apotheosis in Western capitalist society" (Rappaport 1976:33). Farmer-philosopher Wendell Berry ([1970, 1972] 2012:81) agrees: "Our only real freedom is to know and faithfully occupy our place—a much humbler place than we have been taught to think—in the order of creation. . . . The principles of ecology, if we will take them to heart, should keep us aware that our lives depend upon other lives and upon processes and energies in an interlocking system that, though we can destroy it, we neither fully understand nor fully control." Robin Wall Kimmerer (2013:276) puts a fine point on the potential effect on the environment, noting that lichens may "cover the rocky ruins of our time long after our delusions of separateness have relegated us to the fossil record."

It has been posited that some aspects of the evolution of language separate humans from nature and militate against an understanding of the human's actual place in nature. Language and its manifestations have affected our epistemology—our way of knowing. Jan Van Baal (1971) has hypothesized that from the beginning of language there has been a subject/object separation. In his view, the felt separation of humans from the world around them (of which they actually are a part) arises from their ability to use symbols. The ability to objectify experience into symbols causes the symbolizer to perpetually be the subject "totally different from his world, the world of objects." With symbols, a human's knowledge becomes "roundabout, and he conceives of reality not by dealing with it in the raw but by removing himself from it through symbolization. . . . He re-presents in symbols, conceptual and [at first] verbal, what is present on other grounds" (Ong 1967:137). Conscious, rational reasoning reminds the human "again and again of his otherness" (van Baal 1971:220, 226).[1] It is especially "through the linear alphabet, with its necessity for ordered spatial arrangement, that "the possibility of control and organization of the world represented through thought and word becomes overpowering." The human, the subject observing objects, "will be a kind of stranger, a spectator and manipulator in the universe rather than a participator" (B. M. Wilson 1980:44; Ong 1967:136, 73).[2]

At the same time as written language imparted a sense of order and pushed us farther into observer mode, it pushed toward individualism and discursive ways of knowing—rationality, knowledge, fact, technique, secular, science, at the expense of the nondiscursive—nonrational, intuitive, expressive, emotional, metaphor, myth, ritual, sacred.[3] Fostering the alter ego search, Marshall McLuhan (1977) said that cultures that still had strong oral traditions, like the rural Irish and like Appalachia, were bastions of the nondiscursive ways of knowing, which McLuhan championed. Wendell Berry ([1970, 1972] 2012:76) describes how discursive and nondiscursive modes of understanding interact with the environment: "The corporations and machines that replace [small farmers] will never be bound to the land by the sense of birthright and continuity, or by the love that enforces care. They will be bound by the rule of efficiency, which takes thought only of the volume of the year's produce, and takes no thought of the life of the land, not measurable in pounds or dollars, which will assure the livelihood and the health of the coming generations." T. S. Eliot asks: "Where is the wisdom we have lost in knowledge? Where is the knowledge we have lost in information?" If we hope to hand a healed planet to our children's children, it will be necessary to understand our place in nature in both modes.[4]

Wisdom That Sits in Places

Anthropologist Keith Basso (1996) discovered "wisdom that sits in places" among the Apache people. Western Apache people use stories connected with particular places to reinforce moral lessons.[5] In fact, the mere mention of the place recalls to mind the moral of its story. In Brazil and among Aborigines of Western Australia, too, anthropologists have found that "indigenous people use spatially anchored narratives for moral teachings" (Downing 1996:39; Low 1994; Fabian 1992). In these rural Appalachian counties, the connection between place and the cultural good is not expressed in a fascinating shorthand like that of the Apache. Most Appalachian

Englishes are known more for their volubility than their sparseness (for example, "You come on up from back down in under there" [C. Williams 1980]). But place, people on the place, and how you should treat this place and its people are all of a piece in the stories people tell. The stories that we heard exhibit intergenerational ties to the land, lay down values for how to behave in this place, and display the worth of country knowledge.

How do these land lessons get "into" a child? Being an anthropologist, I am not willing to submit that they are "inborn." Unlike birds, whose nest-building ability is not taught, or mollusks, whose genetic codes tell them how to extrude their shell homes, humans must learn their various attitudes and feelings toward space and place, land and legacy. An anthropologist would say that a baby born in a far-off land and transported to these communities when it was tiny to live with a family here would grow up with this community's attitude toward land.

Sociologist Robert Coles tells of the ten families he observed over ten years in western North Carolina, eastern Kentucky, and West Virginia and maintains that in these rural areas, "learning about one's roots, one's place, one's territory is a central fact, perhaps *the* central fact of existence" (Coles 1967:208, emphasis his). In Coles's analysis of pictures drawn by the children, he finds that they rarely draw themselves or people they know; instead, their pictures represent the environment that surrounds them. Children explore the land at a tender age. They learn specific knowledge about the land and take on their parents' feeling for it. In a scene reminiscent of Alex Haley's *Roots* where Kunte Kinte raises up his baby daughter Kizzie and dedicates her to the moon, the world, and her people all at the same time, Appalachian Laura Workman tells that when baby Danny's father first came to see him,

> Ken held him high over his head and pointed him around like he was one of the guns being aimed. I heard him telling the baby that here was the corn, there was the beets, and there was cucumbers, and here was the lettuce, and there was the best laying chicken we've got. Next thing he told the baby to stop the crying and he did, he just did. . . . and then he just took him and put him down over there, near the corn, and the other kids and my sisters all stood and looked. . . . Ken said did I mind the little fellow lying out there near his daddy's farm, getting to know Deep Hollow, and I said no, why should I. (Coles 1967:213)

(Compare this to a friend of mine who, in his first encounter with his son, sang the University of Michigan fight song to him.) When baby Dottie Workman began to crawl, her mother said, "It's good, because now she'll get to know her daddy's land—where he does his growing and where he keeps his baskets and his tools, and the bushes over there, they'll stop her from getting into anything too steep" (Coles 1967:214). This is reminiscent of the pastoralists of East Africa, or the buffalo-hunting Indians of the North American plains where a baby is wrapped in hides at birth, spends his life in homes furnished with hides—literally eating, sleeping, living the products of the animals—and when he is old and death overtakes him he is wrapped in hides for burial.

The Workmans contend that they want their kids to "remember their first years later on as . . . when they learned all about the hollow and how to take care of themselves and go and do things out there up the hills and in the woods and down by the stream." "At three Danny Workman had been all over his father's land, and up and down the hollow. . . . He collected rocks of all sizes and shapes; they were in fact his toys" (Coles 1967:215–16). I can picture little Danny carrying a handful of rocks he collected and sleeping with them in a clenched fist, the way my own nephew carried a basketful of Matchbox cars with him everywhere, and slept with two or three tiny cars clutched in one hand. As if he knew that he was growing up one hundred feet from a four-lane state highway and eighty-seven miles from the Indianapolis 500 Speedway; as if he knew that he would send himself though college buying and selling cars; as if he knew he would build a business customizing Land Rovers and make it his livelihood.

Culture Teachers and Teaching Places

> I feel like I know every acre on that farm and I heard my dad talk about it.
>
> Interview 9/15.BF

Anthropologist Edward T. Hall (1959:69–74) defined three different ways of learning. Only one of these—which he labeled "formal learning"—makes a tight connection between the teacher and the taught, and in this case, between the culture teacher, the culture learner, and the teaching place. Formal learning occurs with the teacher and the learner face-to-face. It is a process of precept and admonition. The learner tries, makes a mistake, and is corrected. Formal learning tends to be suffused with emotion. Another type, informal learning, is a process of imitating models that the learner chooses. "Sometimes this is done deliberately, but most commonly it occurs out-of-awareness. In most cases the model does not take part in this process except as an object of imitation." The third, technical learning, is a process of transmitting a logical, clear, and thorough analysis to the learner. "The very essence of the technical is that it is on the highest level of consciousness." Personal contact is not necessary in technical learning. The teacher may put the analysis in a book or on a video or website.

An example of formal and informal learning is the way I learned to plant and care for flowers. This is one of my earliest memories. I am on my knees beside my mother in the garden dirt beside our house. She is on her knees, too, and she has a trowel, a bucket of fertilizer water, a little cup, and petunia plants. She shows me how to dig the right-size hole, put the petunia plant in, fill in the soil and tamp it down. Then we pour a cup of fertilizer water over the whole plant. As the plants grew, she showed me how to pick off the dead blooms, and when I started to pick off new blossoms instead, she showed me how to tell the difference. I could have learned all of this information from a book (after I learned to read). That would have been learning it the "technical learning" way. But I would not by that means have learned anything about my relationship with my mother, or our relationship together to the land around our house, because technical learning excludes the subject, her relationship with the knowledge, her relationship with her teacher, and her feelings.

Coles (1967:243) gives an example of formal learning from Billy Potter from Rocky Creek in Logan County, West Virginia: "The first thing [Daddy] taught us was what to call the different trees and bushes and vines. He takes us walking and he'll see more than anyone else. He knows where the animals live and where they're going and why they want to go over here and there." Another example of personal and meaningful formal and informal learning comes from farmer Daisy Simmons, an eighty-seven-year-old retired teacher from Linwood Fork in Woodrow County who remembers what her grandparents taught her, and where. The water she refers to is the sap from maple trees.

> In the beginning, they had about fifteen trees that produced the water. They took the water and made the syrup. . . . Granddaddy let me collect water and bring it in and pour it through a strainer, a sack he'd made. He had it fastened to wooden bars across a barrel. You first poured your water through there to take any insects, bark, or trash out. And after that then, he wouldn't let anyone go into his syrup house and handle the water at all. He did it himself because it had to be clean. And he didn't want anybody else risking it. It was handled just like making sorghum molasses at the last. It was boiled down in a vat and when it began to get fairly thick, he let the fire die down and poured that water or thin syrup . . . in buckets and we took it to the house. When we got to the kitchen with it, we poured it into those big preserving kettles through a strainer and then it was all cooked down. Grandmother would cook that. She could test it in a cup of cold water and tell when it was thick enough to use as syrup. When some of it would get too thick, she would give it to me and tell me, if there was snow on the ground, . . . to go out and drop it on the snow. And she said that as soon as you drop it, take this spoon and pick it up and put it in this dish and you had a nice little piece of candy to suck on and chew on, play with all evening. (Interview T326 12/24.BM)

Another example, told by retired military officer Howard Tucker, who returned to Greenly County where he grew up, describes being taught how to hunt in the personal formal and informal modes. In this one story he shows an admiration for his father's knowledge and foreshadows themes of many stories that we heard about the native versus the newcomer, and about the country person's knowledge trumping the city slicker's bravado:

> I can walk all over our land and neighbor's land too and when I got old enough to hunt and my dad liked to hunt and the first hunting I did, he took

me squirrel hunting. And I don't know if you know anything about squirrel hunting or you ever did, but squirrels like hickory and right now is the squirrel season and they're cutting acorn nuts. And usually if you find a squirrel or two of them in the hickory nut tree eating hickory nuts—in fact there's a lot of foliage—and if you're quiet you could get right up there close to the tree and then wait until they move. And when they go to get another nut, you can see them. But squirrels are real aware and they're real smart and they detect you. And they'll get on the other side of the tree, where you can't see them. And my dad, that's the first thing I remember about hunting with him. I didn't have a gun. He had a shotgun and was getting a couple of squirrels up the tree. And that's what they did—got up the other side so we couldn't see them. So, he knew how to squirrel hunt so he gave me the gun and told me exactly what to do. And he went to the other side out a ways and shook the bush. And the squirrels, they thought there was an enemy force and they come around my side where I could see them. That was the system we used and I enjoyed that tremendous. Because that was a sense of achievement for a little kid. I was probably eight, nine, ten years old.

He taught the real firearm safety, which the rules are pretty simple, really. He said—and he was exactly right—you treat every gun like it was loaded until you know it's not, until you *know* it's not. Because somebody said, "It's not loaded," you don't accept that at all. You view it as a loaded gun until you yourself know it's not. And you never point at anything that you're not gonna shoot. You want to make positive identification what you're shooting at before you shoot it. He said once you pull the trigger, you can't get it back. You can't do anything about it; it's history then, so you want to make absolute sure that you know, not just think, "Well it looked like a deer." You don't just think, you make absolute sure—any doubt at all—you don't shoot. (Interview T58 09/16.KLM)

As if he had just heard Howard's story, a man from Wellsboro, Pennsylvania, in the northern section of the Appalachians, interviewed by National Public Radio (1999), said: "It's one way you can bond with your [son]. He [my father] was there when I shot my first deer. That's an important memory to me. If I had a son, I would want to be there when he shot his first deer. Those are precious moments as far as raising children." A memory of a habitual activity with her mother on the farm ties seventy-nine-year-old lifelong resident Dorothy Spencer of Harwood in Farlane County to her grandparents: "My grandpa, my grandmother, they would work with their horses, plow their ground, raise their chickens and turkeys and things like that. . . . And they would go and plow away and my mother and I would fix their lunch and carry it to them every day at twelve o' clock" (Interview 9/23.AER).

Thus specific cultural knowledge of how to gather and use native plants and how and where to hunt animals is taught. Broad themes of the culture—the attachments to the land itself—are also passed down from father to son, mother to daughter, grandparent to grandchild. When Diana Sled, a young woman with children of her own, rides around on the farm with her father—which she names as her favorite thing to do—she recalls memories of past times spent there together: "He would make me scoop silage. But I didn't have to lift hay bales. I would drive the tractor or the truck for the men to load the hay on" (Interview 6/29.LC).

Later in the interview, her father chimes in: "Right here is what she done. Got a hold of that pocket when she was a little bitty girl, and I'd walk and she'd be pulling. Here we'd go, just like that. . . . She'd go up here—we have a silo up here. She'd go up there and lay the silage in. She'd come to me and say, 'Now, Daddy, I laid the silage in. Take me to the store'" (Interview 6/29.LC).

Some stories connect work done by family members with the material evidence of that work. A woman in her sixties whose gardening has been temporarily slowed by illness shows me the area beside her house, and says: "This used to be real pretty. This was our patio. I've got four children . . . they went to the top of the mountain and helped me get these rocks to build the patio with" (Interview 6/14.MBW). Diana Sled's mother and father, Frank and Beatrice Tucker, tell of working with Beatrice's grandfather.

> Frank: The locust posts that we got off the north of the mountain are the best.
> Beatrice: And this side was made with oak. And the wind has made it do that. We have to replace it and I just dearly hate to. Because my grandfather sawed all that wood. . . . Paw-Paw cut all that lumber and sawed it on his sawmill.
> Frank: And the buildings we built together.
> Beatrice: The two outbuildings that we have, they sawed the lumber for those, too, and built them. (Interview 6/29.LC)

Places where cultural knowledge was passed down provide a continuing link to deceased forebears. Stanley Patrick, a fifty-two-year-old man who has lived in Swanson in Farlane County all his life, says, "My father was so fond of the . . . farm I that when I go back there on the farm I almost feel a closeness to him, that he's still around . . . he loved the farm so much" (Interview 9/20.BRC). Christopher Turner, a younger resident of the same area, twenty-three years old, has similar feelings: "Granddaddy taught me how to mow the yards, things like that. And dad taught me how to play catch on that land. I killed my first deer on that land. Just too many firsts on that land. That's a tie alone that can't be broken . . . I wouldn't feel the same if I lived anywhere else . . . I don't have the tie or history I've got with my land" (Interview 9/18.CMH).

A young college administrator, a white man who has always lived near "the line" where the Black community of Clearview begins, describes a favorite place and what he would do there. This time, he is the culture teacher, bridging the generations between his parents and his daughter:

I think I would take my daughter and we would go for a walk in the mountains behind our house. . . . There's a place that we've always called Hawk's Knob. . . . But it's almost at the top of the mountain, and there are the most unusual rock formations there, even one place where you can crawl down in a rock that's almost hollow. And it has the most wonderful echoes, and so I would teach Susan the beauty of the echoes here in our mountains and the most beautiful sights. And you can see the Deays River Mountain tunnel from there, and you can see all of the homes up and down this beautiful valley. So I would teach my daughter the value of how this place we call home has been special and let her experience some of those same senses of wonder that I remember as a boy. (Interview T308 12/20.JD)

Cultural Rules

Went out there and here's this deer—huge big buck—and his head is cut off right behind the ears. And so I come in the next morning and Leo was mad.

Interview 6/7.MBW

David Evans's story—prompted by the sight of a certain area while driving by—combines an emphasis on a certain location and what should and shouldn't be done there, an example of neighbors pitching in together, a desire to conserve nature, and a sanction against people who break the rules regarding how to manage culture's relationship with nature. The men in the story are all hunters. Hunting itself isn't at issue; breaking the rules is.

See that little house there. I'll tell you a funny story. About six or eight years ago, Leo [elderly neighbor he was staying with to help him out] and I were sitting on the porch one evening and just about ready to go to bed. We had done pulled our shoes off. It was toward the end of September. [Deer hunting season begins with archery in October, muzzle loading in early November, and general firearms in mid-November.] We'd been seeing four big bucks out in the end of the meadow. Every evening you could see those big bucks out there.

We knew people watched from the road. [Spotlighting is considered unsporting and is illegal.] This particular evening just about dark I heard a big rifle shot. I said, "Leo, somebody has done shot one of those deers." He said "You think so?" I said, "I know so." I said, "That's exactly what they're shooting at." So barefoot and all we hit the truck and out the road we go, and we seen a woman go by in a little white car by herself and she was flying. And I told Leo I seen that car about fifteen or twenty minutes ago go up the road, turn around and come back. And I said there was *two* people in that vehicle when I seen it. So we just sat there on the road a minute and directly here she come back up the road. So we just sorta got in behind her and we went down to the church and stopped and got behind and got the license number.

I told Leo, "That boy is somewhere over behind the cornfield with that deer." So we opened his gate and turned in and went down in the field and around the cornfield. And about that time here she come back down the road flying and when she got on the other side of the corn, we heard her slide to a stop and heard the car door slam.

So we hunted and hunted and it was dark by this time. We couldn't find any dead deer anywhere. So Leo just sorta gave up. He drove out there the next morning. Said he looked around. I had to go to work the next day. He didn't see any deer, and about the middle of the day his brother and step-brother and people were putting up hay on the side of the mountain. They come over and said, "Leo, go out and look at that deer; it looks like an awful big deer lying out there dead." Went out there and here's this deer—huge big buck—and his head is cut off right behind the ears. And so I come in the next morning and Leo was mad.

In the meantime I had called the license number in and got who the car was issued to and all. So when I got in over here the next morning, here's that big dead buck out there. Flies had done—you know how they get in hot weather. And Leo said, "Maybe we'll go out and get that durn deer and take it to the woods." And my son said, "I've got a good idea; they've got the head off of it," he said. "I think they ought to have the body." So we took Leo's pick-up and drove out to the field. And slid that dead carcass up in it.

They lived in this little white house; they were renting it. We turned around in the road there and come back down to their driveway. The three of us got a hold of that deer and walked up to their driveway and pitched it right in the middle of their driveway. Well, a woman came out on the front porch—the same woman that was driving the car the night before. And, oh man, it scared her to death. She run back in the house. We got in the truck and drove back home. Took the hose and washed the gore out of the truck.

Went in and sat down, was eating our lunch. And directly heard a noise outside. Went out there, and there was a game warden. And he was looking all in the back of our truck, smelling and looking around. And we all walked out onto the porch, all three of us. And he said, "Did you guys just haul a dead deer over and put it in some woman's driveway?" I looked at him and said, "We sure did." I said, "How did you know?" He said, "I just happened to come by and had a call to come out here. And I come by and here's a dead deer with no head lying in that driveway. And so I went to the house. And so a woman told me three men in a brown pick-up truck just threw it out and drove off." So I told him, "Let me tell you the whole story." So I told him. . . . So he went straight to town, evidently, and got a search warrant, and brought the sheriff. And I told Leo and Tom, "I'm just curious, let's ride over by and see what's going on."

About two hours later, drove over here and I saw the sheriff behind the house. They went in the house with this search warrant. The woman had panicked and she'd went wherever her husband was at; left the house open.

And they went in the house, and there was that big buck head in the freezer. The whole thing. Head, horns and everything in this big chest freezer on the back porch. So you know what happened to them. They wound up down in court and I think it cost about six or seven hundred dollars. I think they found, a lot of grouse, wild turkey. Somebody told me a bag of marijuana and I don't know what all. (Interview 6/7.MBW)

In an earlier chapter, we discussed the residents' care for the histories of these communities. A story being passed down in the Swanson and Harwood communities of Farlane County underscored the cultural importance of protecting the tangible remains of the community's heritage.

One day some Pagans came through here. I guess there were four motorcycles, and went on the covered bridge . . . and they were kicking the slats out. . . . Whitesville cares a lot about its covered bridges, that's probably something you'll find out. And so Tom went down and asked them to stop, and they said, "No, we're not going to stop." And he said, "Well, I called the sheriff, he's coming." And they said, "We're leaving." And he said, "No, you're not." So he pulled out his gun and shot the tires off their motorcycle. Well, they didn't like that so then they started shooting at him. And so nobody hit anything but motorcycle tires. . . . The sheriff came and took them all to Burksville and Tom got to come home. And the motorcycle people got to spend a little bit of time in jail for vandalism. (Interview 9/22.GAS)

Natives versus Newcomers

We had never had a problem and still haven't with people who grew up here.
                                                    Interview T58 09/16.KLM

Tension between natives and newcomers is expressed in a saying that became a cultural motto as we heard it again and again in slightly different versions. It sets out the rules of handling cattle that have broken out of their fences, a persistent problem. The saying—prompted by the sight of a fence that looks breached—goes, "a good neighbor will stop and put your cow back in; a neighbor will call you and tell you your cow's out; these brought-ins [newcomers] just drive by." Seventy-one-year-old Howard Tucker told about differences in cultural skills between natives and newcomers:

Other people—native people—maybe not native, but the descendants of the original settlers, they all had to know guns and shoot. They had to; they used that fur. It was some of their livelihood to kill deer, a bear or a squirrel or whatever, you know, and so everyone knew how to shoot.
    We had the deer season in Greenly County—we killed deer and we have hunt clubs and all and had a good time and killed a lot of deer and for years

there was never a gun accident. There was never a hunting accident in Greenly County. The first one was two people from —— City and they had just heard some people they knew who killed deer and heard them talking about it—at the beer hall or church, or wherever, I don't know—and they got interested in hunting and they got—anybody can buy a gun, and a hunting license. You could go hunting and they did. They came down here, and they decided, "One of us will go around this way and the other one go around this way." They shot each other. Yeah, that's what happened, they were gonna go and they said, "One of us may spook a deer to the other one," and they got around there and met and they didn't identify themselves, one of them. I don't know what the deal was, but one of them shot the other one and that was the first hunting accident—so-called accident—in Greenly County. There's been others since, but all of them had been from other people who came in here than the natives. I keep saying, but the people who lived here had to, had to, live with guns, you know. And they knew how to use them and they knew that you had to treat guns with respect and they did so. We had never had a problem and still haven't with people who grew up here, grew up with guns and all. But some of our people who have come in, you know, and have come in the last twenty, thirty years—some of them have gotten involved in accidents. (Interview T58 09/16.KLM)

Country versus City

It's nice to be able to come home and have a sense of peace and security.

Interview T308 12/20.JD

"Places are locales of intense emotional attachment, thick with meaning and memory, shaped by both local and translocal phenomena; they possess the 'power to direct and stabilize us, to memorialize and identify us, to tell us who and what we are in terms of where we are (as well as where we are not)' (Casey 1993:xv). . . . Place making needs to be understood not just in terms of the practices and representations that contribute to the production of a sited identity, but also in relation to the siting of difference (Gupta and Ferguson 1997)" (P. Thomas 2002:368, 373). The sitings of difference we heard contrasted urban and rural life, with urban visitors always portrayed as ignorant of rural living, unable to withstand its hardships or enjoy its pleasures.

This kind of story may function as boundary maintenance—to define one culture by putting in relief its differences from another culture. Creed and Ching (1997) would analyze these stories as expressions of identity politics, made necessary by urban hegemony. Farming itself could be viewed as a form of "resistance" to the 9–5 world (Fisher 1997; Handler 1994).

In their descriptions of life on this landscape, residents readily differentiate rural areas from urban settings. In all of these comparisons, residents make favorable allusions to their smaller communities while listing what they do not like about metropolitan localities. Words carrying negative connotations such as *crowd, noise, crime, pollution,* and *stress* were ascribed to urban areas. In contrast, *a slower pace of life, peace, beauty, seclusion,* and *security* were used to define their homes. Taking turns speaking, a newcomer couple explains, "Another thing [to cause] someone like us to come out here is for a certain sense of peace and privacy and isolation. . . . You sort of want to get away from civilization. And commune with nature. . . . And that's a pretty fragile thing" (Interview T004 06/09.ABM).

Their thoughts are echoed by other residents who are new to the area, who have lived away for a time, or have visited urban areas:

> Whenever you factor in the quality of life in northern Virginia, the Washington Metro area compared to the quality of life here, I think that there's no comparison between the two. I mean, you've got the crowd, the noise, the pollution, the gridlock—the traffic gridlock along the Beltway. . . . There's just no comparison between the two areas. When you come back here, it's beautiful, it's quiet, the community is friendly. It's a good place to raise children if you're planning to have a family. (Interview T338 02/13.RUCart)

> Where I lived was a small development far away from the freeway and even at night I could hear the traffic on the freeway. I could hear sirens. I could hear car alarms. I could hear dogs barking. I came here and the first night the only thing I could hear was a train off in the distance and the crickets . . . outside. . . . It's peaceful here. It's a slower pace. . . . It's a lot different and I enjoy it. And I'd hate to think of anything happening here because, like Mom, I grew up around here. (Interview T333 01/05.DCM)

These transplanted urbanites might agree with Sigurd Olson (1958:151), one of the advocates for setting aside the Superior National Forest and Boundary Waters Canoe Area in Minnesota, who said, "Only through my own personal contact with civilization had I learned to value the advantages of solitude."

We so often heard that doors remained unlocked here that it became a symbol of the security of rural life. Clearview resident Alvin Underwood said:

> Knowing all of your neighbors, knowing that they watch out for each other. Living and having parents who have lived at the same place for over thirty years and have never had anything stolen from their land or their homes, that means a lot in today's society. Living in a place where you feel somewhat secure leaving your car unlocked, and being able to go outside and not have to fear who may be out there. And in a time when there's much fear in the world and much reason to fear, it's nice to be able to come home and have a sense of peace and security. That everything's going to be stable when you get home, regardless of what kind of day you've had at work. Knowing that you can find that solitude in your home and the place that's your community. (Interview T308 12/20.JD)

George Settle, also from Clearview, associates the fast-paced urban life with stress, and describes his desire to return home to leave this stress behind:

How did I decide to move back? . . . Well, that's a long story. . . . I worked in the steel mill, and they closed down . . . and then I went back to work, and then while I was working on another job, I had a heart problem . . . and I had open heart surgery. . . . They opened me up and went in me three times, and I didn't even know nothing about it—when they discovered what I had. So, when they brought me back around, the doctor come in and asked me, said, "Mr. Settle, you gave us a pretty good scare." Said, "You know what happened?" I told him everything happened to me, and I said, "Well that was a Sunday." I said, "I guess today is Monday." He said, "You're right about everything but one." I said, "What's that?" He said, "Today's Thursday." And I was out four days. . . . I said, "Well I tell ya doc, Christ was out for three, I was out for four, he must have brought me back for a reason." And so, after I got myself straightened around a little bit . . . . there's one thing left for me to do. . . . I'm going back to the land that I can live on, be on, don't have to worry about nothing, not nobody, no stress, no pressure. This is paid for, my grandfather left it, my daddy left it and gave it to me so I come back here . . . I just like to be happy and live on my little land here that my grandfather left for me. (Interview T309 11/14.JD)

Urban dwellers are assumed to be ignorant of nature's ways:

We'll get back to talking about the beagles. I heard an old fellow up the road talking—he was sorta like me; he likes to hear the beagles chase the rabbits. And his cousin from the city came out to visit him, and his dogs was out takin' a run, and he said, "Just listen to the music; just listen to that music." And the guy said, "I don't hear any music." And he said, "Well, just *listen* to the music." He says, "I can't hear anything but them darn dogs barkin'!" (Interview 9/24.TC)

Residents of the largely African American community of Clearview express the same kinds of people-place-culture connections as other residents, but they also add ties to land that have grown out of their community's unique history. Alvin Underwood, who is white, has returned to Clearview with his young family. He wants to pass on childhood experiences to his own children:

Well, my family still lives here, and a consideration of my parents keeping the children while we work was of great value. Plus the experience of having the influence of not only my parents, but [before coming home] I lived in a part of the country where there were only white people; and I wanted my children to have the same experience that I did of having another culture. Of experiencing a place where I had experienced good relations with neighbors, regardless of color. And I truly wanted my children to have that same experience and I didn't want to have to leave Woodrow County to have it. And Clearview was the only place where that would occur and the opportunity was there for land and I took it. (Interview T308 12/20.JD)

Residents of Clearview have been called upon to prove their legal relationship to their land. For example, the father of the head of one of nine Black families who purchased land on Clearview Creek between 1879 and 1883 was listed in census records as the servant of a wealthy landowner, who in his will "left $1,000 each to three colored servants 'for their faithful and devoted service to me.'" The purchaser himself was born into slavery and freed at age eleven. He purchased 201 acres in Clearview from a white man in 1879. In 1886 the white man's heirs brought suit against the Black landowners of Clearview, alleging that the lands had not been paid for. The purchaser purchased his land again on the courthouse steps for $214.02 by taking out two bonds of $107.01 each payable once a year dating from 1887. He was finally issued a deed on February 4, 1891 (Lion 2000). This history has figured into the places residents deem important, as a seventy-nine-year-old descendant of the original purchaser who returned to Clearview after working in the Midwest says:

Well I like it all. Right truthfully, I like it all. I like the part that I grew up as a kid in and traveled with my daddy, and I like it all, but I like Woodrow County. I'd go to the courthouse. That's where I would take you, because I like this here, since I done got older and learned about life and everything and what I was taught. If you were anything that really means something and worthwhile, you started at the courthouse. You started at the courthouse. You learned the courthouse. That's your business part of your county. (Interview T309 11/14.JD)

Using Metaphors to Portray the Right Relationship to the Land: Land as Family and Land as Sacred Space

It may not be heaven but it's close.

Interview 7/20D.MS&SS

Anthropologists recognize that a reliable tool for understanding the relationship between people and their culture is discovering the metaphors that people use. That's because the use of metaphor is itself a powerful means of creating identities for ourselves: "Metaphors move us, and their aptness lies in their power to change our moods, our sense of situation" (Fernandez 1974:129). The metaphors that we heard portray the culturally accepted relationship to the land. They are of two types: one likened the land to a family member; the other gave the land a religious or spiritual essence. Viewing the land as family fortified wanting to keep the land in the family:

"[The land] is like another member of their family. It's almost as important to them as one of their children." "To me this family thinks more of their heritage, their ancestors, and since the farm has been in the family for so long, they love it. You know, it's more than just a farm" (Interview 9/16.LU; 9/16.JH). Our recent interviewee farmers from Borden County also expressed a family-like connection to the land:

> I guess you could say it's in my blood. My grandparents put their blood, sweat and tears into getting that going. It just feels like a part of me. (Interview 02 10/1.RW)
>
> It's a special feeling and—until you're there or do it, it's hard to explain how you get—almost married to the land. And you appreciate it and you try to take care of it, because you're counting on it to help take care of you. So it's a two-way street there. That probably sounds silly—the married part— but you do—you learn to love it. (Interview 07 10/10. LG)

Residents described their area as "just a paradise," "the garden of heaven," and "heaven" itself. A woman native to Greenly County with long genealogical roots there says, "My husband and I sit in the swing and my sister and her husband do, too, and we'll sit up there on a Saturday night and my husband'll say, 'It may not be heaven but it's close'" (Interview 7/20D.MS&SS). A newcomer says, "This little county is just a slice of heaven." A resident of seventy-five years says, "This is the garden of heaven." "It's just heaven on earth and I hope I get to live here until my dying day." Another labeled it "My paradise." And of course, we heard the land called "God's country."[6]

One of the questions we asked was where residents would go if they had to leave this county. Some interviewees joined their concern with death, burial, and the afterlife with their answer to this question. They answered, "I hope it will be heaven" and "I want to go to heaven. That's where I want to go." "I feel that the land we own is a gift from God. For as long as we live." "[If I had to leave where I would go is] as close as I can find to this place! Really. I just hope I'm never forced to leave. I think that the only place that I could go that would be nicer than this would be heaven" (Interview 9/16.JH; 7/20.SS&MS; T325 11/28.RM; 6/21.MBW).

This language may make us conclude that "land is sacred" to these farm families. But Keith Basso (1996), writing of North American Indian people, reminds us that the appellation *sacred* should be used carefully when applied to attitudes toward land.[7] His cautionary tale could also be applied to the Appalachian region. The hard, violent moonshining hillbilly image is sometimes replaced by a soft, romanticized, close-to-nature one. What do the data show us? To determine whether land is close to sacred we used the usual definition of *sacred*, implying "separate," "distinct," "special."[8] We searched to see whether land is spoken of and treated in a special, different way by these residents. We found that more than a nuance of the sacred—the set-apart, distinctive, special quality—flowed through the words of farm families in southwestern Virginia. These references to things sacred fell under certain repeated themes. Metaphors connected the land with heavenly spaces; the land was a player in rites of passage; the sacred figured in the reasons for land stewardship; something akin to religious experience occurred on the land; land was featured in conversion narratives.[9]

Rites of Passage through the Life Cycle

One theme drew a connection between the rites of passage through the life cycle and the land upon which they took place. Residents saw it as important to tell about birth, baptism, death, and burial on this land. Laura Dell, a newcomer to Greenly County, thirty years old, said: "Yeah, I claim this as home. Jonathan was born in this very house, right in our very bed, [he comes to her and she smooths his hair while he peeks out and hides his face against her], and he was conceived there, and grew there, and came out there!" (Interview T005 06/09.SLV). Seventy-five-year-old native Phyllis Watson, when asked, "Do you want to tell me a little bit about yourself?" began with, "I was born in the old white house over there" (Interview T054 09/22.RAF). Another said simply, "I was born down the road" (Interview T004 06/09.ABM). Residents knew the genealogy of the land, whether it had been in their own families or not, and would point out who was born in this room or in this house or on this land.

Newcomers to the county of course couldn't tell of being born there (although they could and did tell of intending to be buried there), but they could tell about how they found and bought their land. When one of our interviewers asked: "How did you decide to move here? What made you choose this county?" a woman answered, "I would say God probably told us [about this place] because a rainbow came out when we were looking at it" (Interview 6/21.LC). A newcomer couple who were eventually able to purchase an old state-owned business when it was finally deemed legally abandoned said that finding this place "was just—it was just an answered prayer. . . and this was just meant to be our home. That's all there is to it" (Interview 6/21.MBW). Another couple notes:

> We've lived in other parts of the world and when we came here we just feel like God had really showed us a special place. His hand has been in it every step of the way. As a matter of fact we are in this home right here and right now because we believe God placed us here.
>
> I like to take people up in that area because to me that's the mountains. You know you've got beautiful brooks that are just cascading across stones that have been there forever. Completely undisturbed. You feel very close to nature and to God. . . . The things that are undisturbed is what we like to show people. (Interview T109 11/01.ASY)

When asked to show the interviewers around their places, some residents took us to a cemetery. We discussed the importance of being buried in this ground in an earlier chapter. Of course, cemeteries are almost always hallowed ground. But in Appalachia, along with large town and church cemeteries, there are many small family cemeteries, located on the family land itself. Newcomer Laura Dell and her family had plans to make a new cemetery:

I love this place. I love this place. I've never felt more at home anywhere else. And we've investigated and decided we're going to put a family graveyard on our property, and it'll be back up that way [points to the right and beyond us]. None of us are ready to be planted yet, but we have some older people in the family—in their 90s—and I kind of want them to come here and live when they die. And I hope to live here and die here. . . . We're going to put [in] our *own* graveyard—our own family—and we've already invited all of our relatives to come die here. And just come and be planted. (Interview T005 06/09.SLV)

A man who had lost his wife placed an engraved granite marker for her on the top of his mountain, even though her remains were actually buried in the cemetery of the church where both of them were, and he still is, an active member. He also placed markers for a nephew and a niece on the mountain, even though they were buried in the cities in which they lived (Interview T003 06/07.MBW).

Stewardship of Sacred Space

Some residents connected the need to care for the land—stewardship—to its sacred quality. Some newcomers joined their description of how they found their land to a discussion of why they take care of it. "When we moved in here, we named it 'God's little acre.' That's all we have here. . . . But we feel like it's a gift, we try to take care of it the best we can. This is God's world and this is God's land" (Interview T056 09/23.CSL). Laura Workman from Deep Hollow, Wolfe County, Kentucky, says, "There's a God in Heaven, and He gave us this hollow, and it's the nicest place in His Kingdom, it must be. I want the children to remember that in addition to us owning this, it's God's" (Coles 1967:219).

Others see future generations as part "owners" of the land: "The land doesn't really *belong* to you. Some day you'll be gone, and the land will still be here. You shouldn't do whatever *you* want." Elizabeth Ward, a twenty-seven-year-old life resident of Greenly County, picks up the stewardship theme. "There's no reason people should come and trash [it] or do anything to hurt their land, because the land is sacred. And it is. And there is no reason to do anything. Then it will be gone. Nobody does anything. Everything is real good aside from a Pepsi can, that's all—which is not good—but that's all. . . . Most feel respect for the land and don't mess up somebody's land. You respect it" (Interview T063 09/17.AV).

Six-year residents of Swanson, Harold and Janet Warren said:

Basically what we do on our land is work, geared towards providing for our home. We cut firewood. We don't kill anything we don't eat. We hunt for meat. We grow vegetables for the food we use. . . . What I would want you to know about what we do with our land is we respect it. We keep it clean and we don't abuse it and destroy it and litter it. We don't use a lot of unnecessary chemicals. . . . We want things to stay like they have always been, and we don't want to be disturbed. But we do want to get the God-given benefit of firewood, and growing vegetables, and enjoying the serenity and the peace and beauty of it. (Interview T109 11/01.ASY)

Religious Experience

Residents' descriptions of their time on the land were at times reminiscent of religious experience. William James (1958) and others associated religious experience with a feeling of oneness with the surrounds—a oneness that breaks through the separation that individuals typically feel from their environment and from other people and living creatures.[10]

> One of the most, as far as senses go—sight, smell, feel, and everything—one of the most, well I don't want to say sensual experiences: I was on top of the mountain one day and it was foggy and I couldn't see a thing, and I hiked up there and I was on top of the rocks overlooking everything and I could see the fog. You could just see the fog and the mist just blowing past you, and the wind picked up and it just—like within two seconds—it blew it out. It blew it completely clear and you could see everything all the way around you. Plus you could see through the clouds. You could see right underneath them. I was right eye level with them. And that was, that was an experience. And that is something that I will never ever forget, is that right there. (Interview T023 07/19.MS&SS)

Another resident told us:

> And we've had some unusual spiritual experiences as a matter of fact. . . . [In] the garden and I would be praying. This is a very special place. It's a very spiritual place. . . Coming here for us, like I said we had always lived in town. . . . You're going to think I'm weird when I tell you about this. A little cloud came over real low, and we're kind of high up here, and the cloud was actually about the same level as I was and a little rainbow came out of that cloud below me right below that garden as I was praying. And you know a rainbow is a sign of God's promise. (Interview T109 11/01.ASY)

There is in many of the interviews, if not a description of feeling one with the surrounds, at least a feeling of well-being, of serenity: "If you ask me a favorite place. Somewhere beside the creek looking at the water and looking at the mountains. That's very relaxing. If I could get a day off and listen to the water and look at the mountains. It kind of gets your head right again" (Interview T034 09/14.HZ).

The Land in Personal Religious Narrative

A student-run survey that asked local residents when they felt closest to God brought a response that "hunting gave him this feeling of closeness which he could not achieve anywhere else because he was up in the mountains with just the birds and the animals" (Bielo 2000). Another set of interviews that plumbed the place of religion in the daily lives of former coal miners who lived in rural areas showed that the land and the Lord were connected for them. "I get up every morning and say 'Lord, this is the day that you made.' I used to roll out on my knees before I got too old but now I'm too stiff. So now I get up and pull the curtain back and I look at that old mountain. Look at that mountain and say 'Lord, this is a new day. I'm yours, whatever you want to use me for today, you work through me.' And every day is a joy" (Interview T011 SP.KSB). "See, a church to me—some people think a church is part of a building and a certain place you need to go and all. The Lord said two or more in my name and I'll be there. A church can be out in the mountains, in a field, anywhere. . . . I was actually saved in the mountains. I go to the mountains and pray" (Interview T014 SP.MAM).

8

Using Place to Confront Threats to the Environment and Culture

My mother's father owned [this piece] at one time. . . . [And when I inherit it, it will be] in this stage, just the way it is. There will be no development.

Interview 6/29.LC

Highlighting the crux of the Progress versus Preservation culture war, Virginia Foundation for the Humanities and Public Policy grants director David Bearinger (1998) says, "In many ways . . . such basic American ideals as Prosperity, the Free market, and Progress seem to be at odds with the goal of maintaining strong rural communities." Folklorist Mary Hufford (1998a:8,10), studying in West Virginia, suggests that cultural activities that have the local landscape as their focus—talk about native plants and places, suppers that use a native plant, and roaming the mountains—function "as touchstones to a shared past, and as thresholds to a future in which a historic, mixed mesophytic landscape continues to form a hedge against social, environmental, and economic crises." They "are resources for holding together a way of life that is continually dismantled by plans for progress."

Hufford's area of study is most threatened by deep mine closings and mountaintop removal (to get at the coal underneath). Our study area of Appalachian Virginia faces different progress problems: the threats felt most keenly here are degradation of rural environments caused by population pressure (housing developments and malls), newly proposed interstate highways, and the needs of distant urban areas for electrical and natural gas power, waste management, and paper products, along with culture clash with agriculture-averse newcomers.[1] Protests are mounted to keep these threats at bay. My file of clippings of people protesting attempts to flood their land, to plant 765,000-volt-carrying towers on their land, to bury natural gas pipelines in their land, or to otherwise condemn their land has grown thick in the forty-four years that I have lived here. Common knowledge of place, common talk of place, and activities in common places have helped residents confront perceived threats.[2]

Collective Place and Community Resiliency

A collective sense of place can become part of a community narrative that fosters resiliency. Recent social science research has highlighted "narrative" and the identification of "core values" or "sensemaking" as critical elements that promote community resiliency. The concept of resiliency has expanded from identifying "protective factors" for individuals touched by disaster or abuse, to discovering elements that help sustain communities affected by ongoing cultural change and persistent negative stereotyping. Clauss-Ehlers and Lopez-Levy (2002) conceptualize community resilience as "a process rooted in cultural values and practices." A recurring theme in the discovery of community-sustaining factors is "the importance of cultural knowledge and identity." This is akin to the concept of "collective remembering," which is "similar to the memory of an individual—it provides cultural identity and gives a sense of the importance of the past." Researchers find "mechanisms of protection" in "themes of connectedness, spirituality, cultural knowledge and tradition." "Reestablishing expressions of [cultural] identity that connect the land, the language, and the spiritual and cultural practices of a people may . . . result in an increase in health and well-being" (Sturken 1997:1; Kirmayer et al. 2009:80; Feiler 2013a, 2013b; Collins 2001; Panelli and Tipa 2007; Brendtro, Brokenleg, and Van Bockern 1990; Clauss-Ehlers 2004; Masterson et al. 2017; see also Foucault 1988).

On the other hand, for persons for whom place is culturally significant, failure to conserve place brings serious consequences: "Without place conservation, the contents of culturally meaningful behaviors and processes of place-making disappear, cutting us off from our past, disrupting the present, and limiting the possibilities for the future" (Low 1994:66).[3] Locally, an insightful pastor had this to say during a study of pastors' views on health. He commented on a place that had lost its community resiliency: "I use the phrase 'the culture of anxiety.' . . . We've lost that deep rootedness to place and to a community, and I think this also contributes to this anxiety. So many people only know part of their story and they don't know their history and they don't have that foundation to draw back on and to remember. . . . We don't seem to be rooted in tradition" (Presbyterian Pastor 2013).

The Specter of Internal Colonialism and the Destruction of Place

They're going to peddle power over us.

visitor to "APST 460" class, 1993

Internal colonialism is a concept that has been applied to inner-city ghettoes, to Indian reservations, and to Appalachia. It "results from the way in which United States' urban centers of finance, political influence, and power have grown at the expense of rural areas" (Jorgensen 1971:85).[4] Like traditional colonialism, where a mother country gains resources (and a captive market) from a colony, with internal colonialism urbanized highly populated areas gain, for example, cheaper electricity by sacrificing rural landscape. Current scholars recognize Appalachia as a national sacrifice zone (Fox 1999; Scott 2010).[5]

Although internal colonialism and national sacrifice zone are concepts of social science, the kernel of their truth, and even the labels themselves, are reflected in these thoughts by Greenly County residents: "We are a thinly settled rural relatively poor area lying between surplus generation in the west and growth area in the east." "It's the large corporation seeking to increase or maintain profits . . . they try to roll over poor rural people . . . destroy people and environment for a profit. They're making us a national sacrifice area" (Interview 2/20.DW).

Several years prior to the power line proposal, anthropologist Stephen Foster (1988) wrote about another controversy concerning the same electrical power utility's plan to build a dam on the New River in Ashe County, North Carolina. Foster says that the damming of the river became a potent symbol for culture change in general, and for outside interests versus indigenous culture. The same thing occurred in the 765,000-volt power line controversy. The decision as to whether the power line can be built rests in the hands of the State Corporation Commission of Virginia (SCC)—the government body that regulates utilities and corporations in general. In his forty-three-page summary of some three thousand pages of testimony from public hearings regarding the need and routing for the proposed power line, the hearing examiner writes: "Primarily, the public witnesses viewed the proposed transmission line as a symbol of corporate greed imposed at the expense of the cultural attachment of the people to their land and the scenic beauty of the region" (H. P. Anderson 2000:3).

As Foster notes for Ashe County, not everyone who lived in the area was on the same side in the controversy. In the case of the power line, the SCC examiner lists officials from four towns and counties (not in the path of the proposed corridors) and some local chambers of commerce and businesses who had come before that body to testify for the building of the line. On the other side, boards of supervisors of six counties and towns protested against the power line (some changing their minds from earlier support of the line) along with eight citizens' protest organizations.

We have several times in our study made the point that this is not a throwback area—not a place that time forgot. We have noted that the people in these counties are not frozen in a frontier time-warp. But the individual decisions they have made—such as commuting to a job off the farm—have often been conservative ones in the sense that they have had as their goal the ultimate protection of pieces of land in their present (and past) condition. Foster (1988:160) said that "the difficulties these transformations pose for Ashe County people do not derive from an inability to cope with change as such or from a rigid adherence to tradition; they have sought change from time to time in their own ways. Instead, the difficulties reside mainly in the particular nature of these changes: they are perceived as imposed without choice from the outside."

The five-county residents' talk reflects a desire to protect the land from changes stemming from biological and human agents. We heard discussion of acid rain, "some kind of disease that is harming sycamores," chestnut blight, damage done by deer and beaver, and hurricanes and ice storms. We heard about the pine beetle and the spongy moth killing trees, and increased haze indicating air pollution. We heard concern about environmental effects with unknown antecedents; for example, residents mentioned that they used to see certain species of birds that they no longer see, and, on the other hand, that they are seeing new species not seen before. We heard about coyotes killing sheep, cattle polluting creeks, creeks being dammed (which warms the water, making it unfit for fish), and people muddying spring water while exploring in caves. We were told of trash left by hunters and erosion caused by hunters' vehicles.

Active county planning commissions and resident-approved zoning regulations—rare in rural Appalachian areas—are also signifiers of the value of land stewardship in this area. Residents noted that farmers are increasingly aware that their own actions can become threats to the environment, and most have taken steps to limit these consequences: "The farmers now are a whole lot more careful about what they throw down the sinkholes. They used to throw their garbage down the sinkholes and their abandoned cars and their abandoned trucks and dead animals and stuff down the sinkholes. Like I say, they're a lot better about it anymore, because they realize what their impact is going to be down the road" (Interview 6/21.MBW).

Judging by the number of farmers applying for cost-sharing help from the US Farm Service Agency's Environmental Quality Incentives Program to undertake conservation projects, many farmers want to do more to protect the environment. But four out of five farmers who applied in recent years were denied for lack of funds. One of the rejected farmers, from eastern Washington State, said, "Most of these things don't really have any monetary advantage to the landowners. The benefits are the clean air, the clean water and the wildlife habitat. It's the general public that reaps all the advantage."

Interviewees described how the land should be treated with "respect" and "consideration." The land was discussed as if it were an extension of the landowners; respect for the land and respect for the landowners were one and the same. They defined rules for conduct on the land, differentiated between individuals who would or would not be allowed on land, and listed ways they personally cared for the integrity of the land. Residents expected people on their land to behave in certain ways: no littering, no destruction of natural or cultural features, no rowdiness, following proper hunting tactics, and leaving the land in the same condition it was found.

> You know, well, I don't want anybody throwing trash on my land. I think we try to keep our land nice and pretty, and I don't want anything or anybody destroying our land and putting stuff . . . that's going to hurt us—on our land. (Interview T320 12/02.BB)
>
> I don't mind people bringing kids to my place. I hate people driving over my property, knocking my grass down. I hate spot-lighters, road-hunters, people who seem to like to destroy. They don't respect the nature. They—I just don't like people like that. If you're going to hunt, do it in the woods. If people treat me with respect, then I have no problem with it, but when they act like it's okay that they can do whatever they want, that's when we lock horns. (Interview T315 12/30.JB)

> We try to preserve our land and take care of it and keep it clean. We
> don't want people throwing down cans or trash, climbing over the fences
> and tearing them down, destroying the scenery. This is some of the ground
> rules when people come on the farm, to leave it in as good or better shape
> than they found it. (Interview 12/22.BM)

The detailed knowledge of precisely how much land is owned by which residents
and exactly where these boundaries are located illustrates the concern for retaining
the land unbroken. This is evidenced in the *scale* with which people discuss the land.
George Settle didn't want to let go of a piece of land as small as a two-foot right-of-
way. His reaction is also stimulated by what the African American community of
Clearview remembers as a past injustice:

> They blacktopped that road all the way up to right there [the boundary
> between the white and Black communities], and when they got to the line
> fence down here between Gene and Joe Settle's property, they couldn't go no
> further. They wanted two foot of land to widen the road out to come the rest
> of the way through. . . . They couldn't come through it because they need my
> signature on that paper to give them the right-of-way and give them the
> right to take two foot of ground. . . . I wouldn't sign it because I was angry. . . .
> I said, "My mother walked this road when I was a kid, carried me along with
> her in the mud" [when she was petitioning to get the road paved before the
> state eventually decided to]. (Interview T309 11/14.JD)

One of the largest looming threats was subdividing the land. Yet, even with all the
talk of keeping the land intact, the local newspapers are not devoid of classified ads
for "Land for Sale." Families who need the money, or families who have suffered the
loss of an older generation where the younger generation doesn't want to—or can't
afford to—farm, will sell the land. Ambivalence arises when residents are caught in a
cruel choice between the cultural rule of retaining the land as is, and the temptation
to take advantage of the high prices to be gained from selling the land—not for farmland, but for housing developments. Often the family doesn't subdivide the land
themselves but sells it to someone who does. Frequently (but not always) this middleman is not a native. A neighbor of mine told me she works at home for a business
that "buys up raw land all over the country." What is raw land? Raw—the definitions
include uncooked, and being in a natural condition, not processed or refined. In
other words, ripe for cooking or processing or refining—or developing. My guess is
that it is farmland, or maybe forestland. Not developed. Not yet.

This ambivalence about the land—wishing to retain it in its present state but
wanting to take advantage of the economic opportunities that it increasingly
affords—is not new. Anthropologist George Hicks (1976:60–61), studying in North
Carolina in the 1970s, quoted a storekeeper: "Our mountains are just being ruined.
And we let 'em do it." "Less than ten minutes later," Hicks reported, the storekeeper

"was enthusiastically discussing his plans to build and operate a motel and camp-ground. His attitude, a vague, disturbed sense of loss combined with an eagerness to exploit the financial possibilities of the land, is quite widely held." As I was writing this chapter, I received a phone call from a realtor who said: "I showed that piece of property [in Greenly County] to a developer, but he didn't want to pay the price that the owner was asking. And the owner won't go down on his price. It's been in his family for over fifty years, and I'm not sure how bad he wants to sell it, anyway" (Field Notes 4/11.MBW). Sociologist John Stephenson (1995:337–38) studied in the same North Carolina area in the 1960s and again in the 1980s. He wrote:

> We see in this one small Appalachian community a case of rural invasion and succession. Local families are leaving Shiloh in search of improved lives in towns and cities, and urban refugees are taking their places in the country, also in search of better ways of living. The machinery of this complex exchange is oiled and operated by a combination of local and outside entrepreneurs—all brokers of one kind or another. And the consequence is an uneasy acceptance of change on the part of natives—an eagerness to take the money and run, coupled with as yet ill-formed questions about messes of pottage.

This boils down to an ambivalence between "land as social space" and "land as property." Stephenson quotes a native who said "unsentimentally, 'You've got to have progress, but after you reach a point you lose what you had and you can't get it back.'" In their study of the history of Clay County, Kentucky, Billings and Blee (2000:24, 275) show that local elites "were major actors in regional industrial development and were prime beneficiaries of the plundering of local resources by outside corporations at the turn of the century," when they "acted as the agents" of those corporations.

The literally looming proposed 765,000-volt power line was seen as a threat to beauty and historic continuity—"seeing the same things the ancestors saw" would be no more. It would tear at the serenity residents praised, and thus be "just too costly in the human spirit" (Interview T009 06/14.MS&SS).[6] Residents planted signs along the road that said "Go to hell, ApCo," which might be said to be a profane way to strike out at a threat to the sacred (or semi-sacred) (Interview T020 06/29.LC). One resident was certain that a deity is watching and protecting this space: "I don't think God is going to let that power line come through here and destroy any of this" (Interview. T109 11/01.ASY).

While some thought God might provide protection, others had a sense of fatalism, as did the man described in this anecdote from a Harwood woman: "When our fight against the power line started, I was out in the community collecting money, I think for the historic work. An old-timer said to me, 'Little girl, there's no use to fight AEP, they're too big.' But I say, especially to young people, our way of life is worth fighting for. At least I can tell my grandchildren and great-grandchildren I did all I could. Too bad the battle has to be fought over and over. By the way, the gentleman did give me $10.00" (Link 1999). John Gaventa, building on his earlier work inspired by Lukes (1974, 2004), developed a nine-part "power cube" to illuminate levels, spaces, and forms of power. The man's brush-off of the fundraiser was an expression of "invisible power . . . the internalization of powerlessness. . . . In such a situation, visible conflict or public engagement is preempted because people may not see a need to act at all or, just as effectively, may not believe in their own capacity to do anything about the status quo" (Gaventa 2018:100; 1980; Powercube.net; IDS 2011). The person the man was speaking to was a grandmother, but calling her "little girl" fit his embodiment of powerlessness.

Despite the "it's no use" refrain sounded by this man, hundreds of people spent time, money, and effort to create organizations to protest the proposed power line. Natives and newcomers came together in these organizations—sometimes for the first time. Their protests had to fit into the mold already created by the states' approval processes. That meant that they had to be formal, and "scientific." They went to public hearings before the State Corporation Commission to testify themselves, but they also found specialists to study the need for the power line, potential dangers of high-voltage power lines, the presence of endangered species of animals and plants, the characteristics of karst (limestone and cave) topography—and cultural attachment to land. In so doing, the citizens participated in Gaventa's (2018:102) "claimed spaces" where people talked informally on their own terms and then developed more formal citizens action groups. They used social capital by calling on professionals who would be recognized as experts. The citizens then took their work into "invited spaces," "public consultation and public hearings [which] have become an accepted part of the American regulatory process." We will discuss this process more in the next chapter.

9

The Culture Wars, Anthropology, and the Law

Legislating Diversity

[To] preserve important historic, cultural, and natural aspects of our national heritage, and maintain, wherever possible, an environment which supports diversity and variety of individual choice.

National Environmental Policy Act, Section 101(b)(4)

A theme struck early in our discussion was the need to preserve diversity—biodiversity and cultural diversity. It is threatened by "the urbanization of the globe" (Thompson 2000:50). Legislation supports diversity in the United States. Cultural conservation, which requires both preservation and encouragement of culture, is mandated by federal laws. The most often cited legislative supports are the National Historic Preservation Act of 1966, the National Environmental Policy Act (NEPA) of 1969 and the American Folklife Preservation Act of 1976. Yet the report on cultural conservation, required by the National Historic Preservation Act as amended in 1980, lists thirty federal statutes that relate to cultural conservation, dating from 1889. So there has been concern for cultural conservation in the United States for well over a century.[1]

Mandates to include *intangible* aspects of culture, alongside material cultural *properties,* have been buttressed more recently. During the 1980s, artificial distinctions in federal heritage policies were challenged and changed: "The [old] language of the laws upheld distinctions between 'nature' and 'culture' and further divided cultural heritage into 'tangible' and 'intangible' aspects. Yet natural land forms and wildlife species could serve as touchstones to community life and values as readily as structures of the built environment could" (Hufford 1994:2). The House of Representatives report on the 1980 amendments to the National Historic Preservation Act (Title 3, Section 502) stated the aims of the legislation as assuring that the "intangible elements" of our national heritage be "identified and afforded appropriate protection and benefits, such as those protections now accorded tangible historical resources" (United States House of Representatives 1980). This concern for cultural conservation is echoed in the National Environmental Policy Act of 1969, in which the "human environment and traditional lifeways" are considered a part of the total environment, worthy of protection (Loomis 1983:25).

In the section below, we will demonstrate that, despite these legislative efforts, it was hard to give voice to rural people's concerns. It was hard for the people themselves; it was hard for expert witnesses. In the chapters following, we will show that recent government changes have moved the needle from difficult to nearly impossible.

The Place of Anthropology in the Culture Wars

In practical terms, the issue is whose values should inform the choices. Who ought to sit at the table when the big decisions get made?

Liebow 1998/1999:18

The National Environmental Policy Act requires environmental impact assessments for federal projects that affect the quality of the human environment. Guidelines for how to do this stipulate that "'human environment' shall be interpreted comprehensively to include the natural and physical environment and the relationship of people with that environment" (CEQ Regulations 1978:S 1508.14). Social science research methods function to help meet the NEPA requirement that "presently unquantified environmental amenities and values may be given appropriate consideration in decision making along with economic and technical considerations" (NEPA Sec. 102[2] [B]). How-to-do-environmental-impact-assessment manuals make it clear that social science data about intangible culture are to be a part of this process.[2]

Our project to study cultural attachment to land was mounted in the hope of making a contribution to how to discover, measure, and analyze a cultural intangible. Environmental actions change the culture, as well as the ecology in which human beings live. Indeed, the concept of "place attachment" has potential as "a 'new' defining dimension for natural resource management concerns" and environmental policies (Hull 1995; Norton and Hannon 1997).

Jain et al. (1993:200–201) correctly note that there are "specific approaches documented and required for assessing effects on biophysical parameters such as air quality, land use, and water quality," and that, on the other hand, a variety of methods have been used to assess social impact. (In cultures where the culture and the natural environment are inextricably bound together, the division between natural impact assessment and social impact assessment presents a false dichotomy.) The ethnographic research methods of anthropology are recognized as especially well-suited to this kind of research because they meet a criterion that social impact analysis be connected to an "internal" view of the affected community.

Ethnographic methods are well known for eliciting information from the insider's/native's/culture bearer's point of view. Ethnographers label this an *emic* perspective, and lay it alongside an *etic*, or observer's/analytic perspective for a fuller description and explanation of a culture's most important values and processes.[3] Francis McManamon, chief of the National Park Service Archaeology and Ethnography program, notes that "cultural anthropologists tap the traditional knowledge that makes these places what they are" and "systematically illuminate local perceptions."

Indeed, the Environmental Protection Agency and the Society for Applied Anthropology joined in a project where "anthropology has demonstrated the relevance of the social aspect of environmental protection. It has shown the value of local versus expert knowledge, and it has provided opportunities to test the applicability of the anthropological approach, with its rich and specific detail, to national policy" (Johnston 1998/1999:27).

Giving Voice

Its methods of discovering a local cultural mind, then, are one reason for anthropology to be a recruit in the culture war. Another is giving voice—"the need to ensure the genuine participation of local people in conservation programs" (Furze, De Lacy, and Birckhead 1996:back cover). "The singular contribution of anthropologists has been in equipping communities to take part in making the decisions," fortifying "inclusion, collaboration, and acknowledgement of local insight," especially from "groups historically excluded from the dialogue." "Finding acceptable answers [to environmental issues] involves value laden, conflict-riddled choices over who will bear the burden locally in order to achieve a widespread benefit." "Who makes the big decisions?" "Whose values should inform the choices?" (Liebow 1998/1999:18–19).

The last phase of the power line project took us into new territory and gave us new ways to give voice. Our earlier research reports on cultural attachment to land had been submitted to citizens' groups, to use as they liked in their efforts to conserve their cultures and preserve their environments. This time I was asked by representatives of two counties to present our report directly to the state regulatory body for utilities, the State Corporation Commission (SCC), and to testify in a hearing before this body. This brought us face-to-face with the legal arena and carried with it the new role of expert witness. Colleagues like Benita Howell at the University of Tennessee contended that whereas a governmental regulatory commission might dismiss the emotional testimony of residents, carefully collected and analyzed ethnographic data might be attended to.

Over time, the proposed routes for the 765,000-volt power line kept changing. As these two additional counties lay in its potential path, more data needed to be collected. Stringent deadlines for citizen input were imposed by the State Corporation Commission. Thus, the very short time allowed for this phase of the cultural attachment to land study demanded some changes. It would not be possible for a cadre of trained students to compile extensive participant observation field notes and to conduct and transcribe interviews, undertake analyses of these texts, and write reports, as we had done in the past. Citizens suggested that they themselves could conduct and transcribe the interviews. They did not want to attempt analysis, leaving this aspect to the Radford University team. This was a new level of citizen science: previously residents with whom we worked had provided orientations for me and the student researchers and smoothed our entrée into their communities; this time residents would be collecting data themselves. (A model for participatory research/citizen science is the Appalachian Land Ownership Study conducted in 1978–1981 by the Appalachian Alliance and administered by Appalachian State University and the Highlander Research and Education Center.)

Both old and new trends in anthropology helped to assuage my concerns about this new level of partnership: (1) collaboration with the people that we are learning from has been advocated in anthropology since modern-day methods of fieldwork were formed; the trend today is toward ever more collaboration;[4] (2) the National Park Service in its Applied Ethnography Program headed by anthropologist Muriel Crespi mandated collaboration with natives in learning about the relationship between culture and environment; (3) the Environmental Protection Agency's (EPA) Community-Based Environmental Protection program advocated citizen involvement and citizen data collecting. The EPA explained that "these community-specific activities can be effective because: They take into account local social, economic, and environmental concerns. They create a sense of local ownership of issues and solutions and encourage long-term community support and accountability."

If our experiment worked, perhaps it could serve as a model for allowing citizen input in the legal arena, especially for communities with little money or in situations with little time allowed. To help resident interviewers with data collecting, we provided a comprehensive project manual developed with my colleague Mary LaLone— which included open-ended questions that had been tested in my previous research—and conducted workshops on ethnographic interviewing. My colored glasses became even rosier, and I wrote, "The objective of this project is to create ways in which citizens' environmental concerns—such as cultural attachment to land— are rendered audible in a legal venue by being articulated through scientific means."

Our use of anthropology in a legal-like context echoed Borofsky (2000), who said that "public anthropology" should "challenge the framings that support particular definitions of a problem."[5] Three of these frameworks that underpin many decisions made in the environmental culture wars are: (1) economic language and thought predominate; (2) science is valued, but for whom and from whom?; and (3) if you do attend to culture, it had better be unchanged and "traditional." Our experience with studying cultural attachment to land that lay in the path of the proposed 765,000-volt power line suggests that questioning frameworks is easier said than done.

Framework: Economic Language and Concepts Predominate

Land use and environmental impact assessment is an area in which the marketplace has intruded to the detriment of protecting citizens' basic human rights to—in the words of the United Nations Declaration of Principles on Human Rights and the Environment—"a secure, healthy and ecologically sound environment," to be "free from any form of discrimination in regard to actions and decisions that affect the environment," and to have the "right to active, free, and meaningful participation in planning and decision-making activities and processes that may have an impact on the environment and development."

In words that echo our discussion of internal colonialism and sacrifice zones, Barbara Johnston (1998/1999:24) says: "Environmental problems create winners and losers. Winners profit from exploiting resources. They are rarely 'local,' and their status typically insulates them from the discomfort.[6] Losers suffer from lost resources, health, and livelihood. Their powerlessness is often tied to poverty, ethnicity, or religion." Anthropologist Setha Low (1994:68) adds that "within the politics of place, poor people's neighborhoods are always the most vulnerable because the local constituency does not have the political and economic power to struggle against the definitions and decisions of governmental officials and private entrepreneurs." These definitions tend to be economic in idiom, and are at odds with understanding the complexities of an ecosystem and the cultures that are attached to it. Anthropologist Roy A. Rappaport (1994:265) says: "Under these circumstances essential public concerns which cannot be put into economic terms remain not only inaudible but even unarticulated."

Our rural Appalachian examples of Setha Low's vulnerable populations spoke out at meetings on the power line: "As Bill Mitchell, a retired railroad engineer, put it, 'It's nothing but an electric interstate in the sky that's going to dump cheap Midwest electricity into the East Coast market'" (Pritt 1995:23). They spoke at State Corporation Commission hearings. The residents whose thoughts the hearing examiner encapsulated when he said they "viewed the proposed transmission line as a symbol of corporate greed imposed at the expense of the cultural attachment of the people to their land and the scenic beauty of the region" would not have been surprised by a startling photograph that shows the United States at night. Cities show up as a white brightness. West Virginia and southwestern Virginia are nearly dark (H. P. Anderson 2000:3; A. Wilson 1992).

Rappaport (1994:263) observes the incompatibility between commodity and ecology: "The logic of commodity on the one hand and biology, both organic and ecosystemic, on the other, are not only at variance but at odds. . . . It follows that decisions guided by the terms [of commodity] . . . are likely to simplify, which is to say to degrade and thus to disrupt, the ecological systems in which they are operative." These words are foreshadowed in the writings of conservationist Aldo Leopold (1949:210) forty-five years earlier: "One basic weakness in a conservation system based wholly on economic motives is that most members of the land community have no economic value." These generalizations echoed many times in the power line case, as in this instance when geologist William D. Orndorff wrote about karst topography and rare, threatened, or endangered species that are associated with it, like bats:

> Landowners in the —— areas have traditionally been good stewards of the land with regard to the north slope of —— Mountain in the allogenic recharge zone of the —— Cave System. An example of this is the seasonal closure of caves to protect the hibernating bats. Approval of a power line corridor across the watershed sends a message, whether intended or not, to

the landowners. That message is that economic development takes precedence over conservation interests. Construction of the power line corridor could result in an increase in other activities (for instance, forest harvesting) in the area that produce severe impacts on the rare, threatened, and endangered species of the —— karst. (Lion 2000:Appendix A:3)

What should take precedence? Rappaport (1994:266, 272) says, "[With regard to] the relationship of the economic to the biological-ecological, generally speaking, ecological and biological considerations, being more fundamental, should take precedence over economic considerations and, in general, economic systems should be adjusted to the requisites of the biological-ecological systems on which they are contingent." Violating this relationship "subordinates long-run ecological, biological, social, cultural and other aesthetic considerations to short-run economic interests." Not one to mince words, Wendell Berry ([1970, 1972] 2012:164), says, "short-term practicality is long-term idiocy."[7] Nowhere is there a clearer example than power lines that are purported to be a seven-year solution built on 250-million-year old-mountains.

Rappaport (1994) asserts that today's American English is overwhelmed by words centering around the economy. There is little room for a nonquantifiable value such as sense of place or cultural attachment to land. Just as Bellah et al. (1985) told us that we have much language that reflects individualism, just so we have much language that supports an economic outlook and evaluation. Just as individualistic language militates against a communal impulse, just so an economic idiom is at odds with understanding the complexities of an ecosystem and the cultures that are attached to it: "Ecosystems and landscapes, [then,] reduced to concatenations of commodities, tend to become simplified, degraded, decreasingly distinctive, and decreasingly capable of maintaining themselves" (Rappaport 1994:265).

There is no way to assign monetary value to cultures. They are, as we say, priceless. More generally many of the things humans take to be most important are, in their nature, beyond the reach of quantification. . . . Living systems—plants, animals, societies—are complex beyond full human comprehension. . . .

When subordinated to a logic of commodity and a monetary metric, ecosystems are conceptually fragmented into local agglomerations of more or less discrete "natural resources." Actions informed by such conceptions realize such fragmentation.

In sum, an ecological logic, which is based upon relations of mutual dependency among qualitatively distinct things, and which is fully compatible with the values of cultural and aesthetic preservation is displaced by a monetary logic incapable in its nature of recognizing qualitative distinctiveness per se, but which subordinates all distinctions to simple-minded calculi of more/less. (Rappaport 1994:272)

In the power line case the hearing examiner's report discussing various routes said: "certainly for the people affected by the —— route the environmental impact of the proposed transmission line is devastating. However, the —— alternative has fewer environmental impacts in virtually every parameter evaluated" (H. P. Anderson 2000:29). The environmental impacts are counted separately and totted up.

Often the desire to preserve natural resources and to conserve cultural resources are at odds with one another. For example, it may be that to preserve a fragile riverine ecosystem, farmers who have lived near it for generations would have to be moved off the nearby land.[8] But in this case, preservation of natural resources, conservation of cultural resources, and protection of future economic resources would all be served by the same action. The natural resource of water running through karst topography could best be preserved by not putting a situation requiring use of herbicides on top of it. Conserving the cultural trait of the use of springs as the primary water supply could be served by the same action. Conserving folklore that has the power of the area's many "bold" springs as its locus could be served by the same action. The natural beauty of the area could be preserved by not dotting it with power towers. Conserving the cultural attachment to the land that has this natural beauty as one of its pillars is served by the same action. Protecting the economic aid promised by nurturing tourism in the area is served by the same action.

The overweening impact of economic language is revealed in the report of the State Corporation Commission hearing examiner, in which he summarizes lengthy testimony and gives his recommendation to the three-judge panel comprising the Commission. Words like *cost* (*cost-effective, costly, costs*), *develop* (*developed, developing, development*), *economic* (*econometric, economical, economically, economics, economy*), *expense* (*expensive*), and *industry* (*industrial*) were used a total of 149 times. All uses of the words *grow* (*growing, grown, grows, growth*) referred to growth in power needs, and economic growth, industry growth, technology growth, and internet growth, except for three uses referring to population growth, tumor growth, and tall-growth plants (a problem for power lines). Words such as *culture* (*cultural*), *family* (*families*), *farm* (*farmed, farmer, farms*), *history* (*historic, historical*), and *home* (*homes, homeowner, homeowners*) were used a total of forty-seven times. (To be sure, as we discussed in chapter 3, the culture and the environment are inextricably linked, so residents were also very interested in the impact on the environment.) All uses of the word *need* (*needs, needed*)—sixty-one uses—referred to the need for electricity generation. This is not a criticism of the hearing examiner, who faced the daunting task of distilling three thousand pages of testimony into forty-three well-organized pages. It is a criticism of the framework in which he works, and ultimately the larger economically dominated culture in which this framework was born.

In yet another prime example of cost-benefit analysis gone amok, in November 2000 the US Supreme Court was asked to consider ordering the federal government to change decades of clean-air policy and begin considering compliance costs—not just health benefits—in setting nationwide air-quality standards legislated by the 1970 Clean Air Act and regulated by the Environmental Protection Agency (see US Supreme Court 2001.)[9] (We'll have more to say about the continued use of this kind of analysis in chapters to come.)

Framework: What Is Science, and Who Is Scientific?

While we in the social sciences see the newborn interest in attending to the intangible aspects of culture in environmental impact assessments as a foot in the door, the corporations and utilities that are required to undertake the studies see it as the camel's nose under the tent. And one way the camel will be kept outside is via the definition of science.

In the State Corporation Commission hearing examiner's report, words implying expertise and science are applied only to certain activities and persons (and not others). The six uses of the term *expert(s)* referred to those who studied real estate values, karst topography, and bats. Likewise, *research(er, ers)* referred to health, real estate values, and bats. All uses of *science* referred to studies of health-related issues. As the attorney for the protesting residents wrote in his "Exceptions to the Report," "the Report details the qualifications and professional experience of the witnesses supporting the Examiner's findings while failing to provide similar information for witnesses with opposing views" (Lion 2000:2).[10]

One of the latest techniques used to determine routes for things like power lines is geographic information systems (GIS). Using this same 765,000-volt power line case, geographer George Towers (1997:123, 116) made the point—also made in other case studies in places as far-ranging as South Africa—that a tool as scientific- and objective-seeming as GIS is actually subjective and political: "GIS-made maps often assert scientific authority with precise geometry, elaborate mathematics, complex methodologies and simple graphic designs." But the decisions regarding what to put on the maps, and how to weight each item, are inherently subjective. "The value judgments that comprise the weighting system should include those of the community [whose] lands are to be judged"; they do not. On the GIS-generated maps that purported to lay out the best corridor for the power line, cultural resources were defined, as is typical, as "historic districts and sites on or eligible for listing on federal or state historic registers."

Defining cultural resources this way misses "[humans'] *world*" as opposed to "[humans'] environment. [Humans'] world is a fabric of ideas and dreams, some of which he manages to give visible form"—what we have been calling the mental landscape (Tuan 1967:16–17). In the power line siting process, eleven potential effects, such as communication interference, effects on geologic features and impact on proposed, endangered, threatened, or sensitive (PETS) species were identified as significant issues. For purposes of the GIS process they were given ranked importance weights by the federal agencies involved (the Forest Service, the Park Service, and the Corps of Engineers). They ranked water quality ninth out of eleven. Residents, on the other hand, were very concerned about the potential effects of herbicides used on power line corridors since in this area of karst topography they rely on springs and private wells for household and farm water, for fish hatcheries, and for commercial water bottling operations. What is bound to be missed without ethnography is that residents are proud of their spring water—telling stories of how long their families have used it, how "bold" the flow rate, and how good the taste; offering interviewers spring water to drink was a cultural pattern.

In the environmental impact assessment required because the power line could cross federal lands, cultural attachment to land was identified and studied as a significant issue. It was not, however, included on the geographic information systems (GIS)–generated maps that ranked the various corridors. Towers (1997:119), citing other geographers who have studied GIS methodology, notes that "knowledge of the landscape, they argue, is difficult to operationalize mathematically and is therefore often ignored in GIS. Ironically, GIS's failure to include the subjectivity of sentiment renders it partial and all the more subjective."[11]

So geographic information systems is seen as scientific, whether it is or not. On the other hand, ethnography is seen as not scientific, whether it is or not. As I took the stand in one of the sumptuously appointed hearing rooms in the large State Corporation Commission building in the far-from-home state capital to defend ethnography in general and our study of cultural attachment to land in particular, the weight of legal definitions pressed in. As folklorist Mary Hufford has said, there is a suspicion of storytelling and a separation of storytelling from science. Michael Orbach (2000) noted that policy managers use the stories of natural history—for example, the life history of a fish—and treat it as science, but stories about people are a different story.

Although I think Eric Wolf's/Alfred Kroeber's often-quoted "Anthropology is both the most scientific of the humanities, and the most humanistic of the sciences" captures anthropology's strength, it was clear that in this court-like atmosphere it is necessary for ethnography's image to be as scientific as possible.[12] For example, ethnographic sampling is bound to be criticized. A survey of half a dozen textbooks on qualitative research showed that all recognize that the overall purpose is providing in-depth detailed understanding, which is generally acquired by means other than random sampling. The textbooks recognize that true random sampling would be prohibitive in an in-depth interview study, and that the self-selection that inevitably accompanies an interview situation militates against randomness. However, random sampling brings with it the imprimatur of science, and may be the only way— certainly the way that seems to be most accepted in court—to support our methods. Otherwise, even with purposive sampling, critical case sampling, what-have-you, we will be accused of choosing to talk to certain people for ulterior motives.

The next issue to raise its head was bias. For most of the hour and a half that I was on the stand the opposing attorney and I talked past one another concerning bias. Bear in mind that ours was not a study of attitudes toward the power line. Our study was an ethnography of particular aspects of culture with the guiding question, "Is there cultural attachment to land here, and if so, on what is it based?" Thus, the only way the study could be biased, as far as we were concerned, was if it had been done in a way that demonstrated that cultural attachment to land was actually there when it wasn't, or vice versa.

For the ethnographer, bias may arise in two ways:

1. The researcher may hold unconscious points of view that prevent her from seeing certain things or cause her to see only certain things at the expense of others that are equally present. Our methods avoided these pitfalls by using a standardized although open-ended set of questions and by analyses that utilized a good deal of quantification.
2. Data could be collected in such a way that the interviewer might lead the interviewee to information, making it appear that the interviewee had more cultural knowledge than he or she actually had. Or the interviewer might interrupt the interviewee, not affording the opportunity to display cultural knowledge that was actually there. Again our methods painstakingly controlled for this through an evaluation process that scrutinized the interviews before analyzing them. Thus, from our point of view, careful controls against bias had been an integral part of our methodology. I said this in several ways from the witness stand.

But for an attorney, bias is a different breed of cat, and the legal definition of bias can be used to endeavor to discredit our science. To avoid the appearance of bias in the legal sense—that is, having a prejudice for or against one of the parties in the proceedings—I had avoided becoming a member of or appearing at meetings of any of the protest groups or talking with the media, and caused the student researchers to do the same. Nevertheless, the opposing lawyer's several specific questions culminated in this summary question: "Was this not power line opponents interviewing power line opponents for the purpose of opposing the power line? Is that not biased?" The attorney also noted with disdain that interviewers had sometimes interviewed their relatives.[13]

Questions about the power line were not included in our set of questions asked. Since we were plumbing the culture of the area, the power line did come up in interviewees' discussions. That is not surprising. The interview transcriptions themselves were acquired by the opposing attorneys under a motion to compel discovery, and one of their staff members had diligently gone through the 449 pages (for the two newly threatened counties) and located three uses of the term *power line*. On the stand, I told them about seven more that they had missed, because to me this did not constitute bias. Instead, concern about the power line was an emerging part of the culture, and just one of several components of a larger cultural theme that the student researchers had discovered through coding and thematic analysis, namely "Protecting the Land." Other components of this theme were concern over trash being left on property and fences torn down, active county planning commissions, and resident-approved zoning regulations, for example.

The lawyer for the counties in which we had studied asked me, in redirect testimony, to discuss each of the uses of the term *power line* that the opposing attorneys had located in the interviews. The counties' attorney then asked: "Is there bias introduced into the process by this answer [that mentions the power line]? There's no way to avoid that [kind of answer], is there?" I answered: "Right. It's unavoidable and it doesn't interfere with the goal of learning people's cultural knowledge."

What does our experience suggest with regard to collaboration with our informants? Collaboration is one of the central features of ethnography and surely an asset in learning about cultures. But when we cross over into the world of power relationships, where to be heard as a witness we must carry the banner of science, is our closeness with informants, our collaborators, a limiting factor? Does this collaboration translate into contamination in the legal setting? If, in providing testimony in a situation where herbicide use were proposed, a geologist asked local residents about their knowledge of spring waters in order to learn about water flow through rock, then presented his findings in court, would he or the citizens be subject to the appearance of bias? If residents asked their neighbors the same questions and presented the answers to the geologist who analyzed them and presented the findings in court, would the specter of bias loom larger? If citizens collaborate with scientists in areas of controversy, must the citizens then abstain from exercising their rights to protest in order to keep themselves free from appearance of bias?

If indeed citizen science is problematic in a legal setting,[14] and time is of the essence as in this case, the techniques called REAP (Rapid Ethnographic Assessment Profiling) may be a viable alternative. As used by the National Park Service (1997), REAP is "a project-driven study and battery of methods including focus groups, transect walks, and community mapping. . . . Work should be completed in four or fewer months, but these need not be consecutive." Furze, De Lacy, and Birckhead (1996:56) in Australia describe a similar approach, Rapid and Participatory Rural Appraisal, in which "social research methods are chosen which maximize the development of key social knowledge, . . . optimize the cost-effectiveness of rural social research and ensure the participation of local people." The Park Service warns, however, that "REAP does not substitute for the more detailed ethnographic overview and . . . may indicate the need for more prolonged work."[15]

Framework: If You Do Pay Attention to Culture, It Had Better Be Unchanged and "Traditional"

Anthropologist Benita Howell (1999:7) identified the same power line situation as a "path-breaking and potentially precedent-setting case" because cultural attachment to land was designated a significant issue in the environmental impact assessment process. She evaluated a study of cultural attachment to land contracted for the environmental impact study. Subcontractors conducting that portion of the study fell back on modernity theory to assert that rural communities could be characterized as either folk—isolated from outside influences, relating only to kin, attached to the land in sentimental and not economic ways—or as urban/urbanizing—not isolated, absorbing some nonkin residents, and making a living via non-land-based means.

The folk were viewed as "culturally attached" to their land and thus worthy of saving from environmental impact. The urban/urbanizing were seen as not culturally attached to the land and not worthy of saving from environmental impact. As Howell (1999:6) said, "If these [subcontractors'] descriptions index anything, they index isolation, which is *not* the same as cultural attachment to place" (emphasis hers).

Former president of the Society for Applied Anthropology Robert Winthrop (1999), alluding to this power line case, points out that these subcontractors were not acting idiosyncratically; indeed, "U.S. cultural resources policy overvalues 'tradition' in a rather narrow, static sense of that term ('traditionalism'). . . . The system is strongly biased toward demonstrations of cultural continuity, rather than its creative adaptation." Haley and Wilcoxen (1997:767) note that this "conflicts dramatically with the fluidity researchers now recognize in cultural identities and traditions." Cultures are better seen as processes rather than particular static forms (Batteau 1983).

> The focus of our [cultural resource management] policy effort should not be on protecting places as much as on sustaining the communities that organize themselves in relation to particular places. We should not emphasize the preservation of particular cultural forms as much as encourage their creative appropriation and adaptation. As the Appalachian [power line] example suggests, however, this would be a difficult step, for in principle it would represent a far greater challenge to what is currently a largely unfettered engine of American industrial development. In any case, envisioning how we might better nurture the critical linkages between place, culture, and community in the face of rapid environmental change represents an important if daunting task for both culture theory and American social policy. (Winthrop 1999)

Although citizens may bring any concerns before the State Corporation Commission (SCC) (they must hire an attorney to negotiate the system), the Virginia State statute setting forth the mandate for the SCC's work states:

> Commission to consider environmental, economic and improvements in service reliability factors in approving construction of electrical utility facilities. . . . As a condition to approval [of construction of electrical utility facilities and certain electrical transmission lines] the Commission shall determine that the line is needed and that the corridor or route the line is to follow will reasonably minimize adverse impact on the scenic assets, historic districts and environment of the area concerned. . . . For purposes of this section . . . "environment" or "environmental" shall be deemed to include in meaning "historic," as well as consideration of the probable effects of the line on the health and safety of the persons in the area concerned. (Code of Virginia: 56–46.1)

No mention of living culture per se. Again, we see, inscribed in law, a concern for history that does not allow for current culture's dynamic use of history.

The scoping process required during environmental impact assessment can, however, uncover cultural concerns, as it did in the power line case. According to Hiss (1990:174), the first time a state transportation department "looked into the question of how a work of engineering will alter a way of life with the idea of actually protecting an ongoing, living culture" was in 1988 in Lancaster County, Pennsylvania, when more than a thousand Amish people, who generally do not participate in government, came to a meeting to collect testimony concerning a proposed road, and sat silently.

The legal/court system doesn't seem to be the place for settling the Preservation versus Progress, Place versus Property culture war.[16] Early on in the power line "battle," one of the main opponents expressed his regret that, due to being decided in this system, the situation indeed became an adversarial battle. Confrontations of this sort can be particularly abhorrent to cultures that do not generally value confrontation in communication styles, such as Appalachian cultures (Wagner 1994/1996). Although Don Barger, regional director of the National Parks and Conservation Association, says: "A lot of rural people are so polite that they will allow you to push and push and push, but they all have a line somewhere. If you go over that line, watch out. They've just decided, 'I have to take action now. This person can't push me any farther.' What I saw trigger that reaction more than anything else was a sense that their community was being disrupted—not community in the physical sense but as a sense of place and belonging" (Woodside 1995:5). The procedures of the court-like system separate need from route and hear these as separate issues. Each proposed route has separate hearings in turn, which promulgates NIMBYism (Not in My Back Yard). An attorney for one opposing county said he couldn't be the attorney for another, without fear of conflict of interest. This one-at-a-time process hammered away at early coalitions until they dissolved into individual groups with "just don't put it here" philosophies.

Besides bringing into focus the concerns and values of local people, loosening the grip of economic language, and demonstrating that cultures are not static, I would like anthropology to be in a place to raise the bar of need—or at least the bar of awareness—for development of new projects. Do we need a power line that will serve electricity needs for seven to eleven years that will change the face of 250-million-year-old mountains forever and have an impact on cultures that have called the mountains home for more than ten generations? The human dimension—in all its fullness and all its messiness—has to be attended to. The stories have to be listened to. "As soon as our attention turns from a community as a body of houses and tools and institutions to the states of mind of particular people, we are turning to the exploration of something immensely complex and difficult to know. But it is humanity, in its inner and more private form: it is, in the most demanding sense, the stuff of community" (Redfield 1960 [1955]:59).

Will we end this chapter by saying that the university-citizen collaboration was 100 percent successful: citizens were duly empowered, ethnography brought its usual purpose—to help people understand each other's cultures better—into the arena of the court-like setting of a government regulatory body, and all lived happily ever after? The project described here was certainly worthwhile. A county administrator wrote letters to the student researchers, saying:

> Those who have seen the study are most impressed with your work that reflects an overall perspective gained from the interviews that tell the story of the attachment that the citizens of the county have for their land. . . . Your interpretation of the interviews will be helpful to the future goal setting in the county—to develop the land for tourism, recreation, and wildlife conservation. . . . We wish you much luck in your future endeavors as an anthropologist. May your enthusiasm continue to provide you with challenges that will make differences in the future of our country. . . . You provided us with a document that will prove to be invaluable to the county in many ways.

How empowering for the citizens was this project? It was empowering with regard to demonstrating to the culture bearers that others valued and were interested in their cultures. It chipped away at the accretions that years of stereotyping of rural Appalachian people have built up. When students presented a play they had created using words from the interviews to a local historical society, an audience member commented that she had never before felt proud of her heritage. A local historian said the families in her area "knew they had been here forever, but no one had presented that as something to brag about."

Was it empowering in the sense of making a difference in the decision-making process of a government regulatory body? In a victory for the utility of anthropological methods in environmental research, the State Corporation Commissioners disagreed with the hearing examiner regarding the worth of our research, writing:

> With respect to the testimony of public witnesses and certain parties, it is readily apparent that residents along the possible routes have a strong attachment to the land that would be affected by the Project. In their testimony before the Hearing Examiner, many spoke of generations of a family living and working on particular farms. Their words by themselves conveyed the strong attachments the witnesses have. In addition to individuals' testimony, the study sponsored by Protestant witnesses —— documented the particular attachments to the land of the residents of the —— community in —— County. Further, Protestant witness Melinda Bollar Wagner collected additional expressions of attachment to particular farms and communities and of continuous habitation in her study of cultural attachment of residents of —— and —— Counties. The Commission disagrees with the Hearing Examiner's conclusions on bias in Ms. Wagner's study. We give weight to the study's conclusions that residents of the two counties, especially the —— and —— communities, have individual and communal ties to particular pieces of land. We

accept her conclusion that these residents have "emotional, economic, and social connections to their surrounding landscapes."

This is the only instance in the sixty-two-page document where the commissioners disagreed with their hearing examiner. Academic reviews of our work labeled it "precedent-setting." Was it a Pyrrhic victory?

10

Culture Wars Continued, Environmental Crises

The National Forest superintendent declared "No Build" for the 765,000-volt power line based on the NEPA-required environmental impact assessment and supplemental data submitted by residents' organizations for two of the studied counties. Two more were not spared.[1] When the last tower went up, the two sides met at the terminus. Like the last railroad track spike joining the Central Pacific and the Union Pacific in 1869, American Electric Power crews set a charge that fused the last connections with a ceremonial flourish in 2006. The two governors of Virginia and West Virginia stood in a celebratory attitude. It was billed as a dedication program for the ninety-mile, two-hundred-foot-wide corridor, a $306 million project that was the largest electric transmission project of its kind at the time. Chairman of the Federal Energy Regulatory Commission, Rep. Joe Barton, Republican from Texas, said, "Never again will it take 15 or 16 years to build a project like this, if it's a necessity." He was referring to 2005 congressional legislation easing restrictions (Dellinger 2006). His words would be prophetic of things to come in the culture wars of Preservation versus Progress.

The power line case is "crisis-like," in the words of Stephen Foster (1988:220), who studied protests against the same power company's plan to build a hydroelectric dam in North Carolina. Crisis-like situations continue to arise in the region, including buried pipelines to carry fracked natural gas (gas recovered from shale rock by hydraulic fracturing). The Mountain Valley Pipeline's planned path runs from West Virginia into North Carolina (where it becomes the Southgate Extension) crossing through Virginia. The pipeline would travel about 303 miles and was originally estimated to cost $3.7 billion, with projections now at $6.6 billion. Mountain Valley Pipeline's website (featuring a beautiful scene of forested mountains on its home page) says it will provide "transmission capacity to markets in the Mid- and South Atlantic regions of the United States." Pipeline construction in Virginia has racked up nearly four hundred violations of state erosion and sediment control regulations and fines of more than $2 million since work began in 2018. But although the pipeline has encountered permitting issues and investor cold feet, it is still on the table. Proponents are using a tightened global energy market caused by Russia's 2022 invasion of Ukraine to push for the pipeline's completion.[2]

In the power line case, the residents whose area was in jeopardy received no benefit. The electric power was to be wheeled to East Coast cities. The line was estimated

A cartoonist's rendering portrays residents' response to the high-voltage power line. (© 1998 *The Roanoke Times*)

to become outdated seven years into the future. In the case of the fossil fuel gas pipelines, the ultimate users of the product may be even farther from the unprotected area. Just as in the case of the 765,000-volt power line, for the gas pipelines, preservation of natural resources, conservation of cultural resources, and protection of future economic resources would all be served by the same no-build action. For the gas pipelines, the natural beauty of the area could be preserved by not blasting a corridor into the earth, much of which is underlain by karst (limestone) topography. Conserving the cultural attachment to the land is served by the same action. The natural resource of running water could best be preserved by not polluting streams with eroded topsoil. Protecting the tourism economy in the area is served by the same action. Leaving the fossil fuel in the ground as a reservoir for future need—which would lessen with increased energy conservation and more reliance on renewable energy sources—would be served by the same action. The benefit to those whose places are affected is even more tenuous, since the "United States has transformed itself from a gas importer to an energy superpower looking to build export terminals to ship oil and gas overseas. Exports of liquefied natural gas (L.N.G.)—natural gas cooled to a liquid state for easier transport . . . has boomed in recent years, more than doubling in 2019 and fast making the country the third largest exporter of the fuel in the world, trailing only Qatar and Australia" (Tabuchi and Plumer 2020).

For the gas pipelines, the Federal Energy Regulatory Commission (FERC) is the permitting agency. FERC wrote an environmental impact statement (EIS) for the Mountain Valley Pipeline "in compliance with the requirements of the National Environmental Policy Act (NEPA) and the Council on Environmental Quality regulation for implementing NEPA." The 930-page document, released in June 2017, addresses "impacts and mitigation" of geological, biological, socioeconomic, and cultural resources.

The subcontracted report on cultural attachment to land discusses our earlier work and describes similar findings from research of current archival records, including citizens' comment letters, public scoping meeting transcripts, and other documents, and field research in November 2015. Included in the report are "the following quotes from stakeholder letters, FERC public scoping meetings, and meetings between ACE [Applied Cultural Ecology] researchers and local residents [that] exemplify the people's cultural attachment in ways that paraphrasing would not" (Bengston and Austin 2016:33, 29–30):

> For those of us who call —— Mountain home, it is a very rare and special place where the mountain watches over us. It is sacred. It provides both peace and protection. Its power is not to be disrupted casually. [Landowner, West Virginia, Impact Report and EIS Scoping Recommendations 2015]
>
> First, the forest surrounds me with the world of nature, which I can't live without. The barred owls, the wood thrushes, the cool morning mist drifting down the slope, the sounds of roaring wind, the clean water that feeds my spring, the earsplitting silence on a snowy day. The views of the mountain slopes in their pastel buds preparing for spring are food for my soul. [Resident, Virginia]
>
> I love my precious lands. I care for the soil with my very soul, and all creations. Indian Burial grounds, ancient oaks in direct path of gas pipeline, spring fed pond—we use every inch of our lands in all aspects of life—pristine views. Water is our life. We have the best water in the world. [Resident, West Virginia]
>
> The domestic water supply for my household comes from a permanent spring on my property, very close to the boundary of the [National Forest]. Spring water that originates in the [Forest] has provided the water supply to the farm on which my family lives for more than 100 years. . . . Please do not allow a private company to destroy this century-old connection between federal lands and your neighbors and mine who live adjacent to the National Forest. [Resident, Virginia]

Like the residents opposing the power line, the groups opposing the gas pipeline cite degradation of a way of life, including "effects on scenic and recreational areas, loss of property values, threats to pipeline integrity from seismic activity and karst terrain, contamination of groundwater, wells and surface water and threats to public safety." But they also raise their concerns to the global plane. The pipeline to carry fossil fuel represents "reckless development that exacerbates the ongoing climate catastrophe" (Fitzsimmons 2019). A protestor in West Virginia said: "The Mountain Valley Pipeline is one of the worst possible things we could build at this point in time. . . . All the science suggests that fossil fuels are killing us. . . . A 42-inch gas pipeline is the complete opposite of an appropriate response to the greatest threat our planet has faced" (Hinton 2019). In a letter to the newspaper, Virginia Tech professor Dr. Emily Satterwhite (2019) quoted young Swedish climate activist Greta Thunberg's analogy, "our house is on fire," and likened pipeline opponents to firefighters.

Likewise, opponents of the six-hundred-mile underground Atlantic Coast Pipeline that would go from West Virginia to North Carolina, traveling through Virginia, brand it a polluting project that would "worsen the climate crisis, destroy water resources and degrade public forests and wildlife habitat." To these concerns is added "harm to environmental justice communities," with African American communities in the pipeline's path (H. P. Anderson 2020; Fjord 2021a, 2021b). More than seventy-five organizations have opposed the pipeline. As of June 2020, this pipeline proposed by Duke Energy and Dominion Resources lacked "eight required permits that have either been rejected by courts or suspended by agencies." The US Supreme Court took up one of the court cases and overturned a lower federal court decision that had blocked the pipeline "from crossing beneath the Appalachian Trail on National Forest land" (H. P. Anderson 2020). But the US District Court for the District of Montana ruled (in a case linked to the Keystone XL pipeline coming from Canada) that the US Army Corps of Engineers could not use the 2017 Clean Water Act Nationwide Permit 12 (NWP 12) to authorize dredge and fill activities. NWP 12 is used "to avoid the lengthy process of obtaining site-specific Clean Water Act 404 permits. . . . Project-specific permitting not only takes time, but also may trigger public participation opportunities for project opponents." "NWP 12 is vacated as it relates to the construction of new oil and gas pipelines pending completion of the consultation process and compliance with all environmental statutes and regulations" (Bell 2020b, 2020a). Subsequently the proposal for the Atlantic Coast Pipeline was withdrawn on July 5, 2020. The pipeline website said that the cancellation "was a necessary decision given the legal uncertainties facing the project" (atlanticcoastpipeline. com). Former vice president Al Gore and civil rights leader Rev. William Barber, who had visited African American communities in Virginia that would have been affected by the pipeline, said: "The courageous leadership of impacted community members who refused to bow in the face of overwhelming odds is an inspiration to all Americans." "The cancellation comes despite [then-] President Trump's efforts to bolster oil and gas pipelines across the country by weakening enforcement of some of the country's landmark environmental laws, including provisions of the Clean

Water Act, the Endangered Species Act and the National Environmental Policy Act" (Cox and Schneider 2020).

Citizens' groups opposing the still-on-the-table Mountain Valley Pipeline "are taking a number of actions." Emily Satterwhite says:

> Citizens have appealed to the courts and to state control boards, citing environmental damage, including erosion-polluted waterways. Hundreds and hundreds of people all across West Virginia and Virginia and now North Carolina are working every day on every angle. There are people working on the health effects of the toxic coating on the pipeline. There are people working on Federal Energy Regulatory Commission. There are people monitoring the work that the pipeline company is doing. There are lawyers working pro bono. There are people living in trees . . . who've been there for more than a year. (Yale Climate Connections 2019)

Barbara Ellen Smith (2018:65) notes that, "by trespassing on selected sites of private property and seats of power, contesting corporate practices that are destructive of place, . . . organizers in Appalachia are refusing to be locked down or locked out even if it means they are temporarily locked up."[3] Some citizens have performed tree sit-ins in the path of the Mountain Valley Pipeline; some have chained themselves to excavating equipment. Satterwhite locked onto an excavator above a large banner declaring "WATER IS LIFE." She described the experience to Yale Climate Connections (2019): "I was on the mountain for fourteen [hours]. That day, I climbed up an excavator and wrapped my wrists in chains and locked them inside a metal encasing onto the hydraulics of the equipment and waited for Mountain Valley Pipeline to show up." Fourteen hours later, state police cut away the locking mechanism. Satterwhite was charged with interfering with others' property. A plea agreement required two hundred hours of community service and a year of probation.

A theme of our research has been "Who gets to sit at the table" when energy and environmental decisions are being made. One way to downsize the table is to define protesting a serious criminal offense rather than an act of civil disobedience. The Mountain Valley Pipeline protestors who sat in trees, built barricades, and chained themselves to earth-moving equipment were arrested. They were usually charged with misdemeanors. The sentences they were given were generally from community service to fourteen days in jail. But as of June 2019, at least three people who did similar things were charged with threats of terrorists acts, a felony. The Trump administration proposed that the penalty for this type of anti-pipeline protest should be up to twenty years in prison: "Transportation Secretary Elaine Chao asked Congress to make several changes to the laws governing her department's Pipeline and Hazardous Materials Safety Administration." There is already a federal law against "knowingly and willfully damaging or destroying" natural gas pipelines, with a penalty of up to twenty years in prison. How did the Trump administration propose to change this law? One part of the proposal amplifies the definition to include "vandalizing, tampering with, impeding the operation of, disrupting the operation of, or inhibiting the operation of" a natural gas pipeline. Another change is to add "under construction," so that the law would apply to "a facility under construction." "When you combine provisions that vague to penalties that extreme, that creates uncertainty about what is and isn't legal" (Editorial Board 2019). And it most certainly would act as a deterrent to protesting, which, of course, is the point.

Another way the decision-making table can be cut down in size is to truncate the time allowed for public comment, the types of comments allowed, and the length of an environmental impact assessment document. In 2017, President Trump issued Executive Order (EO) 13807 to the Council on Environmental Quality (CEQ), the White House office established at the same time as NEPA to oversee its implementation. The order "directed CEQ to review its existing NEPA regulations and modernize and accelerate the Federal environmental review and decision-making process." The title of the executive order sets the tone: "Presidential Executive Order on Establishing Discipline and Accountability in the Environmental Review and Permitting Process for Infrastructure." The words *time/timely/timetable/timeline* appear twenty-four times in the order.[4]

The executive order and CEQ's subsequent proposal affect the NEPA environmental impact assessment process by shortening time, limiting pages, allowing applicants to play a role in the process, truncating the environmental impacts it can take into account, and deleting analysis of cumulative effects (such as climate change). Taking up its executive order charge, the Council on Environmental Quality said, "The increased costs and complexity of NEPA reviews and litigation make it very challenging for large and small businesses to plan, finance, and build projects in the United States." The CEQ "found that the average length of an EIS [environmental impact statement] is over 600 pages, and that the average time for Federal agencies to conduct these NEPA reviews is four and a half years" (CEQ Fact Sheet). Both would need to change, as per Trump's executive order. To "Modernize, Simplify and Accelerate the NEPA Process," CEQ proposes to "establish presumptive time limits of two years for completion of environmental impact statements (EISs) and one year for completion of environmental assessments (EAs)" and to "specify presumptive page limits." To "Reduce Unnecessary Burdens, Delays," the CEQ proposed to "allow applicants/contractors to assume a greater role in preparing EISs under the supervision of an agency" (CEQ 20200110). What can be included in an environmental impact assessment is also to be truncated.

> Require comments to be specific and timely to ensure appropriate consideration. . . .
>> Simplify the definition of environmental "effects." . . .
>> State that analysis of cumulative effects is not required under NEPA. . . .
>> Clarify that "reasonable alternatives" requiring consideration must be technically and economically feasible. (CEQ Fact Sheet)

"It is CEQ's intent to focus agencies on analysis of effects that are reasonably foreseeable and have a reasonably close causal relationship to the proposed action"

(CEQ 20200110). (Climate change need not apply.) The Obama administration directed agencies to attend to climate change in their project reviews. Trump's executive order and CEQ's operationalization of the order reverse and block that attention.

The executive order even has teeth. The "performance accountability system" for the agencies coordinating environmental impact assessments, will evaluate the degree to which the agency hits these marks of timetables and costs, and this will be considered by the Director of the Office of Management and Budget (OMB) "during budget formulation and [will] determine whether appropriate penalties . . . must or should be imposed" (Trump executive order 13807). One would be forgiven for concluding that Trump's executive order and the CEQ's proposal were weighted to the Progress–economic–investors side of the equation.

The responses to the CEQ proposal align perfectly with the culture war Preservation versus Progress sides. On the "Progress" side is a letter from Competitive Enterprise Institute (CEI) representatives of ten "free-market organizations [that] strongly support the proposal, which will expedite reviews of major agency actions with significant effects, minimize litigation, and roll back NEPA's misuse as an anti-development weapon." The free-market signees decry the Environmental Protection Agency's (EPA) role in upholding the Clean Water Act sometimes independently of the NEPA process, and hail the "One Federal Decision goal" that would make that additional oversight impossible. They ask for an even clearer "rejection of NEPA's use as a climate policy framework." They call for the CEQ to add that these new regulations "limit the scope of NEPA review" by stating:

> NEPA analysis is not merited for potential environmental effects that:
> Are not significant (because they do not discernibly "affect the quality of the human environment");
> Are not reasonably foreseeable;
> Lack a close causal connection to the proposed action; or
> Are beyond agency's ability to prevent and would occur regardless of the agency's action.
> The final Updated regulations need not spell out how those determinations constrain NEPA's role in climate policy. The attentive public will surely get the point. (CEI 2020)

What Trump and the CEI signatories want to do is to turn NEPA's "invited space" for public input to "closed or uninvited spaces of participation: spaces where bureaucrats, experts, elected representatives, and others make decisions with little consultation with or involvement of citizens. . . . Power remains unaccountable and often opaque" (Gaventa 2018:101–2).

We have used the term *culture wars* to characterize the two sides of Progress and Preservation. The CEI letter used the term *climate wars*. The conclusion makes clear which side the authors are putting their money on, so to speak:

> Mitigating climate change one project at a time is a fool's errand akin to draining a swimming pool one thimbleful at a time. Worse, the economic losses from blocking individual projects based on greenhouse gas considerations are bound to vastly exceed the speculative climate benefits. Moreover, because affordable energy and economic growth are critical to human mastery of climate related risks, and because the climatological significance of any infrastructure project is for all practical purposes nil, blocking energy infrastructure or other private investment requiring federal agency approvals in the name of climate protection is bound to do more harm than good. (CEI 2020)

This flies in the face of Hazlitt's (1946:5) description of "the art of economics," which "consists in looking not merely at the immediate but at the longer effects of any act or policy; it consists in tracing the consequences of that policy not merely for one group but for all groups."[5]

On the other side of the ledger is a letter from the US Senate Committee on Environment and Public Works, Minority Office. They note that the CEQ's new rules would "fundamentally re-write the National Environmental Policy Act regulations": "In particular, we believe that proposing to no longer require federal agencies to account for cumulative environmental impacts and indirect effects and allowing companies to prepare their own environmental impact statement is short-sighted, counter to the law, and fails to protect Americans from the public health and economic threats of climate change. . . . Instead of taking steps to respond to the growing risks, this proposal is untethered from our climate reality."

The senators note that fifty years of legal precedent uphold the view that NEPA requires analysis of the overall cumulative impact of the proposed environmental action: "Federal actions that trigger the NEPA process can impact generations, so it is imperative that cumulative environmental impacts, and direct and indirect climate effects more broadly, are included in the NEPA environmental review process" (Senators 2020).

One of President Biden's first acts was issuing Executive Order 13990, "Protecting Public Health and the Environment and Restoring Science to Tackle the Climate Crisis." This executive order rescinded Trump's Executive Order 13807. But the rescinding only goes so far. The Council on Environmental Quality had already changed NEPA regulations in 2020, and those regulations are congressional, not executive, matters. The infrastructure bill, HR 3684 – Infrastructure Investment and Jobs Act, as passed by the Senate weakened NEPA's safeguards. The word *efficient* occurs sixty-one times in the bill's October 1, 2021, text. One of the "key architects" of the infrastructure bill, Sen. Kyrsten Sinema (Democrat-Arizona) said, "Simplifying burdensome permitting processes will ensure efficient, timely completion of critical infrastructure projects that will fuel jobs, boost renewable energy production, and expand economic opportunities for communities across Arizona." In July 2021, a dozen conservation leaders noted in a letter to Congress that the bill's provisions "underscore a misplaced focus on limiting the environmental review and public input process, which threatens to undermine the principles of racial and climate equity that should guide an infrastructure package." It remains to be seen whether the House of Representatives' version of the bill ultimately reinstates the vigor of NEPA, which is described by Democratic representative from Michigan Debbie Dingell as "the Magna Carta of environmental law" (Grandoni and Fears 2021; White House Briefing Room 2021; Barho 2021; Greene 2021; Parkin 2021).

It looks like the decision-making table is shrinking—who gets to sit at the table is being scaled back. Conservationist Gary Paul Nabhan (2018:17, 18, 22) and mediator E. Franklin Dukes (2011; Dukes, Frederick, and Birkhof 2011) agree that local communities should not be left out of decision-making: "If we are to have communities sustained ecologically, socially and economically, it is essential that a capacity for productive, collaborative, place-based decision processes be developed. . . . Changing this dynamic [away from top-down decision-making] is key to a kind of community-based restoration that benefits us all (and other species as well). . . . It's time we engage rather than alienate the diverse voices in our rural and urban communities. . . . To regard everyone—farmworkers and loggers, cafeteria cooks and wild foragers, hunters and fly-fishers, teachers and preachers, ranchers and career professionals in agencies—as equal partners in collective efforts to 'stitch back together' our damaged landscapes and communities." In 2018, Nabhan was optimistic, but I ask, is this a Sisyphean effort, given the current political chasm?

11

Cultural Conservation and Cultural Confrontations

Wildwood Farms
Ridgewood Farms
Heatherwood Fields
Horseshoe Bay Farms
Spradlin Farm
Wyatt Farm
Strawberry Fields
Governor Floyd's Farm
Greenfield
Greenfield Crossing
Old Orchard
Orchard Run
Woodfield
Wilderness Woods
Pine Meadows
Twelve Oaks
Majestic Pines

Sounds like a slice of rural America, doesn't it?

Wildwood Farms is a housing development, colored light gray, beside Interstate 74 east of Indianapolis—"2 Models Now Open."

Ridgewood Farms is a housing development in Salem, Virginia.

Heatherwood Fields is a maintenance-free community north of Chicago.

Horseshoe Bay Farms is a golf course community in Door County, Wisconsin.

Spradlin Farm is a sixty-two-acre mall with Home Depot and Target anchor stores in Christiansburg, Virginia.

Wyatt Farm is a subdivision in Blacksburg, Virginia.

Strawberry Fields, formerly Scott's Pick-'Em-Yourself Strawberry Farm, is a subdivision just outside the city limits of Johnson City, Tennessee.

Governor Floyd's Farm is residential lots available for purchase in Pulaski, Virginia.

Greenfield is a subdivision beside Interstate 57 near Monee, Illinois.

Greenfield Crossing is the name for apartments on Interstate 70 east of Indianapolis; the logo is green plants growing in a farm field.

Old Orchard is a shopping center in Skokie, Illinois, near Chicago.

Orchard Run is a subdivision in Grand Junction, Colorado.

Woodfield is a mall in Schaumburg, Illinois.

Wilderness Woods is a golf club in Wisconsin Dells.

Pine Meadows is another golf course in Eau Claire, Wisconsin.

Twelve Oaks is suites and apartments in Arlington Heights, Illinois.

Majestic Pines is a casino near Black River Falls, Wisconsin.

These names symbolize urban and suburban sprawl.

Confrontations of citizens versus energy projects—dams, power lines, fracking, gas pipe lines—are "crisis-like." But our concern for cultural conservation of rural places and ways of life would be incomplete without discussion of another threat to rural life and farming that is on a slower, but nevertheless detrimental roll. "The insidious disarray of metastatic development" has little protest against it, precisely because it is not crisis-like (Foster 1988:220). Yet sprawl *is* increasingly recognized as a problem.[1] There is a "sprawlwatch" website, and the National Trust for Historic Preservation and the American Farmland Trust advertise books and articles with titles such as:

"Sprawl Guide"

"Legacy on the Line"

Changing Places: Rebuilding Community in the Age of Sprawl

Challenging Sprawl: Organizational Responses to a National Problem

"Alternatives to Sprawl"

How Superstore Sprawl Affects Communities (And What Citizens Can Do About It) and "Better Models for Superstores"

Development claimed at least 31 million acres of prime agricultural land between 1992 and 2012, according to a 2018 report from the American Farmland Trust. Virginia has not been immune to the loss of farmland experienced in other places. The American Farmland Trust designated the Great Valley of Virginia one of the most threatened regions in the United States. Putting farm, forest, and other rural land into one basket, Virginia lost more than 312,300 acres to development between 2002 and 2012. "Of all the development that has occurred in the last 400 years, more than a quarter of it has taken place just in the last 15 years" (VDACS 2020; Virginia Performs 2017). "Early in Virginia's history, land devoted to farming and forestry covered most of the state. By 1960, only 13.5 million acres of Virginia's approximately 25 million acres remained in farmland. In 2012, the total was 8.3 million acres, a loss of more than 5 million acres of Virginia farmland in 52 years. Statistics tell a similar story for Virginia's forests. In 2003, Virginia had 15.8 million acres of forestland, which represents a decline of 180,600 acres since 1992" (VDACS 2020). More than one-third of Virginia farmers are over sixty-five, and 70 percent of the state's farmland is expected to change hands over the next fifteen years, with farmers hoping those hands will be their children's.

Farming here has traditionally taken place on a blend of field, pasture, and woodland, with utilization of the flora and fauna of the forests alongside farming (Hufford 1998b). Appalachian Virginia holds part of the world's oldest and biologically richest forest. The counties we learned about provide a good case study because, "while land development activities and consequent scenic degradation have increased dramatically in the Southern Appalachians the means for protecting public interests in this uniquely scenic region have not, and the preservation of scenic quality has become a largely defensive effort responding to a series of crises." The Blue Ridge Parkway, a national park, surveyed the six counties in southwestern Virginia that lie along its path and found that they are "experiencing a rapid rate of change from agricultural to single family homes and commercial development. These counties also contain the greatest number of views of scenic farm lands that lack formal direction through zoning, vision documents or economic incentives, to encourage them to remain in farming" (Fels 1995).

The power of eminent domain plays a part in the loss of farmland. These days, the power of eminent domain is being used more often, and for more purposes. Governments have taken land to power urban America and industry, for tourism and recreation, and in the national defense (*Southern Exposure* 1995; Horning 2000). Many governments now use eminent domain as an economic tool. More and more frequently eminent domain decisions—and land use decisions in general—are economic decisions. The degree to which the economy frames and dominates the Preservation versus Progress debate is symbolized by the near-fate of George Washington's boyhood home, the eighty-five-acre Ferry Farm, in Stafford County, Virginia (where he allegedly chopped down the cherry tree). It was slated to become a Wal-Mart store and parking lot in 1996, and county "officials welcomed the retail giant because the county needed more tax revenue." (Eventually preservationists bought the land for $2.2 million, the same amount offered by Wal-Mart) (Ginsberg 2000).[2]

Along with gobbling up land that had been farms, development brings an influx of newcomers who, although they have sought to live in a rural area, may be at odds with its nature. But "community" is "in" among exurbanites. When urban dwellers contemplate moving to a rural area, they claim they are seeking to connect, not just with the land but also with the neighbors. What relationships among neighbors will they find in their new destinations? When compared with neighboring in rural areas, a guide to how to deal with neighbors in urban/suburban areas is laughable, although it's meant to be practical instruction. For example, "make written agreements any time you and your neighbor share responsibility for common property like plants, trees or structures." If dogs bark, "Keep a record—a logbook—of bothersome noise.... Present your evidence to the pet's owner and threaten to go to court if necessary." If neighbors' teenagers are a problem, "hire security guards" (Harder 2000). Interviewees described newcomers on a continuum from those who came closest to fitting their own "good neighbor" criteria to those who were more than a nuisance. Although NEPA and FERC do not play a role in determining the outcomes of these confrontations, they are increasingly being adjudicated by the courts.

We have alluded to the newcomers' versus natives' perspectives in previous chapters. We heard about it most when interviewing Borden County farmers in 2013. For this project we took as our starting point the findings of a Land Policy Task Force on the county's future. The Task Force found that "What Matters Most" to county residents is "preservation of rural character, Appalachian heritage, and community identity." Partnering with a local government office and a nonprofit organization, with Appalachian Regional Commission Appalachian Teaching Project funding, our project, "Sustaining the Community Mind for Long-term Community Resiliency: Appalachian Values Assessment," had as its mandate discovering what elements constitute "rural character, Appalachian heritage, and community identity." The project researched what residents want to preserve and perceptions of potential threats to those efforts.

Fourteen Borden County farmers were interviewed. The interviewees were selected by our community partners using a purposive sampling technique. Thus, full-time, long-term farmers were selected. One of our interviewees works a full-time job as well as farming. Three own and run a store as well as farming. (For the county as a whole, of the 864 principal operators of farms in the county, 47 percent consider farming to be their principal occupation, while 53 percent consider their principal occupation to be other than farming.) The interviews yielded 922 minutes of recorded talk and 382 pages of verbatim transcription plus photos and 147 pages of field notes, methods journals, and content logs for photos and transcriptions.

When we asked, "What parts of life here do you wish could be preserved for future generations?" maintaining the county's rural nature was uppermost in the minds of the farmers. Keeping the open landscape was seen as key to sustainability, as shown by the farmer who coined the term "open-land lifestyle." "Well maybe that means [keeping] the open land, not developing it. We've got a conservation easement on our farm and you know being able to go out and walk through the fields and watch the leaves change or the grass come up in the spring. Little things like that are interesting" (Interview 11 10/07.LL).

A second question, "What would make you sad if it happened to the land?" explored farmers' perceptions of threats to the desired open-land lifestyle. They expressed fears of development, a taking (via eminent domain) or having to sell land because "the economy or the situation gets to the point that the farm cannot sustain us—the family—making a living here" (Interview 07 10/10.LG). Development causing farmers to lose land and/or the ability to farm the land is a long-standing serious concern for Borden County farmers. In this county, "ownership of land has been moving out of the hands of long-time resident families for at least fifty years" (R. Cox 2017:1).

New residents who move in from outside of rural areas typically have more wealth, thus driving up land prices and pricing out local landowners, especially young first-time buyers: "[Hobby farms] compete with commercial farms for the same land and drive prices up beyond what working farmers can pay. Hobby farmers are likely to view land as a consumption item, enabling owners to enjoy a rural life-style rather than providing them with a livelihood" (Spain 1993:156; Buttel 1982; Healy and Short 1979). This creates a "disincentive for agriculture. As land prices are driven up by demand for residential property, farmers find it harder and harder to expand, and almost impossible to start from scratch, simply because traditional farming operations can't generate enough income, per acre, to pay for land priced for potential residential use or development" (R. Cox 2017:3). The newcomers don't pay the freight, when compared to farmers. A Borden County Planning Commission Comprehensive Plan found that "on average for each $1 in revenue from residential properties, the county spent $1.09 providing services to those lands. . . . For each $1 received from farm/forest land uses, only 35 cents was paid out to provide ser-vices. . . . While residential development contributes the largest amount of county revenue, its net fiscal impact is negative because the total expenditures for residential land use exceed its revenues" (Powers 2010:166).

Farmers gave passionate answers to the question, "What do you think about the increasing interest that people seem to have in visiting Borden County and living in Borden County?" Although both positive and negative answers were given, it was clear that former urban dwellers who bring their expectations and demands to Bor-den County are a source of distress and resentment. This aspect of newcomers, as well as land being taken over to house them, are seen as threats to sustaining rural open-land farms and farming culture. Some respondents recognized the reasons Borden is deemed a desirable place but still noted that the actions of some of the non-natives do not mesh well with farming in Borden County.

> Well it can be good and it can be bad. I can see why they would like to live here, but then again if everybody moves in, then it's—the Eagles had a song, they said, "Call someplace Paradise, kiss it goodbye," and that's about right. I don't know—don't really have that much of an opinion on it. Parts of the county's really overrun out toward —— and ——, but there's nothing you can really do about it. (Interview 11 10/07.LL)

> It's kind of a double-edged sword. It's good and it's bad. It's good from the economic standpoint especially for the little town. But I'm not sure it's helping county wide. . . . Tourism is a different kind of deal a little bit. But with more houses, it's kind of hurting the county as far as tax rate and amount of taxes that's having to be paid. (Interview 09 10/14.VC)

> It's those ones that come in here to get away from something, then want to change this to just like what they got away from. (Interview 06 10/14.HS)

> They moved here to get away from the lifestyle they had and now that they've got here, they want to bring their lifestyle to us. (Interview 04 10/13. HW)

> I guess it bothers me more than anything that people move in and they want it like they had it before. In other words they come in and they want to

change it like they want it. A neighbor comes and he builds close to our property, but our cows' manure stinks. He wants us to get rid of our cows because he moved close to us. (Interview 12 10/11.KC)

The neighbor complained about tractors [on the road]. These farms have been around here longer than you [neighbor] have. I don't know where you're from, but if you want me to, I'll rent you a U-Haul, and I'll pack it for you. This is where I've lived all my life. There's cattle runs around here. Cattle's going to bawl. There's dogs. They bark. If you want a quiet ordinance after midnight, what you need to do is pack your [bags]. . . . If you want to live in Borden County, accept the way Borden County is. You come to the country, expect the smell. (Interview 10 10/21.MBW)

I was at a meeting, and there was a man wanting to build four lanes so that you wouldn't have the traffic congestion. And I wasn't so sure that we didn't just need to build three, one coming in and two going out, so that everyone knew how to get out. But as more people come, [there is] more traffic, more congestion and then sometimes that doesn't necessarily fit the rural character and the farming. They enjoy the peace and quiet and rural nature until they [notice the] smell and the inconveniences. So sometimes that's not compatible. But it's all good. (Interview 13 10/11.AR)

Off the record, we heard even more stories recounting newcomers' complaints about tractors on the roads and animal sounds. Some newcomers want to change the rural area to have the infrastructure and services of the places they came from. They want paved roads, sidewalks, trash pickup. Surprised by the interviewees' descriptions of some newcomers' lack of appreciation for the rural life they had recently chosen, one of the student analysts remarked, "That'd be like me going to Italy and saying, 'That's just too Italian!'" A real estate agent told me that the local realtors were writing a booklet to explain to potential buyers what they should expect in rural Borden County. Later, when I asked her if I could have a copy, she said they had decided not to write it. (Its impact on sales might not be in the positive direction.)

Farmers in Appalachia are not the only ones who have this problem. Stephen Bloom (2000) wrote about "a clash of cultures in Heartland America." Sonya Salamon (2003) wrote *Newcomers to Old Towns* about rural Illinois. Brian Hoey (2014) learned about migrants and locals in Michigan. The pressure from nonfarm neighbors can get so bad that the farmer has to sell out. Tony Caligiuri, president of Colorado Open Lands, which handles conservation easements, "watched as his father had to sell three different farms in southeast Pennsylvania, in part to escape homeowner complaints as suburban sprawl surrounded each operation" (Oldham 2020).

In fact, farmers in the United States are not the only ones who have this problem. In Britain, "relatively few rural dwellers now have any direct linkages with the productionist countryside . . . which is leading to a series of high profile challenges to taken-for-granted smells, sounds and sights of agricultural activities." This includes, for example, "the court injunction taken out against the owner of Corky the Cockerel in

1993 for crowing too noisily" (Milbourne 1997:2). In France, second-home owners brought a lawsuit against Maurice, another cockerel who, in their view, crowed too early. In a different French region, "a case was brought against the owner of fifty ducks and geese" that made noise. In the village of Foix, a new resident filed a complaint "because the church bells were too noisy." These complaints have prompted defenses. The mayor of one village posted a sign "warning visitors that they are entering a risk zone. Church bells ring often. Tractors make a racket. All because 'farmers are working to give you what you eat.'" A legislator introduced a bill to protect France's "sensory heritage," "the crowing of the cockerel, the noise of cicadas, the odour of manure." The legislation passed the National Assembly unanimously (*The Economist* 2020).

The complainers have pushed for various ordinances against sounds and tractors, but their grievances have not generally risen to nuisance lawsuits against farmers. All states in the United States have "Right to Farm" laws that limit nuisance litigation. Usually it is landowners near a large "factory" concentrated animal feeding operation (CAFO) who have brought nuisance suits. The laws typically make a distinction between insiders and outsiders—people who moved into the situation they are complaining about (National Agricultural Law Center 2020). "Existing residents often have many more rights, since they've been there for a long time, whereas new arrivals are considered to have 'moved to the nuisance' and are afforded considerably less protection" (FindLaw 2016). However, at least one lawsuit in Borden County was brought against a farmer with cattle on open pasture, very far from the Environmental Protection Agency definition of a CAFO as a confined situation with more than 1,000 animal units, such as 1,000 head of cattle (USDA 2020). In the case of this lawsuit, the judge limited the number of head of cattle that could be maintained on the pasture.

One of the Borden County farmers conveys the need for balance in the culture war of Progress versus Preservation:

> I will say this, some of that people pressure for places to live and spaces—spots—to build houses is what's putting pressure on the farm land. And it's what's taking some of it away and it's what's making it difficult in some cases for farms to remain farms. So I'm not against it, but the fact is that that interest in Borden has made the farming community have a little more difficult time in being able to sustain and remain here. So it can be a balance there, but it's going to be a little bit of a tricky balance to keep—to keep our rural lifestyle and our farms and still have folks move in and live here. I mean it's possible. It's been happening and it will continue to, I'm sure. But I think that's going to be one of the biggest challenges we have in Borden County—is to try and balance that—so that we don't lose all of our rural lifestyle. It's going to be a balancing act. It's going to be difficult. (Interview 07 10/10.LG)

In the next chapter, we will review some strategies for balancing Preservation versus Progress.

12

Culture War Strategies

But the question arises whether, by some slight amelioration of the impending changes, certain values can be preserved that would otherwise be lost.

Aldo Leopold, *A Sand County Almanac*

The family farm and open land are on the national mind: "Since Pew Research Center began polling on environmental issues in the early 1990s, public support for environmental protection in general has remained high. Seventy-four percent of Americans believe the country should 'do whatever it takes to protect the environment' compared to twenty-three percent who said the country has 'gone too far' in environmental protection efforts" (Richman, Lotze, and Loza 2017). In this chapter, we will look at balancing acts performed by governments and citizens.

Solutions that ignore the culture war that America is fighting in the environmental trenches are doomed to failure: "The forces of change whose emblem is the bulldozer, and the forces of preservation whose totem is the tree, are everywhere at war in this country" (Garreau 1991:11). Kolodny (1975) and Garreau (1991:13) document the varying land perspectives of early European comers to America's shores. The Massachusetts Bay Puritans saw a scary wilderness of wasted land, in need of using. The Virginia Cavaliers saw a wonderful pristine wilderness.[1] These regional biases are gone, but the warring views remain throughout the country: "One sees the untouched land as an object of veneration, a source of spiritual strength. The other sees the land as a commodity to be used and exchanged for money."[2] As Rotan, Texas, librarian Dani Day said about controversies surrounding ranchland, "It seems like there is a real division between the people who are connected to the land and the people who aren't. It's not animosity really, just a cluelessness about one another" (Tomsho 1998). Conservationist Nabhan (2018:11) says, "And if we know anything at all, it is that those different cohorts of voters looked through very different lenses at legislative actions like the Endangered Species Act, the Paris Climate Accord, offshore oil drilling, the Sage-Grouse Recovery Plan, the designation of national monuments." Put another way, Theresa Trainor (1998/1999:22), member of the Environmental Protection Agency during the Clinton administration, said: "There are many situations where competing economic, environmental, and cultural values are creating complex challenges for people trying to reach agreement about the best use of our nation's natural resources."

The far-reaching and sometimes subtle character of this war can be seen in the language and rhetoric used to support *developing* the land versus *conserving* land in its natural state or for traditional uses. Anthropological linguists have long known that words carry deep and broad connotations and affect perception and behavior (Sapir 1921; Whorf 1956). Those who stand on the Progress side "are also likely to believe it obvious beyond challenge that 'more' is better, that 'growth' is good, and that 'change' means progress." They see undeveloped land as vacant, empty, and wasteful. John T. (Til) Hazel, the famous and infamous developer of Tysons Corner, Virginia, saw land as "no different from coal or oil; it is a natural resource. . . . The most fervent swear word in his vocabulary was 'waste'" (Garreau 1991:367, 387). Hazel would find an ideological kinsman in Carl Karcher, founder of Carl's Jr. restaurants, an early competitor to McDonald's in Anaheim, California. An interviewer inquired whether he missed the old Anaheim of ranches and citrus groves, now replaced by fast-food restaurants, subdivisions, and strip malls. "Well, to be frank about it, I couldn't be happier," he said. "I believe in Progress" (Schlosser 2001:28). Another soulmate is multimillionaire Arthur M. Ratliff, mine operator and real estate entrepreneur in Tazewell, Virginia, who says: "God created us to conquer the planet. He created us for victory!" (M. E. Long 1983:796). For coal operators, the land is merely "overburden." They see it as a shame—as in fact sacrilege—not to use the land. "God gave us this coal to *use*. To not use it would violate God's laws" (Appalshop 1979). Midwestern farmers, too—those Salamon (1992) would label entrepreneurs—can see God's command in "unused" land. A Lutheran minister in an Iowa farm county said, "I believe God waits with bated breath for us to use some of the gifts that he has given us—to develop what, by itself, would be waste, into something productive" (Dudley 2000:8).[3] A lawyer for the Coal Association of Kentucky said that strip-mined land, rendered flat, is more valuable than the mountain land it once was, because the flattened land has more market value (for golf courses, for example). (Reclamation is meant to restore the land, but Frank Kilgore from the Virginia Citizens for Better Reclamation says "grass on a strip mine is like lipstick on a corpse" [Appalshop 1979].)

Compare this Progress talk to our Preservation-oriented rural residents, who see land as legacy, as heritage, as something loaned to them by God to pass to their descendants: "We're just borrowing this land from our grandchildren" (Carden et al. 1993). For some, the land itself has rights; if "the owner of the land [is allowed to decide what will happen to it], then the land and the life on the land have no rights" (Larry Adams, Kentucky deep miner interviewed in Appalshop 1979). Ann Kingsolver (2018:22) asks about mining, "How did it ever come to make sense that corporate rights to minerals under the land took priority over collective and individual rights to the trees and homes and farms on top of it?"

Another aspect of the culture wars is the different conceptions of time held by the two sides. Joined with the much-touted (and true) "slower pace" of rural life is its longer view of time. The rural residents we interviewed talked of time by referring to seven, eight, nine, and even ten or more generations in the past. The Progress side of the culture war is willing to build a 765,000-volt power line that will "provide adequate reliability for seven to eleven years before requiring additional reinforcement"—that's the figure accepted by the power company and the government agency regulating it—across mountains that are 250 million years old (H. P. Anderson 2000:26).

In the previous chapters we have described long-standing and new problems in a Preservation versus Progress culture war. That there is a disconnect between food production and farming in the popular mind was made to clear to me as I taught a cultural anthropology class in a classroom not designed for discussion. Usually enthusiastic, but now exasperated, I thought to ask a simple question to start some conversation. I asked, "Where does our food come from? The answer starts with an *F*." A biology major pictured on flags flying from the light poles around campus as a student exemplar said, in all seriousness, "Factories." Recognizing the importance of rural culture, Wendell Berry and Gary Paul Nabhan say the way forward to an environmentally sustainable future is smaller landholdings with more people in touch (literally) with the earth.[4] That path is strewn with debris that would be hard to clear, though Berry ([1977] 1996:230) says, "The enormous productivity of industrial agriculture cannot be denied, but neither can its enormous ecological, economic, and human costs, which are bound eventually to damage its productivity." Organizations like American Farmland Trust, the Land Institute, the Center for Rural Affairs, and the Land Stewardship Project are working to undo the damage. Others are reaching for strategies for balancing development with preservation of farms and open land.[5] Some of these strategies are used by governments, some by citizens' organizations, and some by individual farm families.

Revitalizing Downtowns

The National Trust for Historic Preservation maintains that "the most successful weapon [against mall sprawl] is a commitment to revitalize downtown." More than two thousand downtowns have requested help from Main Street America, established in 1980 as a program of the National Trust for Historic Preservation (2020). Its mission is to "bring economic vitality back downtown, while celebrating their historic character, and bringing communities together." Another strategy is to loosen "rules that forbid mixing residential and commercial uses" (Mathews 1994). Segregating functions so that residences cannot be mixed with businesses is a move decried as long ago as 1963 by Jane Jacobs in *The Death and Life of Great American Cities*. This decision, made time and time again in cities and towns across America, helped to foster the growth of suburbs and new "edge cities," places outside of cities characterized by a recent conversion from farm or bedroom community to offices, malls, and housing (Garreau 1991).

Development outside of cities and towns is sometimes boosted by economic incentives. After World War II, home loans were given to veterans only if their homes were built on large lots. Through this, says Pulitzer Prize–winning writer Thomas Hylton, "we wasted huge amounts of land. We degraded our cities" (Bishop 1996). "Banks deny mortgages in declining neighborhoods," and it may be "more expensive for a developer to reclaim an abandoned urban site than to build on virgin land outside the city" (Thompson 2000:51). Funding local schools and local projects with local taxes is ostensibly meant to retain local control, but it has had the roundabout effect of encouraging development, because, when municipalities depend on local taxes they are encouraged "to go after development no matter what it is. So you have planning on the basis of 'Where are we getting our taxes?'" To counteract this motivation for development, some policymakers favor statewide real estate taxes that would be divided among a state's communities (Bishop 1996).

Many authors blame the car for driving the road and parking lot construction. The car allowed commuting between homes and workplaces and suburbs and malls. Building good mass transit systems can help conserve open land because "if a city has good rail and bus lines, then development can be concentrated around mass-transit stops rather than spread out all over the countryside" (Thompson 2000:51). A by-product of transit-friendly living—with "compact developments, sidewalks, accessible retail and employment centers and permanent green reserves"—according to public health officials, is that it would also be pedestrian-friendly and could help reverse the effects of car-induced sedentism and obesity, and isolation-induced psychological maladies (Brody 2000; Sprawl Watch 2001; L. E. Jackson 2003; R. J. Jackson and Kochtitzky 2002, 2010; Langdon 1994).

Planning and Zoning

Across the country, zoning or restrictions on land use have a wide variety of manifestations, from Houston's boast of "no zoning," to subdivisions with "restrictive covenants" regulating house color and dictating when Christmas decorations can be displayed. Historically, rural areas have been notoriously averse to zoning restrictions. Most of the time rural people seem to go by the maxim, "When you own land, you own it from heaven above to hell below" and can do anything you want with it (Appalshop 1988). A retired farmer was reported in the newspaper as saying about a proposed zoning ordinance in Andrews County, "Someone tries to make me move my dogs, they're going to the graveyard." In this case, where a nearby man-made lake has yielded a plethora of vacation homes, the native farmers "were convinced that zoning was little more than a big-money plot to protect pricey vacation homes at the expense of the little guys who are trying to scratch out a living from the land. 'Those Yankees from up North are coming down here and trying to move us out of the county, and we've lived here all our lives'" (Poole 1988).

But Virginia's local governments have tried to obtain more power to curb sprawl. The rural counties we studied *are* planning for their futures. The zoning practices of Greenly County, in place for many years, reflect the residents' determination to maintain its rural, undeveloped, unsubdivided character. Zoning restrictions legislate that certain land cannot be subdivided into pieces smaller than five acres. This legislation was passed more than forty years ago, by zoning boards made up of community leaders. When a newcomer asked one of these board members several years later how they had agreed upon five acres (thinking this large lot size was something of a phenomenon), the former board member replied, "We didn't know if we could get approval of everyone for *ten* acres" (Field Notes 6/15.MBW). A member of the Board of Supervisors of Farlane County drew fire for suggesting that minimum lot sizes throughout the county be lowered from two acres to one acre (Block 1999). (On the other hand, Bob Yaro, former deputy commissioner of the Massachusetts Department of Environmental Management, has said that this kind of zoning doesn't actually work to protect open land, but instead produces parcels that are "too big to mow and too small to plow" [Hiss 1990:214].)

When a subdivision ordinance came to the table of the Borden County Board of Supervisors, speakers at a public hearing noted an economic class distinction between local people and outsiders buying land and driving up prices. Large lot sizes "drive the young people out of the county because they can't afford the cost. If they can't afford it, only the rich can live in Borden County. Is this going to become a retirement center?" (Mannon 2000). These varying citizen and government views point to "a problem of defining the point at which the inalienable rights of the private owner end and the inherent power of the state begins" (Sparks 1971).

In local communities in some of the western states especially, environmentalists, ranchers, loggers, fishermen, and government agencies—who would seem strange bedfellows—have formed collaborative conservation groups and watershed alliances, generally called regional growth management plans. They are local groups focused on taking a "community-based approach" to conserving a particular area (McCarthy 2001).

Creating Historic Districts

Historic districts, whether urban or rural, whether sanctioned by state or federal governments, can be a way of protecting places. Historic districts must generally have standing structures with historic significance. Once so designated, historic sites have standing in decisions concerning environmental use to a greater degree than living culture does.

The residents of Swanson and Harwood in Farlane County mounted a major effort to obtain state rural historic district status. A resident who took part in the process says, "The Rural Historic District nomination process is what brought about my experience as an amateur architect. Some of us took a short training session, created forms for submitting information about properties, and spent countless hours out in the community, looking at houses and visiting folks. Our efforts cost a great deal in time and some funds, but were well worth it if Historic District status helps us hold on to the rural and scenic beauty of our place" (Link 1999). On the other hand, the African American residents of Clearview were discouraged by professionals from trying to obtain historic site designation because the architecture reflected in the residents' memories was not, in their view, sufficiently in evidence on the ground.

Advocating Direct Payment or a Living Wage for Farmers

In Europe, agriculture is supported by nonfarm constituencies, "and at the same time constrained" from, for example, making decisions that would harm long-term ecological health. It is subsidized "because it fulfills important roles in providing food, preserving desirable ways of life, and sustaining a healthy national environment" (Barlett 1993:252). Farms have "public value" (Hiss 1990:118).

In the European Union, a strategy for keeping the land in farming and keeping farmers on the land is direct payment. This maintains the cultural landscape and pays for the ecological services that farms provide to ecosystem conservation. It is a manifestation of Wendell Berry's ([1970, 1972] 2012:97–98) philosophy that "a truer agricultural vision would look upon farming not as a function of the economy or even of the society, but as a function of the land; and it would look upon the farm population as an indispensable and inalienable part of the ecological system." The European Union Common Agricultural Policy (CAP) began in 1962 and has evolved so that beginning in 2003, "farmers now receive an income support, on condition that they look after the farmland and fulfill food safety, environmental, animal health and welfare standards" (European Commission 2019).[6] This strategy has not been tried in the United States. Critics of American federal farm subsidy programs say they benefit most the largest farms (Andrzejewski 2018).[7] It is suggested that they be reallocated to return to the purpose they served during the Great Depression, to assist the middle-sized farms, where most family farmers live.

Eric Schlosser (2001:268) details America's fast-food industry's ties to centralized industrialized farming and ranching, and its impact on farming. He says that McDonald's and other fast-food chains, which already dictate "the sugar content, fat content, size, shape, taste, and texture" of their suppliers' products, could also "demand changes in the way poultry growers are compensated by their processors" and could "use its clout on behalf of Idaho [potato] farmers." The chains could "enforce a strict code of conduct governing the treatment of workers, ranchers, and farmers." And, going one step further up the food chain, he suggests that we consumers of fast food could demand that McDonald's and the others do this. We could vote with our pocketbooks.

Growing New Old Crops and Selling Them in New Ways

Virginia's land grant college is leading workshops in Greenly County to encourage farmers to grow, harvest, and market medicinal herbs and other nontimber products in the forest. The goal is to help farmers diversify their crops and at the same time provide them with "an economically sound use of land that otherwise might be logged clean or sold for housing developments" (Schnabel 2001). Workshops highlight products like shiitake mushrooms and ginseng. At $500 to $800 a pound sold to Asian markets, ginseng is lucrative, but it is difficult to grow, and cultivated ginseng can sell for less than the wild plant. Plants from seeds dropped now would be ready for harvest in ten years, prompting a workshop attendee to say, "Most of the folks here will be planting for their children." Ginseng, though, has the advantage of indigenous knowledge of the plant, and, as another workshop participant who learned about it from his father and has taught his son how to hunt it said, "It has such a tradition in my heart" (Schnabel 2001).

Some organizations are encouraging growing and selling heirloom plants. Others are promoting direct marketing for farmers (Ha et al. 2017; Sustainable 2001; Partners 2001). Fitzgerald, Markowitz, and Billings (2012) describe the mission of Kentucky's Community Farm Alliance to preserve family farming and promote a Locally Integrated Food Economy (LIFE) through efforts such as supporting value-added processing and marketing to a wide variety of consumers, including urban food deserts and institutions, as well as the more typical farmer's markets frequented by more well-off customers. John Deere's trade magazine, *The Furrow*, frequently contains articles about farm families who have devised ways of marketing value-added products that allow multiple generations to stay on the farm.

Housing Green Energy

If you drive into the heart of Illinois and Indiana farmland, you're likely to see something looming in the fields besides and beside corn and soybeans. Farmers have leased their land to wind farms and grow their crops right around them. Wind farms in the United States are paying a total of $222 million dollars to property owners across the country. In a wind farm lease, there is "an agreement between a developer and a property owner that grants the developer the necessary rights to develop turbines at an agreed upon location. In return, the property will receive monthly rental payments from the developer for a set period (typically 35 years)" (LandmarkDividend.com 2020). The monthly rental payment "varies according to the number of wind turbines on the property, their location, and the rate of local competition. On average, a smaller, single wind turbine lease can be valued at around $8,000 per year; a larger turbine, between $50,000 to $80,000" (AppraisalEconomics.com 2018).

Dennis Stein (n.d.), farm management educator for Michigan State University Extension Service, offers some caveats when negotiating a wind turbine lease, via PowerPoint presentation bullet points. He notes that the "Land man [middleman between the developer and the landowner] is paid by wind developer, experienced negotiator, well-educated in his craft, smooth talker." The landowner "may not arrive at an agreement initially—may take years. Use dogged determination. Good leases take time and last a long time." "The lease is actually a sale of development rights—compensation should be adequate." And Stein notes that there are setbacks for buildings and anything that would affect wind transmission.

Solar panels on cropland are another potential means of using land to save land. A study from Oregon State University finds that, "if less than 1 percent of agricultural land was converted to solar panels, it would be sufficient to fulfill global electric energy demand" (Branam 2019). Usually solar panels are operated under lease agreements, although sometimes farmers build them themselves to generate electricity for their own use. The amount of money gained from the lease depends on project size, land prices, substitute uses, and regional supply and demand for solar sites. A range is $500 to $2,000 per acre (StrategicSolarGroup.com 2020; Fabrick 2020).

Mike Carroll (2019), agricultural extension agent for Craven County, North Carolina, offers caveats for solar panels similar to Dennis Stein's for wind turbines. Typically "contracts are written to protect the company, not the landowner. . . . One must remember, the developer/contractor is approaching the agreement to protect himself from as much liability as possible and to make a profit. . . . Solar farms providing 15–20 years of alternative energy, revenue to the landowner, and tax revenue to the county is beneficial. In contrast, abandoned solar farm production, excessive cost of decommission or loss of future land use is a detriment to the landowner and area."

New research suggests that solar panels don't have to take farmland out of production, which is of course a consideration. "The concept of co-developing the same area of land for both solar photovoltaic power and conventional agriculture is known as agrivoltaics." In fact, researchers from Oregon State University found that solar panels work best on croplands, then grasslands, compared with fifteen other classes of land cover (Branam 2019). As a bonus, crops grow well, even under the solar panels. "Researchers have successfully grown aloe vera, tomatoes, biogas maize, pasture grass, and lettuce in agrivoltaic experiments. Some varieties of lettuce produce greater yields in shade than under full sunlight; other varieties produce essentially the same yield under an open sky and under PV [photovoltaic] panels" (Adeh et al. 2019:4). Some twenty-five experiments have included a variety of vegetables, "grazing animals in Colorado and growing tomatoes, potatoes and melons without irrigation in Oregon. Others include raising bees around flowers sheltered by solar arrays in Minnesota and placing solar arrays over cranberry bogs in Massachusetts" (Fialka 2019). One study "found that pasture under a solar panel array produced twice as much biomass and used less water than neighboring, unshaded plants" (Werblow 2020:33). New "semi-transparent PV panels open additional opportunities for colocation and greenhouse production" (Adeh et al. 2019:4).

Participating in Environment Enhancement Marketplaces

When commercial industries use carbon or disturb wetlands, they can gain redemption by buying credits from farmers who sequester carbon or mitigate wetlands in other areas. For example, grasslands sequester carbon, but a high-density, short duration grazing rotation for cattle or sheep increases the amount sequestered. It costs the rancher money—for water, fencing, and infrastructure—to set up that system. Middleman corporations are being formed to help pay those costs (Mintz 2020).

Wetland mitigation banking is meant to assure that there is no net loss in wetlands. Wetlands disturbed in one area are offset by wetlands mitigated in a different area. The user buys credits from the saver: "In many parts of the country, wetland (and stream) impacts are difficult to avoid during new development (industry, businesses, residential, municipal, new/widened roads). Mitigation banking has grown in popularity . . . due to new development and infrastructure projects in major metropolitan areas and in emerging markets through urban sprawl." Several hundred acres are needed to make mitigation banking financially feasible for the saver. The mitigation efforts are expensive for the farmer and might including fencing, and as with rotation grazing to sequester carbon, developing new water sources for cattle, by digging wells or collecting spring water into tanks. "Mitigation banking can be costly, time-consuming and involve dealing with multiple state and federal agencies, ultimately placing restrictions and conservation easements on property" (A. Wood 2018:3). The landowner generally needs a consultant and attorney to negotiate the process. For both carbon sequestration and wetlands mitigation, ongoing monitoring determines the worth of the environmental offset.

Forming Family Partnerships and Corporations

Although farms in the five counties we learned about are not generally large enough to warrant the expense of setting up a family partnership, they can be used to advantage on larger farms. Most farmers want to stay in control of their farms for as long as they can; most need whatever income the farm generates; and most are concerned with its value, especially when it comes to worry over their heirs' estate tax bill. In general, family partnership companies are set up by the older generation, who become the managers of the farm as they begin to transfer legal title to the company. Over time they make gifts of interest in the company to their children and grandchildren. (Currently federal gift and estate tax laws allow transfers of up to $11.58 million during your lifetime, tax free. If more than that is transferred, there is a tax that is relatively high—18 to 40 percent.) Because these gifts do not carry with them voting rights or managerial rights or the right to sell them or the property, the recipients don't have to pay taxes to the extent they would if they acquired interests to the farm outright. Instead, they become entitled to a "valuation discount" on their taxes. For example, farm acreage itself might be worth, say, $1.5 million, but nonvoting, nonliquid interests in the farm would be worth less than that, perhaps in the range of 30 to 45 percent less.

There are other advantages to a family partnership. Parents can choose the next farm managers—and the younger generation can participate in the farm management before actually taking control—at the same time as parents could give equal economic interest in the farm to each heir. If they wanted to, they could by these means avoid giving farmland outright to in-laws where divorce might complicate the farm's future. In most cases the parents can exercise some control from the grave. For example, they can stipulate that the farm will not be sold unless all heirs agree, or they can leave the decision regarding the disposition of the farm in the hands of the children chosen to do the farming.

The disadvantages are that the companies are complex and costly to set up, and the nonfarming heirs get not much of anything unless the farm is eventually sold (when they would obtain their share of the proceeds). Until that time, they get their share of the farm's annual net income, after the managers deduct their managerial fee. But their nonliquid interest in the farm won't serve as collateral for loans, etc.

Another type of entity, family corporations, can be used on large farms to give some of the benefits that other types of industry enjoy. For example, dairy farming is a 24/7 deal. A corporation could be formed that provided fringe benefits to those on call. They could include, for example, meals and lodging, so some living expenses could become business expenses for tax purposes. The corporation could develop health insurance plans, day care, or pension plans that would be paid for with tax-deductible dollars at the corporate level.

Buying to Conserve

One clear and clean, though sometimes expensive, approach to conserving land is to buy it. This is the strategy used, for example, by the Nature Conservancy. A specific example of a government agency buying land to protect occurred in 1988, after public outcry when developer John T. (Til) Hazel changed his plans for a portion of the Civil War Manassas battlefield—from building an edge city on it to planting a mall there. The National Park Service condemned the land under eminent domain and bought it for $81 million from Hazel, who had paid $11 million for it two years before. In this case, unlike most, the developer did not use eminent domain but instead lost to it. Hazel registered his dismay by sending out a plane to fly over a celebration organized by the battlefield's conservation group. The message trailing behind the plane read, "The taking of private land is un-American" (Garreau 1991:422).

Government intervention to protect land is rare, at least in Virginia. Up until the year 2000, "Virginia was one of only three states on the entire eastern seaboard without a dedicated funding source for land conservation." In 2001, the Office of Farmland Preservation was established within the Virginia Department of Agriculture and Consumer Services. Nevertheless, Virginia ranks near the bottom when compared to other states on spending on natural resources. Since 2014, Virginia has spent less than 1 percent of its state budget on natural resources and parks and recreation. Adding together funds from the state's general fund, special funds, and federal funds renders a total of about $41 million for fiscal year 2018 for natural resources and parks and recreation (Field 2000; Fiscal Analytics 2017). On the other hand, Virginia has developed ways to encourage conservation easements.

Making Conservation Easements

One of the farmers in our 2013 study of Borden County farmers succinctly defined conservation easements: "The conservation easement is an effort to try and keep as much rural land rural and not become house sites. And the way it does it is the owner gives up the option of selling that property for housing developments, but in turn has a lower tax liability through a given period of time. Some of it I think is forever—it's the way some of them are written. But that's about all that I know, but that's the basic idea" (Interview 07 10/10.LG).

Conservation easements have as their basis the concept of property rights as it has evolved in Western societies. Our view of ownership of property is certainly not universal. As we mentioned before, hunters and gatherers have no ownership of land.

What sense would it make to own a piece of hunting land into which an antelope or giraffe might rarely stray? Horticulturalists, who live by subsistence farming, developed a concept of right to use, or usufruct. A family may use part of the village's horticultural garden. They can't sell it or pass it down. The garden moves periodically, as the land becomes less fertile, so these are not permanent rights. With usufruct comes an inclusive concept of ownership, so that the gardener, the head of the lineage, and the chief all have rights to use the land. We are more familiar with exclusive property rights. If I own it, you don't, unless your name is also on the deed. When you own land in the Western system, you own rights to the land. "Such rights include, among others, the right to [build on it], to farm, to hunt, to extract minerals, to cut timber, to subdivide, and do anything else with a property that is not prohibited by law" (Hutchinson 2000a). "Any one of these rights can be legally separated" from the others. By entering into a conservation easement contract, the owner gives away or sells his right to do certain things, most commonly to subdivide and/or develop the land: "An easement allows landowners to keep ownership of the land and either pass it on to their heirs or sell it—an important consideration for small farmers, who are counting on their land to pay for their retirement. Because the land stays in private hands, it also stays on the tax rolls. But the easement also sets conditions for future development." The terms of the agreement apply to the current and all future landowners. State and federal tax breaks come along with the conservation easement because of "documentable benefits to the public of conserving water, open lands, forests, and other significant historic and natural resources" (D. Hall 1997; Hutchinson 2000a, 2000b).

Land trusts that negotiate conservation easements are not new, the first one dating from the late 1800s in Massachusetts. By the 1960s, only about twelve land trusts were in existence; by the mid-1990s, more than one thousand had been formed. In 1981 the American Farmland Trust was founded specifically to preserve farmlands. It's not surprising that land trusts expanded in the 1980s, since by then sprawl had become readily apparent, and more than 15 percent of farms were lost during the farm crisis of the 1980s (Houghton 2021).

Conservation easements began in Virginia in 1966, when the Virginia Outdoors Foundation (VOF) was founded as an independent state agency. By 2020, the VOF had protected 860,000 acres, 4,000 miles of rivers and streams, and 150 miles of hiking and biking trails (Virginia Outdoors Foundation 2020). But conservation promotion is often the work of nonprofit organizations like the Blue Ridge Land Conservancy, begun in 1996 as the Western Virginia Land Trust, with two staff members working seventy hours a week each, and managing to protect an acre of land for every thirteen dollars donated to the organization (Field 2000). By 2019, the Blue Ridge Land Conservancy had to its credit protection of 25,000 acres and 60 miles of streams in ten counties (Blue Ridge Land Conservancy 2018–19, Spring 2020).

Tax incentives are a recent phenomenon. "The Federal government has offered a tax deduction for easement donations since 1964, but state tax credits for conservation originated in 1983, and were widely enacted in 1999 and afterwards." "A tax deduction reduces a taxpayer's taxable income, so the value will depend upon the taxpayer's tax bracket." "Tax credits lower a taxpayer's bill dollar for dollar" (Hocker and Maroon 2010:136). The 1997 federal estate tax benefit for conservation "cuts the taxes for those who volunteer to protect their land through easements for wildlife habitat, land conservation or other public benefit." A purpose of the law is to "help families who own land in areas being overtaken by sprawl who would like to conserve it. They often find that the value of their land has risen so high that their heirs could be faced with an estate tax of thousands or millions of dollars, and selling the land for development is the only way to pay for it" (D. Hall 1997; Biondo 2000). "A gift of easement can sometimes provide enough tax savings to prevent a family from having to sell land it would rather keep and protect for future generations" because, since development is blocked, the market value is reduced. This lessens the value of the owner's estate and reduces estate taxes for the heirs. Since the market value of the land is reduced, when the owner sells it or passes it on to children, capital gains tax (the tax on the sale of something that has appreciated in value, like land or stocks) is lowered. For federal and state income taxes, the difference between the land's value without the easement and its value with the easement may qualify the donor for a charitable gift deduction. In some areas of the country, there may be a reduction in property taxes. The tax benefits from lowered local real estate taxes occur because generally assessments are based on "fair market value" for their "highest and best use," "which assessors equate with full development potential." Since a conservation easement "reduces or removes the potential for development," the assessed value is also reduced (Hutchinson 2000b).

Although government intervention to protect land is rare, on the other hand, Virginia (in 2002) and Colorado (2000) were the first states to offer "the most powerful state tax incentives for conservation, the transferable tax credits," now also available in Georgia, New Mexico, and South Carolina. "In these states, if a landowner donates an easement but doesn't owe enough tax to use the full credit, [which would be the case for most of the farmers in our five-county study,] they can sell [at least part of] the remaining credit to another taxpayer, generating immediate income" (Land Trust Alliance 2020).

However, recent changes in federal tax law threaten to take a bite out of tax incentives for conservation:

> In June 2019, the IRS issued a final regulation regarding contributions in exchange for State and Local Tax credits. The regulation is intended to prevent states from bypassing a cap on the federal deduction for state and local taxes that was included in the tax bill signed into law in December 2017. However, it also impacts other tax credits, including those for conservation. It will erode state tax incentives for landowners who donate land or conservation easements to land trusts. The finalized rule directly undermines state tax credits created to provide an incentive for donations of land and conservation easements. (Land Trust Alliance 2020)

Although we have decried making environmental decisions solely based on economics, conservation easements do make economic sense for governments. Acquiring land that needs protection in "fee simple" (i.e., purchasing *all* of the property rights) can be very expensive. In Virginia, it is estimated that acquiring conservation easements on these same lands would cost about a third as much (Hutchinson 2000a). Easements that encourage keeping land in farms can help local governments financially because in, for example, Williams County, a fast-growing area that neighbors Borden, Farlane, and Greenly Counties, farms use only eleven cents in government services for every dollar they pay in taxes, "while houses require $1.15 in services for every $1 their owners pay in taxes" (Chittum 2000; Cagle 1999).

Cooperation among land trusts and government agencies is increasingly common. Maryland's Chesapeake Bay area, New York's Adirondack Mountains, Wisconsin's Door Peninsula, and Colorado's Yampa River near the Steamboat Springs ski resort are examples (Biondo 2000). The Blue Ridge Land Conservancy also works with government agencies, for example, by negotiating with thirteen landowners and the Department of Game and Inland Fisheries to buy 8,300 acres of undeveloped mountain land paid for by $3 million borrowed from the state treasury, to be repaid by hunting, fishing, and outdoor revenues.

The overall benefits to the public might be viewed as the "macro" reasons for promoting conservation easements. A micro reason, "We're all God's creatures. We're part of this land. We need to take care of it," was the motivation for a sixty-six-year-old grandmother who put her land in southwestern Virginia under a conservation easement (Cagle 1998). This interview from a sixty-six-year-old man from Greenly County highlights reasons for undertaking conservation easements:

> The way I understand it, it's possible to do this and if it's ever sold it can't be subdivided and it has to always stay in one piece. I mean no matter how many times it's sold it'll always stay together. That makes me feel good because Leo Bradford owns the land that his grandfather and my grandfather and another brother of theirs was willed by Thomas, Jr., my great-grandfather. Of course each of them had added a little bit. One of them got 116 acres and each one of them has added a little bit to it. I think Leo has managed to get that all back together and I think that's just great. (Interview 6/24.MBW)

A Borden County farmer said: "I think it's a good thing because it keeps people from trying to put up houses, like big housing developments, keeps them from coming around and bothering you all the time about the land. Gives them a reason to just stay away. That way you know later on that it will always be something agriculture related. And, I think it will stay like that forever as long as laws don't change. Once you sign the papers it's pretty much set in stone" (Interview 02 10/12.RW).

A seventy-six-year-old farmer from the Finger Lakes region of New York has a different reason for doing the same thing: "We put a lot of effort into building up this place over the years. I laid ten miles of drainage tiles. I picked rocks out of the fields so the land could yield decent crops. We thought it would be a shame to ever see the land broken up into a housing development or something."

Critics of conservation easements, such as a logger in Borden County, who uses the unusual ecologically sound practice of cutting only dying trees and hauling them out with horses, say, "It's wrong to lock land up in easements that prevent use of the resources it provides, such as timber." But actually, conservation easements are flexible and can allow for continued use of resources, and even purposes that the land currently does not have, such as the building of homes for heirs (Chittum 2000). In the contract signed between the grandmother from southwestern Virginia and the independent state agency, the land "can never be subdivided, used for business or industry or substantially altered by blasting or construction." This contract is form fit to allow her to build some new structures and to rehabilitate others (Cagle 1998). The Finger Lakes farmer's contract is so specific that while it allows managed logging, it "specifically forbids cutting two trees—one a huge, beautiful old white pine, and the other a relatively rare American elm" (D. Hall 1997). A rancher's conservation easement near Denver, Colorado, protects shortgrass prairie, so his contract assures that "they can't plow it, they can't build on it, and they can't subdivide it" (Oldham 2020).

In Colorado, ranchers feared development but, like the Borden County logger, were concerned that land trusts and conservation easements worked to keep land "wild," but not in working ranches. So in 1995 they started a land trust of their own, the Colorado Cattleman's Agricultural Land Trust, to keep land in ranches. Not every rancher in Colorado was for it. The opponents to the Land Trust said, "If ranching got so bad that it wouldn't support you, you could sell a small piece of your ranch and for your lifetime you'd have enough money and still be ranching, so why would you give up your insurance policy?" Those arguing for the Land Trust answered, "But every acre that is sold for development makes it so that ranchers will have neighbors incompatible for ranching" (National Public Radio 1998; *Conservation News* 2000). The anti-view looks to your own lifetime, with no concern for the future; it looks only to your own interests with no care for other ranchers and the problems they may have with their new neighbors whom you have sold to.

This old conundrum—either pure wilderness or development—is giving way to deals that protect certain uses of the land, as well as the land itself. They protect two kinds of landscapes: (1) "natural or primeval landscapes" "that human beings haven't altered or interfered with"; and (2) rural "working landscapes" "whose function and look, or character, or feel, have been shaped over time by sequential, ongoing human activities as much as by natural processes." The latter have also been dubbed "working countryside, managed landscape, humanized landscape, historic landscape, ancient landscape, cultural landscape, and heritage landscape" (Garreau 1991; Hiss 1990:114–15 from MacKaye [1924] 1962).

It is working landscapes that have been the focus of this book. They can be the harder of the two types to protect. For example, one reason utility and road building take place on farmland is because other lands are protected. Jim Riggle, director of operations for the American Farmland Trust in the 1980s, explained, "Section 4-F of the United States Transportation Code, drawn up in 1966, soon after the first national alarms had been sounded about the country's deteriorating environment, virtually bars any new highway construction on parkland, on wetlands, and on wildlife habitats." I doubt if any of us want to see roads cut into wilderness. But Riggle says, "what nobody thought about at the time was that by adopting only these restrictions, Section 4-F in effect literally directed transportation engineers to build all future highways on the best farmland—which is predominately flat, and so cheap to build on anyway, and isn't wet, because it drains well, and doesn't have too much wildlife, because farming activities have chased many animals away" (Hiss 1990:173).

Working landscapes deserve protection: They can be buffers and gateways to wilder areas that harbor biodiversity. In the Adirondack Mountains of New York State, "the agricultural lands are the buffers that protect [an area of biodiversity] from encroaching development" (Biondo 2000). This is the case, for example, in Greenly County, which is 54 percent National Forest. The National Forest is a repository of the natural beauty that rural dwellers, urbanites, and suburbanites alike desire. The United States Department of Agriculture, at least in the past, has charged the Forest Service with making every effort to maintain this natural beauty. But it is necessary to *get there* first. The western gateway to the National Forest is through Stanley Valley in Greenly County. The drive through Greenly County to Forest Service land provides a halfway house for the urban, town, or suburban dweller. The family in the car decompresses while enjoying the scenery of Stanley Valley—rolling hills, green pastures, cattle grazing, neat farmhouses, and yards with flowers. The mountains in the distance—signifying the adventure that awaits—grow larger as they approach.

An example of protecting a particular use of land is in Lexington, Kentucky, known for its bluegrass horse farms, where a "purchase of development rights program" preserves farming heritage permanently. It works like this. If an acre of land is worth $4,000 for agricultural use, but $7,000 if it were developed, the city pays the farmer the $3,000 difference to keep it in farm use and retain the distinctive scenery. The program, begun with $25 million from the city government and $15 million from the state, was undertaken because without it, city officials feared that the open spaces that attract visitors would be gone. Not all farmers are for it. One said: "I can't sell ten acres for a house next door. That wouldn't hurt anyone." But even those against it will take the money, if they can't do anything else with their land to make money, since they say farming itself is not profitable (National Public Radio 2000). Likewise, "farmers and citizen activists around Lancaster, Pennsylvania, have used easements to preserve some of the richest agricultural lands east of the Mississippi from the threat of being bulldozed under for shopping malls and suburban housing." A different purpose is served in another area, where Cornell University and a pharmaceutical company are using a 270-acre preserve to discover flora that might yield life-saving medicines (D. Hall 1997).

Sustaining working forests is another purpose that has been served by a variety of conservation arrangements. The Northern Forest—the largest contiguous forest east of the Mississippi—in Maine, Vermont, New Hampshire, and New York has been "vulnerable to timber, pulp, and wood products firms and land developers." But a public-private conservation project for 300,000 of its acres "will keep the majority of the woodlands intact as a traditional working forest available for regulated logging but also open for public recreation. The remainder . . . will be conserved through public ownership" (*Washington Post* 1998). For the purpose of promoting sustainable timber, a different plan was undertaken by the nonprofit Nature Conservancy that backed a Forest Bank in southwestern Virginia. The Forest Bank accepts "voluntary 'deposits' of timber rights from forestland owners, just as commercial banks accept monetary deposits. The timber bank will then grow, manage, and harvest the trees in a sustainable way so harvesting and replanting balance each other. The owner who deposits timber rights keeps the land, but only the bank harvests its trees. The owner gets a guaranteed annual payment from the bank (or a lump sum withdrawal) based on the value of the timber deposit" (Dellinger 1998:B8).

In the western states, conservation easements serve the purpose of "safeguarding areas that connect fragmented ecosystems, sheltering endangered species, preserving soil that acts as a carbon sink and locking up water rights coveted by thirsty cities." "From Montana's sagebrush steppe to New Mexico's Central [Bird] Flyway," "unlikely partnerships between conservative farmers and ranchers and liberal conservationists" have been formed, and conservation easements are so popular that state agencies and nonprofit organizations have long application waiting lists (Oldham 2020).

Some conservation easements even promote a Commons concept—allowing, for example, for hiking trails for public use across private property. They can be written to prevent "cropping the public good." Public value "can be undermined, or cropped, by changes that come to an area." Cropping public value might be, for instance, building a house in the countryside that gives its new owners a spectacular view but destroys the views heretofore enjoyed by the other residents in the area. "In this case, part of a public value would have been stripped from a landscape and converted into cash value for private gain" (Hiss 1990:119–20).

A drawback to conservation easements is that they can be broken—condemned— by the power of eminent domain. This drawback grows more prominent as eminent domain is more frequently delegated to private enterprises and used for purposes that are questionably necessary for the public. We have asserted that the legal system was not the place for settling the culture war. On the other hand, the court system is the place of last resort to hold the line on conservation easements if their terms are broken, generally by new owners. Since conservation easements are relatively new, few have been broken and tested in court. Those few have seen some losses and some wins—for example, a Pennsylvania judge ordered "a new owner to take down a 4,800 square foot house built in defiance of an easement" (D. Hall 1997).

A farmer in Williams County says people have told him "they would pay good money for a view of his farm." But as he says, "the view isn't putting money in [my] pocket" (Clauson-Wicker 2001). Former Blue Ridge Conservancy/Western Virginia Land Trust executive director Michael Van Ness confirmed that "farmers and forest owners have, for two centuries, provided free mountain vistas, wildlife habitat, fresh air, pure water and the majestic sense of place that defines Southwest Virginia" (Field 2000). Editorial writer Elizabeth Obenshain (1996) captured the function of these landscapes: "On my way to work each morning, I savor the rural scenes lining each side of the bypass through [Jonesville]. Cornfields and pastures with a spring crop of leggy foals or a fall crop of lambs add a moment of serenity to a hectic day." (Since she wrote, some of her route has been changed by new road building.) "It becomes a land dedicated to a different kind of harvest." "Farms produce 'landscape.'" "The crop they raise is serenity, an article hard to come by in megalopolis" (Garreau 1991:390; Barlett 1993:252; Gottmann 1961). In a plea for land conservation, Obenshain (1996) observes, "Land is not cheap today, but it will never be cheaper. Views here today will be paved tomorrow."

Conclusion

Preservation versus Progress, Place versus Property

Who knows for what purpose cranes and condors, otters and grizzlies may some day be used?

> Aldo Leopold, *A Sand County Almanac*

We began thirteen chapters ago with protest signs along a rural scenic byway. We listed bucolically named subdivisions and golf courses—pawns in a culture war of Preservation versus Progress, Place versus Property. We took you to a lunch in the country, and asked why you should care about these people who have lived by farming and hunting and gathering on rural land. We have learned that the culture this family and their neighbors carry is a crucible for the cultural diversity that America needs to remain healthy in years to come. It is a vessel holding ways of thinking and ways of doing that may stand us in good stead in an unpredictable future.

We have described the ways land and nature can be *used* to make a living, yet not totally *conquered*. These rural cultures showed how place can fortify people's identities: Land is merged with the people who have lived there; meaning is bestowed on it by the human activities that have happened there; the descendants have a nearly visceral unity with it. Land is legacy; the links in the chain of title forge connections with the historical past on this same piece of ground. The land itself is polestar for a community that talks a language of the land and practices reciprocity when the demands of the domesticated land overwhelm a single family. Place is used to teach cultural rights and wrongs, and is clung to when threats to the environment and the culture that dwells in it are exposed.

We have noted that rural cultures continue to serve a symbolic function; they are urban and suburban America's alter ego. Perhaps, however, the modes of understanding fostered by rural life are more than America's symbolic foil. Conservationist Aldo Leopold (1949:178, 187) implied that a systems perspective—seeing the interconnections among things—was fostered by experiences in nature:

There is value in any experience that reminds us of our dependency on the soil-plant-animal food chain, and of the fundamental organization of the biota. Civilization has so cluttered this elemental man-earth relation with gadgets and middlemen that awareness of it is growing dim. . . . By learning how some small part of the biota ticks, we can guess how the whole mechanism ticks. The ability to perceive these deeper meanings, and to appraise them critically, is the woodcraft of the future.

The value Leopold placed on an alternative way of seeing is seconded by anthropologists like Victor Turner, who implied that there may be an almost biological need for the two parts or "sides" of society that he labeled *community* and *communitas,* and thus for their differing modes of relating to other people and understanding the world around us. He may have been more right than he knew. Anthropologists Roy Rappaport and Gregory Bateson believed that alternative modes of understanding are critical for our continued existence. Our culture's most valued mode—conscious reason—reinforces the humans' conception that we each stop at our skin. On the contrary, we are parts of larger systems upon which our ultimate survival depends. Rappaport (1976:33) contends that "the wholeness, if not indeed the very existence of these systems may be beyond the grasp of ordinary consciousness. Conscious reason is incomplete and so are its unaided understandings." Bateson (1972:444) suggests that the "cybernetic nature of the self and the world tends to be imperceptible to consciousness." This is especially problematic since the advent of advanced technology, which empowers "conscious purpose . . . to upset the balances of the body, of society and of the biological world around us."

We have warned of the culture war of Preservation versus Progress, Place versus Property that threatens the matrix in which these potentially salvation-bringing cultural processes reside—rural landscapes. An early comer to the conservation scene, Aldo Leopold (1949:223, emphasis his) saw the rumblings of the culture war on the horizon and said, "In all of these cleavages, we see repeated the same basic paradoxes: man the conqueror *versus* man the biotic citizen; science the sharpener of his sword *versus* science the searchlight on his universe; land the slave and servant *versus* land the collective organism."

We learned that American culture's economic language and suppositions have played a major role in the culture war. More than seventy years ago Leopold (1949:224), a biologist by training, foresaw this, too: "The 'key-log' which must be moved . . . is simply this: quit thinking about decent land-use as solely an economic problem. Examine each question in terms of what is ethically and esthetically right, as well as what is economically expedient. A thing is right when it tends to preserve the integrity, stability, and beauty of the biotic community. It is wrong when it tends otherwise." Forty-five years later anthropologist Roy Rappaport (1994:263–64, 266) wrote in the same vein:

Monetary standards when applied to ecological systems . . . are in their nature incapable of recognizing qualitative distinctions between and interdependences among the constituents of those systems, and thus cannot take them into consideration in developing courses of action. . . . Economic systems should be adjusted to the requisites of the biological-ecological systems on which they are contingent.

We described a particular battle in the culture war—pitting residents of a five-county area against a powerful power utility. The decision to build a 765,000-volt power line will ever after be used in Appalachian studies courses as one more illustration of the position of internal colony and energy national sacrifice zone that has dogged the Appalachian region since the 1930s up to the present day. The counties and their small populations have little to gain. The counties and their visitors—urbanites seeking respite from their megalopolis life—have much to lose. Struggling to choke back tears, a sixty-six-year-old man who returned to his family's heritage in Greenly County said, "What I was trying to get across was that all my life I've liked to be in nature, and I go out of the way to do it" (Interview 6/24.MBW).

The public utility commission charged with making this decision wrote about one possible route, "the Commission is not unmindful that construction of this transmission line will forever alter the relationship that affected citizens have with their land"; and about another route, "certainly for the people affected . . . the environmental impact of the proposed transmission line is devastating" (State Corporation Commission 1995:18–19; H. P. Anderson 2000:29). But whether the people of these rural counties should be caused to sacrifice, and whether America's citizens should lose one more revitalizing rural respite, is a decision made in the context of our culture's deeply steeped economic motivations.

Now many farm families in Appalachia and elsewhere in rural America face a cruel choice. They are given offers they can't refuse from developers. Continued development without protection for the kinds of places we have described threatens cultural diversity and biological diversity as it renders the landscape level and places generic.

We have reached out for strategies that strike a balance between Preservation and Progress, Conservation and Development. Finding this balance is essential for maintaining choice. It is essential for maintaining cultural and ecological diversity. It is essential for maintaining America's health. If we lose the family farmland and the rural culture, costs to the environment are high; costs to our cultural flexibility are high. Costs, indeed, to individual farmers are high. Suicide rates among farmers are three times higher than the national average (Weddle, Sherman, and Chadde 2020). And "it's like somebody is dying" if the family farm is lost (Keen 2000; Dudley 2000).

Years before our lunch in the country, Aldo Leopold (1949:207, 200) wrote about a land ethic. He said, "Conservation is a state of harmony between men and land." And to achieve conservation, to "see the cultural value of wilderness boils down, in the last analysis, to a question of intellectual humility." More than a decade later, President Dwight D. Eisenhower (1961), a man who had come to prominence as a military general, warned of "the acquisition of unwarranted influence," by "a scientific-technological elite" and "the military-industrial complex"—a phrase he made famous in his final presidential speech to the nation:

It is the task of statesmanship to mold, to balance, and to integrate these and other forces, new and old, within the principles of our democratic system— ever aiming toward the supreme goals of our free society. . . . Another factor in maintaining balance involves the element of time. As we peer into society's future, we—you and I, and our government—must avoid the impulse to live only for today, plundering, for our own ease and convenience, the precious resources of tomorrow. We cannot mortgage the material assets of our grandchildren without risking the loss also of their political and spiritual heritage. We want democracy to survive for all generations to come, not to become the insolvent phantom of tomorrow.[1]

Benton MacKaye ([1924] 1962), father of the Appalachian Trail and cofounder, with Aldo Leopold, of the Wilderness Society, especially saw the worth of the "working landscapes" which have been the focus of this book. He saw them, as he said in words that perhaps seem florid today, as the "barrier of barriers" within a "world-empire of industrial and metropolitan upheaval." MacKaye and those who followed him thought that planning should be regional in scale, and should "treat working landscapes as regional assets." Botanist and Citizen Potawatomi Nation member Robin Wall Kimmerer (2013:338) says: "Restoring land without restoring relationship is an empty exercise. It is relationship that will endure and relationship that will sustain the restored land. Therefore, reconnecting people and the landscape is as essential as reestablishing proper hydrology or cleaning up contaminants. It is medicine for the earth." Yet, "working landscapes today are often the environments that have the least protection and are disappearing the most rapidly." "The wide-open countryside that draws its beauty from the absence of people, attracts people, and then slowly loses its appeal" (Hiss 1990:199, 195; Schlosser 2001:133).

In the past, those who wanted to develop the landscape portrayed rural people as backward Luddites, standing in the way of Progress. As we found in our ethnographic research, the natives of these counties carry a *living* culture—one that has a continuity with the past but that has adopted new means of surviving and maintaining the life and land that they hold dear into the twenty-first century. Although this culture values its past, and nearly reveres the "old people" ancestors, this is not a place that time forgot. We did not capture the "memory culture" of the residents—or a static isolated traditional "community" of modernity theory. Instead, we found an ongoing, living culture, with ties to the past and hopes for the future. The culture has changed to accommodate life in a less agrarian America than the ancestors found in these same valleys generations ago. The culture is anchored in a place that most inhabitants want to maintain unchanged: mountains, ridges, valleys, creeks, springs, sinkholes, caves, culturally carved out meadows, fields, and yards.

Those who are accused of wishing to preserve outmoded lifestyles, to create living museums of "backward" cultures or "yesterday's people," should counter with this question: Can American society afford to lose any means of understanding each other or the world around us—even as we continue to create and discover more and more to understand? Wendell Berry ([1970, 1972] 2012:66) says, "without a complex knowledge of one's place, and without the faithfulness to one's place on which such knowledge depends, it is inevitable that the place will be used carelessly, and eventually destroyed." "The places where we spend our time affect the people we are and can become . . . the kind of work we get done, the ways we interact with other people, even our ability to function as citizens in a democracy" (Hiss 1990).

Acknowledgments

Promises of anonymity do not expire. They do ironically prevent thanking those who deserve the most thanks—the people who asked us to help them with this study, and the families who opened their doors to us and taught us how cultural attachment to place looks and feels. They know that we are indebted. For a portion of the study, citizen scientists, who were also granted anonymity, delivered the backbone.

Teams of extraordinary anthropology students interviewed, transcribed, analyzed, and wrote reports. They brought wonder, insight, and enthusiasm for challenging and exacting work to the multiyear project where we were equal partners. I will list them alphabetically within their teams. They know that this book would not exist without them.

Darlene Carden, Kimberly Comerford, Caryn Ergenbright, Brad Jackson, Brad Nyholm, Amy Sokoloff, Rebecca Taylor, Danny Wolfe; Jean A. Kappes, Megan Scanlon, Shannon T. Scott, Stacy L. Viers; Lola Coleman, Allyn Beth Motley; Meredith Burk, Neil Epperly, Christy Landreth, Sam Linkous, Angela Vaughan, David Wooldridge; Kristen L. Hedrick, Dana Stein; Melissa Lamb, Daliah Macon, Matthew Schrag, Christopher Shedd, Elaine Staab; Kasey L. Campbell, Victoria R. Curtis, Misty L. Daniels, LaTeeka E. Gray, Taylor R. LaPrade, Langley J. Looney, Analise C. Roccaforte, Charles D. Salyers, Haley M. Stewart, Olivia D. Thompson, Hannah M. Watterson, Sarah M. Wood, Ryan M. Woodson.

Students in anthropology "Appalachian Cultures" classes also interviewed, transcribed, and analyzed. They are, in alphabetical order within classes:

Tanya Caspers, Jane Delicate, Bryan Dilday, Brandi Ford, Mark Wilson Gee, Karen Gerlach, Shawn Harrison, Carole Harrover, Robin Henley, John Hovermale, Lesli King, John McEwen, Erika Perdue, Kevin Tomlinson, Lin Usack, Kevin Wingfield, Heather Zollman; Cynthia Callahan, Tammie Cox, Rob Frazer, Eric French, Kim Massie, Regina McGough, Rebecca Prior, Brian Stokes, Ren Talbott, Keppel Wood, Margaret Vowell; J. P. Charbonneau, Brian Corboy, Magdalene Drewnowski, Rachael Eagan, Julia Everett, Michelle Heizer, Christine Hicks, Susan Hudson, Tommy Hunt, Heather C. Krantz, Michelle Matney, Tricia Pugh, Anne Ruifrok, Gregory Souder, Angela Stump; Brad Barrish, Laura Boyce, Shannon Brooks, Kara Burchinal, Jamye Jones, Kathleen Kerr, Jennifer Kline, Elizabeth Layne, Phyllis Lyle, Katie Mackall, Mike Mirro, Ann Newberry, Dawn Richardson, Kathy Shambaugh, Amity Stein, Tammie Thompson; Kimberlee Brown, Akihiro Ebisu, Michael Hall, Rebecca Moles, Rebecca Nieves, Crystal Ramos, Richard Spencer, Amber Yates.

Place Matters series editor Dwight Billings's name has appeared on more than one of my acknowledgment pages. He is a brilliant scholar and a class-act human being who is willing to help others succeed. Anthropologist Benita Howell, a pioneer in the study of place in Appalachia, provided guideposts and aid at critical junctions in this project. Patrick O'Dowd, acquisitions editor, nurtured the manuscript and befriended me in a professional and thoughtful way. Susan Murray is an easy-to-like copyeditor partner. She knows the *Chicago Manual of Style* like the back of her hand, has a keen eye, and makes cordial corrections.

To all the authors whose work is cited here, and to anonymous reviewers—thank you for your work; thank you for your time. Any mistakes or misrepresentations are of course my own.

Notes

1. The Place of Power

1. See Foster 1988 for a top-notch cultural analysis of the dam controversy. See Schoenbaum 1979 for a play-by-play history of it.

2. Early definitions of Appalachia were geographical/geological (the Appalachian Mountain chain), or cultural (a place where more rural cultures resided), and changed from author to author. When the proposal to develop and fund an Appalachian Regional Commission (ARC) was brought to Congress in the 1960s, it was necessary to set precise boundaries to garner support and clarify where funds would and wouldn't be going. Hence, the political/legal definition that is most often used today. As of November 2021, the Appalachian Regional Commission includes 423 contiguous counties in thirteen states from Mississippi to New York. For good discussions of definitions, see, in chronological order, Ergood 1983; Raitz and Ulack 1984; Couto 1994; J. A. Williams 2002. For a discussion of the beginnings of the ARC, see J. A. Williams 2002.

3. The term *cultural conservation* appeared in a 1983 report by the American Folklife Center at the Library of Congress. It refers to efforts to maintain cultural knowledge and the natural resources it is based on. A goal is to preserve cultural and ecological diversity. Efforts that emanate from grassroots concerns are privileged (see Hufford 1994; and Howell 1990, 2002).

4. Although the word *preservation* has come to be associated with a biocentric view of nature, privileging nature over humans, I use the word *preservation*—in this subheading and throughout the book—in a broader sense, more in line with Aldo Leopold's ecocentric approach. To the degree there is an anthropocentric-ecocentric-biocentric continuum of thought in American environmentalism, the discussion here would be ecocentric.

5. James Davison Hunter's *Culture Wars: The Struggle to Define America* popularized the term, referring to the conservative orthodoxy, characterized by "commitment to an external and transcendent authority," versus the liberal progressives, who tend "to resymbolize historic faiths according to the prevailing assumptions of contemporary life" (Hunter 1991:44–45).

6. See also Marx 2000.

7. Conservationist Gary Paul Nabhan (2018:7–8, 12) says that this divide threatens to undermine conservation efforts: "What began as a nonpartisan effort to protect our planet has become one of the most perniciously divisive issues in public life. This division is not only undermining the robustness of our communities; it is also undermining the health of our landscapes, the survival of rare species, the diversity of our foodstuffs, and the food security of our communities. . . . Americans appear to be at war with one another rather than at work with one another. This trend has dire consequences for the health of both our communities and our landscapes."

8. Quote from a visitor to the class (APST 460:1993) that studied the controversy and created a mock town meeting.

9. Stephen Fisher's (1993) *Fighting Back in Appalachia* was our textbook in the "Appalachian Studies Seminar" study of protests and social movements, including opposition to the power line. With Barbara Ellen Smith, Fisher again provides a variety of organizing lessons in *Transforming Places: Lessons from Appalachia* (Fisher and Smith 2012). In *Everything in Its Path,* Kai Erikson (1976) describes in heartbreaking detail the destruction of community when a mining company dam break unleashes West Virginia's Buffalo Creek. In *Power and Powerlessness: Quiescence and Rebellion in an Appalachian Valley,* John Gaventa (1980) deftly theorizes the elements that quash rebellion. Shannon Elizabeth Bell (2016) takes up this question again in *Fighting King Coal: The Challenges to Micromobilization in Central Appalachia.* Jeff Goodell (2006) takes the long and wide view in *Big Coal: The Dirty Secret behind America's Energy Future.* Shirley Stewart Burns (2007) evokes history and current issues in the hardest-hit areas in *Bringing Down the Mountains: The Impact of Mountaintop Removal Surface Coal Mining on Southern West Virginia Communities, 1970–2004.* Eric Reece (2006) chronicles the destruction of the ironically named *Lost Mountain: A Year in the Vanishing Wilderness: Radical Strip Mining and the Devastation of Appalachia.* In *Moving Mountains,* Penny Loeb's (2007) *How One Woman and Her Community Won Justice from Big Coal* celebrates that story in West Virginia. Ronald Eller's (2008) *Uneven Ground: Appalachia since 1945* examines the part government programs and economic development have played in the shape Appalachia is in. Silas House and Jason Howard (2009) raise the voices of Appalachian people who sing and act against injustice in *Something's Rising: Appalachians Fighting Mountaintop Removal.* Tricia Shapiro (2010) describes local, grassroots opposition to mountaintop removal in *Mountain Justice: Homegrown Resistance to Mountaintop Removal, for the Future of Us All.* Kathryn Newfont (2012) eloquently identifies commons environmentalism as a long-held Appalachian sense in *Blue Ridge Commons: Environmental Activism and Forest History in Western North Carolina.* Eve Morgenstern's (2014) documentary, *Cheshire, Ohio: A Question of Power,* tells the story of the town destroyed under the weight of pollution from a coal-fired power plant once owned by American Electric Power (AEP). Eric Lassiter, Brian Hoey, and Elizabeth Campbell (2020) use the collaborative ethnography methods that they have developed (Lassiter 2005a, 2005b) to plumb the many facets of the water crisis caused by a coal-related chemical spill affecting a nine-county region of West Virginia in *I'm Afraid of That Water.* This more-or-less chronological sampling pulled from my shelves is not a comprehensive list of social movement analyses in Appalachia.

10. Jorgensen 1971; H. Lewis 1970; H. Lewis, Johnson, and Askins 1978; Walls 1978; Fox 1999; Kuletz 1998; Scott 2010; S. E. Bell 2016.

11. Appalachian Land Ownership Task Force 1983.

2. The Loss

1. Beaver 1982, 1992; Foster 1988; Howell 1990; Hufford 1998a, 1998b; Stewart 1996. As Puckett (2000:238) notes, "'Homeplace' as a symbol of cultural organization and personal identity permeates the fiction, historical accounts, and folklore of the region." And of course the music. Puckett cites Giardina 1987; M. A. Williams 1995; and K. Long 1994 (see especially Long's "Who Will Watch the Home Place" song). See also Dyer 1998.

2. Compare to Pierre Bourdieu's (1977, 1984) "habitus," which is more closely aligned with the root word *habit* (French *habitude*) than *habitat.*

3. See Reid and Taylor 2010 for the importance of understanding grass roots and grassroots understandings.

3. Using Place to Establish Identity

1. Professor Sam Cook, who has studied mountaintop removal in West Virginia, says that to the natives of the mountains, this form of mining is like seeing a relative skinned alive (Nixon 1999).

2. See also Antonsich 2010; Godkin 1980; Searles 1960; and Wenkart 1961.

3. Hirsch 1995:16; Abram 1996; Basso 1988; Bird-David 1993; Casey 1996, 1997; Driver et al. 1996; Geertz 1983; Jackson and Smith 1984; Ley and Samuels 1978; Lowenthal 1961, 1967; Relph 1976; Rose 1980; Sauer 1963; Tuan 1967, 1974, 1977, 1978; Watson 1968; Weiner 1991; Wright 1947. See also Gold and Burgess 1982; and Weeden 1992. Regarding methods of inquiry, see Bleicher (1980) 1990; James 1902/1982; Kvale 1996; and Merleau-Ponty (1962) 1994. Regarding focus group methodology, see Greenbaum 1993; Morgan 1993; and Templeton 1994.

4. See also Ferguson and Gupta 1992; Gupta and Ferguson 1997; Poe, Donatuto, and Satterfield 2016; and Stedman 2002. "Sense of place is sometimes described as a tripartite construct comprised of place attachment, place dependence, and place identity. . . . Place dependence describes a tangible reliance on an environment while place identity invokes more symbolic or spiritual meaning (Stokols 1990). . . . In other words, place dependence describes a functional relationship between a group or individual and a place, while place identity describes a mental relationship, and place attachment describes a positive emotional bond that develops between an individual or group and their environment (Williams, Patterson, Roggenbuck, & Watson 1992)" (Mullendore, Ulrich-Schad, and Prokopy 2015:68).

Philip Thomas (2002:368) notes that "just how significant place is in the lives of people in a variety of locales is testified to by an impressive range of anthropological works that reveal the manifold ways in which persons, practices, and identities are implicated in cultural landscapes" (e.g., Basso 1996; Feld and Basso 1996; Gray 1999; Hirsch and O'Hanlon 1995; Kahn 2000; Morphy 1993; Santos-Granero 1998).

5. Although Basso (1996) thinks that categorizing the Native American view of land as sacred is too simplistic. See also Callicott 1989.

6. "And God said, Let us make man in our image, after our likeness: and let them have dominion over the fish of the sea, and over the fowl of the air, and over the cattle, and over all the earth, and over every creeping thing that creepeth upon the earth. . . . And God blessed them, and God said unto them, Be fruitful, and multiply, and replenish the earth, and subdue it: and have dominion over the fish of the sea, and over the fowl of the air, and over every living thing that moveth upon the earth" (Holy Bible, King James Version: Genesis 1:26, 28). The earliest taxonomies in the Western world presented the human position as "dominion taker" over the earth. They were hierarchies that listed God at the top, then angels, then humans, then animals. Each was a different order of being; humans were as different from animals as they were from angels.

7. In *Land: How the Hunger for Ownership Shaped the Modern World*, Simon Winchester (2021) takes the reader on a ride through a variety of places to illustrate humans' relationship to land. His discussion of land ownership details cultural clashes and exploitations.

8. Dove and Carpenter (2008) maintain that anthropologists have discovered this for many years and in many places. They use Evans-Pritchard's (1940) ethnography *The Nuer* as an example. See also Davis 2000.

9. Balée and Erickson (2006:ix) say, "The product of the collision between nature and culture, wherever it has occurred, is a landscape." They would call the activities I'm describing here anthropogenic processes of change to environment.

10. Interview 6/14.MBW; 6/21.MBW; 6/23.SLV; 6/24.MBW; 6/29.LC; 8/22.MS&SS; Wagner and Hedrick 2000.

4. Using Land to Make a Living and a Life

The title of the chapter is borrowed from student Melissa E. Lamb's paper, presented at the Society for the Scientific Study of Religion meeting, Boston, Massachusetts, November 5–7, 1999, "'Making a Living or Making a Life' in Off-the-Grid Appalachia."

1. Interviews 6/7.MBW; 6/14.MBW; 6/15.MS&SS; 6/21.MBW; 6/23.SLV; 6/28B.LC; 6/29.LC; 7/04.AM; 8/22.MBW; 9/14.HZ; T312 12/27.JB. See also Mooney 1988.

2. Interviews 6/23.SLV; 6/14.MBW; 6/28B.LC; 6/29.LC; 7/19.MS&SS; 7/20.SS&MS; 7/21.MS&SS; 8/22.MBW; 9/12.JD; 9/14.RH; 9/14.SH; 9/14.HZ; 9/16.JH; 9/16.LU; 9/20.BD; 9/21.MG; 9/24.TC.

3. Interviews 6/7.MBW; 6/14.MBW; 6/24B.LC; 7/4.AM; 7/19.MS&SS; 7/20.MS&SS; 7/20D.MS&SS; 7/21A.MS&SS; 8/22.MBW; 9/12.JD; 9/14.HZ; 9/15.BF; 9/16.JH; 9/16.LU; 9/17.KW; 9/19.KG; 9/25.CH; 9/27.LK.

4. For a discussion of the importance of off-farm jobs for the future of the family farm and rural communities, see Castle 1995; Fitchen 1995; and Swanson 1990 and the studies he cites.

5. Using Place to Create and Maintain Historical Continuity

1. See also Batteau 1982; and Manzo and Nagy 1979.

2. Field Notes 6/14.MBW; 6/21.MBW; Interviews 6/7.MBW; 6/14.MBW.

3. See also Interviews 9/14.RH; and 9/14.SH.

4. Interviews 6/7.MBW; 6/14.MBW; 6/15.MS&SS; 6/23.SLV; 6/24.MBW; 9/14.SH; 9/16.JH; 9/19.LU; 9/24.TC, 9/16.LU 9/24.AMR, 9/18.CMH.

5. Interviews 9/17.JAE; 9/18.DNS; 9/20.TLP; 9/22.GAS; 9/23.AER.

6. Interviews 6/7.MBW; 6/14.MBW; 6/15.MS&SS; 6/23.SLV; 6/24.MBW; 7/18.SS&MS; 7/19.SS&MS; 7/20.SS&MS; 7/21.SS&MS; 8/22.MBW; 9/14.SH; 9/16.JH; 9/16.LU; 9/19.EP; 9/24.TC

6. Using Place to Build and Maintain Living Community

1. Billings and Blee 2000; Davis 2000; Dunaway 1996; Horning 2000; Pudup, Billings, and Waller 1995; Salstrom 1994.

2. See also Gusfield 1967:362.

3. Annette Kolodny (1975), in an analysis of several pieces of American literature, including writings by J. Hector St. John Crèvecoeur, John James Audubon, and James Fenimore Cooper, finds that the "American pastoral impulse" is dominated by a metaphor of land as woman—sometimes the land is glossed as mother, and sometimes as virginal, awaiting exploration and use. This is reminiscent of the emotions behind the Preservation versus Progress debate.

4. Batteau 1990; MacKaye 1924/1962; H. Shapiro 1978; Wagner et al. 1983. Lichter and Brown (2011) say rural America is viewed as America's cultural safety deposit box. See also Harrington (2018) for discussion of "attachment to the rural ideal or rural idyll."

5. See also Putnam 2000.

6. Dumont 1985, 1986; Marsella 1985; Wikse 1977.

7. See also Hostetler and Huntington (1967) regarding the Hutterites.

8. See also Jean Briggs (1970) concerning the Inuit (Eskimo) use of this form of communication.

9. See also Godkin 1980.

10. See also Puckett 2000.

11. Interviews 6/7.MBW; 6/14.MBW; 6/15.MS&SS; 6/17.MBW; 6/21.MBW; 6/23.SLV; 6/24.MBW; 6/28B.LC; 6/29A.LC; 6/29B.LC; 6/29.MBW; 7/04.AM; 8/22.MBW.

12. See Sonya Salamon (1995) for a discussion of these same networks in the Midwest. Kathryn Marie Dudley (2000), in an anthropological study of farmers in a county of western Minnesota who had lost their farms during the farm financial crisis of the 1980s, showed much more competition and jealousy among farmers. Salamon (1992) would categorize these farmers as "entrepreneurial" as opposed to the "yeomen" farmers more typical of those we learned from. At the same time, some of Dudley's interviews—with minor changes due to the different kinds of crops grown—could have been spoken in the rural communities we studied. For example:

> The land is very important. It's like your soul is in it. And you know every inch. And you know how water runs off of it, and you know what's going to grow best on that field. You have such hope every spring when you put that crop in, and oh, it's going to be wonderful, and if it'll just rain. Every day you live with the land. Can you get the field cultivated before the rains come? Can you get the crop up before bad weather strikes? Is the wind going to blow the wheat flat? Every day you work with the land. [Beginning to cry.] And when it's taken away from you, it's like you lose some part of your life. (Dudley 2000:164)

For examples of reciprocity practiced by Missouri farmers, and also lack of cooperation from a "city man who'd moved to the country" who broke the cultural rules, see Rhodes (1989), e.g., 17, 79, 303.

13. See also Eller 1979; Hufford 1998a, 2002; Newfont 2012; Reid and Taylor 2010; and Smith 2018.

7. Using Place to Teach Culture's Ways

1. Some think that language based on hand signals may have preceded verbal language. Hand signals can tell a whole thought; verbal or written symbols set into sentences are linear-digital. Ong (1967:137) carefully traces the history of language and suggests that all symbols "proceed by indirection" because it is the nature of symbols to stand for something other than themselves and thus "demand a lack of contact with reality." But the move to a phonetic alphabet was a move to an even more abstract visual "mode of knowing others and environment" than was true of the previous mode based on oral sounds.

2. See also McLuhan 1962; Porteous 1990; Rappaport 1976; Tuan 1974; and B. M. Wilson 1980.

3. The previous oral-aural language was "rooted in constant interchange of communally possessed knowledge. But writing and printing isolate the individual, or, if you prefer, liberate him from the tribe." "Reading of any sort forces the individual into himself by confronting him

with thought in isolation, alone" (Ong 1967:88, 135). Reading substantiates his ability to think for himself, and loosens the hold of the community. (Of course, other cultural elements also moved in this direction, such as economic forms that required less [obvious] interdependence.)

4. Kimmerer (2013:46, 139, 56), discussing science and traditional knowledge, says, "We see the world more fully when we use both." "I envision a time when the intellectual monoculture of science will be replaced with a polyculture of complementary knowledges." Echoing our discussion of subjects viewing distant objects, she quotes ecotheologian Thomas Berry: "We must say of the universe that it is a communion of subjects, not a collection of objects."

5. Philip Thomas (2002:383) describes a moral geography that is "a spatial imaginary constituted from the interweaving of ideas, idioms, and images of practice and identity, morality and sociality, memory and history, experience and imagination, ... imbued with the vestiges of history."

6. Interviews 6/15.MS&SS; 6/21.LC; 7/20D.MS&SS; 9/21.MG; T013 06/21.MBW; T006 06/15.MS&SS; T341 12/22.ES; T005 06/09.SLV; T052 09/26.ASC.

7. I agree with Basso. I reined in the student researchers, requiring them to use the term *sacred* carefully. But if we hold with Milton (2002:104, 105, 149), we would be more willing to ascribe sacredness to emotional attachments to land. She defines sacred as "what matters most to people . . . those things that give their lives sense, pattern and meaning, . . . whatever we find most emotionally compelling." She asks, "Why should not . . . [any] citizen feel able to state publicly that this mountain, which has been part of his world as long as he can remember, is sacred to him, part of his identity, part of what gives his life meaning?" (Milton 2002:141). See also Wagner (1983) for a discussion of meaning, identity, and the sacred.

8. In Larry Greil and Tom Robbins's (1994:3–4) book *Between Sacred and Secular: Research and Theory on Quasi-Religion,* substantive and functional definitions of religion are discussed. Substantive definitions require that a religion makes "reference to the sacred, the supernatural, or the 'superempirical.'" For functional definitions, on the other hand, the most important aspect of religion is that it provides "an 'encompassing system of meaning' or the ability to 'relate man to the ultimate conditions of his existence.'" When it comes to defining *sacred,* in anthropology and sociology we can hark back to Émile Durkheim, whose substantive dichotomy segregated the sacred realm from the secular or profane one. This fits nicely with Weber's "rationalized" religion, where the sacred, and religion itself, is "apart, above, outside" of ordinary life. It should be noted that it doesn't fit as well with Weber's "traditional" religion, in which the sacred is found everywhere—in the "rooftrees, graveyards, and road-crossings of everyday life" (Geertz 1973:171–75; Parsons 1949; Weber 1948, 1963). Premodern societies are said to practice the traditional form of religion, and modern ones the rationalized type. (However, there are modern and postmodern groups who are removing the distance between the sacred and the secular realms. For example, conservative Christians say, "To the Christian, all things are sacred.")

9. Nabhan (2018:165–66) contends that the faith impulse is not to be ignored in conservation efforts. His "Conservation Couplets: A Manifesto for Moving from Top-Down Protectionism to Bottom-Up Community-Based Restoration" includes: "We once believed that 'science alone should be enough to ensure the rational management and wise use of natural resources for the public good.' We now humbly recognize that 'scientists, policy makers, and on-ground resource managers need to be in constant dialogue with ethicists, faith-based communities, and culture bearers. If we ignore the need for dialogue between science and the spirit, we will not be able to achieve just, equitable, and morally appropriate means to care for creation and for the poor still struggling in our midst.'"

10. See Bellah 1970; Greeley and McCready 1974; and James 1958.

8. Using Place to Confront Threats to the Environment and Culture

1. See also Fitchen's (1991) discussion of New York farmers dealing with "new uses for rural lands: [being a] dumping ground for society," in which she includes prisons, landfills, and low-level radioactive waste facilities.

2. Billings and Kingsolver (2018), Fisher and Smith (2012), and Schumann and Fletcher (2016), among others, include many examples of using place to confront threats to environment and culture.

3. See also Allen 1990; Chapin and Knapp 2015; Downs and Stea 1977; Ellis and Albrecht 2017; Halmo, Stoffle, and Evans 1993; Relph 1976; Sangaramoorthy et al. 2016; and Simonson 1989.

4. See also Frank 1967; and Lewis, Johnson, and Askins 1978. The power line situation provides a good example of internal colonialism or the "metropolis-satellite" concept as it is labeled by Joseph Jorgensen (1971), much as the Four Corners power plant on the Navajo reservation does. Originally built with tax breaks for the utility corporation during the Kennedy administration's attempt to encourage industry to locate near reservations, the Four Corners plant ultimately provided only a few low-paying jobs and used Navajo water to slurry Navajo coal to the plant to produce power for Los Angeles and Las Vegas, while almost 50 percent of Navajo homes have no electricity.

However, internal colonialism by itself is not adequate to explain poverty and exploitation in Appalachia. As Batteau (1983), Whisnant (1992), and Billings and Blee (2000) have pointed out, both internal cultural factors and externally motivated "colonialism" are necessary for explaining Appalachia's situation (see also Wagner 2018). Often missed is the role played by local elites. Billings and Blee (2000) carefully researched the factors that created, maintained, and dealt with the poverty of Clay County, Kentucky. They uncovered the historical impacts of capitalist markets; state coercion at the county and state government levels, including clientelism, corruption, and a public sphere manipulated by local elites; and the cultural strategies implicit in a "patriarchal moral economy." They find that "economic life was structured simultaneously by culture, markets, and power" (Billings and Blee 2000:163).

5. Philip Thomas (2002:384) describes a moral geography for Malagasy people in southeast Madagascar: "A part of people's senses of themselves and their place in the world, the moral geography I have described here is a domain of understanding and imagination that draws on a deeply emplaced identity and ancestral history, the experience of the vicissitudes of colonial rule, and a sense of political impotence, economic marginality, and exclusion from many of modernity's benefits." If colonial were changed to internal colonialism and if exclusion from modernity's benefits were perceived more positively by the residents, as sacrifices willingly made (but for which recognition would be welcome), his conclusion could apply to the residents of Appalachia I am describing here.

6. Nelson, Swanson, and Cain (2018:567) found that in the case of a high-voltage transmission line project in California, the main concerns "were health risks and harm to property values."

9. The Culture Wars, Anthropology, and the Law

1. National Historic Preservation Act of 1966; National Environmental Policy Act of 1969; American Folklife Preservation Act of 1976; President's Council on Environmental Quality, 1978, 1986; National Register Bulletin Number 38, n.d.

2. Andrews et al. 1977; Barbaro and Cross 1974; Black 1981; Bregman and Mackenthun 1992; Canter 1977; Canter and Hill 1979; Cheremisinoff and Morresi 1977; Corwin et al. 1975; Jain and Hutchings 1978; Jain et al. 1993; Orloff 1978; Rau and Wooten 1980; Sherfy and Luce 1989; Smardon and Karp 1993.

A "Community social and cultural profiling guide: Understanding a community's sense of place" written for the US Environmental Protection Agency (1997:1) has as its goal to "help fill a gap in how to address the social and cultural aspects of a place, and the relationship of those aspects to sustainable strategies." And indeed, the handbook is an excellent step. But the distance between the NEPA guide and the *Cultural Anthropology* special issue titled "Space, Identity, and the Politics of Difference" is vast; the distance between the NEPA guide and the *Ethos: Journal of the Society for Psychological Anthropology* special issue "Language, Space, and Culture" is vast in the other theoretical direction (one representing Marxist concern for political economy, the other interpretive understandings). The distance between the NEPA guide and the kinds of post-postmodernist understandings called for by Reid and Taylor (2010) is vast.

3. See, for example, Spradley 1979, 1980; and Tedlock 1991.

4. See Campbell and Lassiter 2010; Howell 2002; Keefe 2009; Lassiter 2005a; 2005b; 2010; and Lassiter et al. 2004.

5. See Wagner 2020. See also Checker 2014; Checker, Davis, Schuller, 2014; Hyland and Bennett 2013; Johnston 2010; Kozaitis 2013; Low and Merry 2010; Moskowitz 2015; and Whiteford and Strom 2013.

6. See, however, Billings and Blee 2000 on the potential complicity of local elites.

7. Berry (1977) 1996:234 says: "To suggest that the health of places and communities might be the indispensable standard of economic behavior is finally to ask how a mere human, whose years are like the grass that is cut down in the evening, can justify on his or her own behalf the permanent destruction of anything."

8. See Howell 1990.

9. Economists themselves have developed the subdisciplines of environmental economics and ecological economics to try to deal with the need to value intangible, largely immeasurable aspects of culture. "Ecological economics is concerned with achieving sustainable outcomes with the minimum economic cost, while environmental economics is concerned with maintaining economic activity with minimum environmental cost" (Furze, De Lacy, Birckhead 1996:40). Biologist Gretchen Daily promotes "natural capital." "The term refers to the soil, air, water and other assets that nature has to offer. As a conservation model, it is rooted in the idea that nature has a measurable value to humans and that protection efforts must go far beyond walled-off reserves and be broadly integrated into development practice and planning" (Root 2021).

10. Toumey (1996:154), in his study of the place of science in American culture, noted: "As an abstract entity, the institution of science is a powerful authority, but individual scientists begin with zero credibility when they represent particular positions in a dispute. They endure a constant burden of establishing and defending their own personal scientific credibility. The usual way to do so is to cobble together a suitable simulacrum of personal credibility from the standard symbols (Ph.D., quantities of publications, faculty titles, and so on), while trying to deny their adversaries the same credibility."

Toumey (1996:156–57, 159) also notes regarding Americans' view of science: "Science should give us certainty, both factual and moral, according to the feelings of many citizens. From this feeling comes a simple moral standard for judging scientific knowledge: it is natural, right, and proper for knowledge to take the form of certainty, but it is highly disturbing—unnatural—for science to conclude that our knowledge of a given problem is riddled with uncertainty. Candor about uncertainty is not what people want. . . . If a little bit of uncertainty equals a very large proportion of doubt, then a lot of uncertainty equals pure incredulity. . . . Individual scientists try to derive their personal credibility from the institutional authority of science, but the pseudosymmetry of scientific authority implies that this institutional authority can be reduced to personal credibility. Science is believed to be a transcendental source of moral and factual certainty, . . . except when a tiny drop of uncertainty or equivocation undermines all the transcendental power of science." See also MacGillivray and Franklin 2015.

11. Like Borofsky's public anthropologists who question frameworks, Towers (1997:124) notes that, even if citizens were allowed to participate in the GIS process, "participating in finding the best corridor could . . . indicate public acceptance of the power line and legitimize its routing," rather than "directly challenging the construction of the power line" in the first place. This is true because of a beginning assumption made by the professional GIS practitioners—that all private lands were available for power line corridors, and the task at hand was merely to rank them. See also Harris et al. 1995; Harvey 2001; and Sheppard 1995.

12. Anthropologist Kay Milton (2002:139) observed similar emphases in environmental controversies in the United Kingdom and Ireland: "But the defence of natural beauty, and the defence of the market interests that threaten it, have to be presented in an idiom that enables decision makers to appear independent. In western cultures, that idiom is scientific." She puts a fine point on the problem of valuing "rationality" over "emotion":

> The opposition between rationality and emotion is a myth, in at least two senses of that term; in the popular sense that it is false, and in the anthropological sense that it is believed in and dogmatically asserted because it protects particular interests and ideologies (Robinson 1968, Milton 1996). All areas of western public discourse are characterized by this myth. We see it whenever people's attachments to non-market interests challenge the operation of the market. Nature protection is just one area of public debate in which the myth is prominently expressed, in which accusations of emotionality are used as instruments of power, as mechanisms for putting down opponents and winning arguments. Does it matter if the opposition between emotion and rationality is a myth? It has, after all, been a very useful device for getting decisions made, for guiding public discourse away from open aggression and towards calm negotiation. But clearly, it matters to those who are disadvantaged by the myth, to those for whom non-market interests matter most, and this, I suggest, is a sizeable proportion of the population in any liberal democracy. The market systematically destroys whatever it cannot encompass. This includes, not only nature and natural things, but also health, family, friendship, spirituality, knowledge and truth. Any failure to put the things that people hold most sacred at the centre of public decision making makes democracies, at best, undemocratic. (Milton 2002:150)

13. See also Ezzell 2016.

14. At the same time as citizen science, or indigenous knowledge, is problematic in a legal setting, it is recognized as essential to sustaining the earth's future by, for example, Berkes (2008); Berry ([1970, 1972] 2012); ([1977] 1996); Kimmerer (2013); and Nabhan (2018). "A healthy *farm* culture can be based only upon familiarity and can grow only among people soundly established upon the land; it nourishes and safeguards a human intelligence of the earth that no amount of technology can satisfactorily replace" (Berry [1977] 1996:43, emphasis his).

15. See also Chambers 1991; and McCracken, Pretty, and Conway 1988.

16. For example, for years real estate developers and environmentalists around Little Traverse Bay, Michigan, fought in the courts. In the words of one of the constituents, "The lawsuits never seemed to end; never seemed to resolve anything." "They took forever, they cost a lot of money and the results were never clear" (Hall 1997). The legal system also did not serve well in the battle to save some of Manassas Civil War battlefield from becoming a mall. Zoning restrictions and contracts with the developer were vague and ironclad. In the end, however, the National Park Service bought the land under eminent domain (Garreau 1991).

10. Culture Wars Continued, Environmental Crises

1. One of the affected counties eventually changed its opposition, seeking "to have as much input as possible into the routing" (Dellinger 2006).

2. Hammack 2022a, 2022b; Litvak 2022; T. Lopez 2019. See Yahn (2016) for a discussion of the problems with fracking "upstream," in northern Appalachia, where fracking of the Marcellus Shale takes place.

3. Other landowners, conceding the overwhelming power of eminent domain (which can advance Gaventa's (2018:202) "invisible power, . . . the internalization of powerlessness") have chosen to protect parts of their farms, by negotiating with the pipeline builders to alter the corridor's route. (This is expensive for companies that want a straight-line corridor, but potentially not as expensive as a possible court judgment of compensatory damages to a farmer. "Just compensation" is required in the US Constitution when an eminent domain taking occurs.)

4. For an account of the CEQ's early years, in which it played a major role advocating for conservation and land use planning, see Rome (2001).

5. See also Siros et al. 2020; and Tai 2020.

11. Cultural Conservation and Cultural Confrontations

1. See Rome (2001) for an account of the origins of suburban sprawl and its role in fostering environmentalism as controversies grew where tract houses were built.

2. On the other side of the eminent domain story are groups like the Defenders of Property Rights, who protest that wildlife protection and anti-pollution laws put strictures on what they can do with their property (e.g., Babbitt vs. Sweet Home, US Supreme Court 1995). Those who have pondered the contentious issue, including the attorneys general of twenty-eight states, think that the new "takings legislation" that the property righters advocate does *not* protect small landowners. Instead, "it seeks to gut legislation, such as the Endangered Species Act and the Clean Water Act" and ultimately "the biggest beneficiaries of the movement are large corporations" (Nixon 1995:42, 44). The group is part of the "Wise Use" movement; documents referencing the group are in Greenpeace's Anti-Environmental Archive.

12. Culture War Strategies

1. See also Cronon (1996) for a beautifully written essay about the cultural significance of wilderness throughout America's history, and the problems it causes for environmentalism. He asks, "What are the consequences of a wilderness ideology that devalues productive labor and the very concrete knowledge that comes from working the land with one's own hands?" (Cronon 1996:21).

2. See Roderick Nash (1967) for the history of the concept of wilderness in America, Marx (2000 [1964]) for the idea of the pastoral in American literature and culture, Howarth (1995) for a brief overview of the land in literature, and Nash (1989) for the history of environmental ethics that extended rights to other-than-human beings.

3. There are, however, conservative Christian environmental efforts. See Spraker 2009; L. Andrews 2010; Ellingson, Woodley, and Paik 2010; Green 2010; Wagner and Spraker 2011. See also Witt 2016.

4. Heading full speed in the opposite direction is this advice for how to "upgrade your outdoor areas" from *Consumer Reports* (2021:33). "Extend the seasonal usability of your backyard or balcony by making it like an extension of your living room. An easy-to-install WiFi extender ensures that you can stream music to a waterproof wireless speaker while reclined in your lounge chair. Timed lighting [enabled by an inexpensive smart plug] can beckon you to step out for fresh air at sunset. A few plants and a heater make your oasis extra-inviting." Total bill, less than $650.

5. See also Steve Nash (1999) for discussion of problems and solutions for the ecology of the Blue Ridge, and the American Farmland Trust website (farmlandinfo.org) for "farmland protection tools and techniques."

6. See also Rescia et al. 2008.

7. Eric Schlosser (2001:266), who writes about the effect of the fast-food industry on American culture, including farming, concludes:

> Any reform of the current system of industrialized agriculture will have to address the needs of independent ranchers and farmers. They are more than just a sentimental link to America's rural past. They are a unique source of innovation and long-term stewardship of the land. Throughout the Cold War, America's decentralized system of agriculture, relying upon millions of independent producers, was depicted as the most productive system in the world, as proof of capitalism's inherent superiority. The perennial crop failures in the Soviet Union were attributed to a highly centralized system run by distant bureaucrats. Today the handful of agribusiness firms that dominate American food production are championing another centralized system of production, one in which livestock and farmland are viewed purely as commodities, farmers are reduced to the status of employees, and crop decisions are made by executives far away from the fields. Although competition between the large processors has indeed led to lower costs for consumers, price fixing and collusion have devastated independent ranchers and farmers. The antitrust laws outlawing such behavior need to be vigorously enforced. More than a century ago, during the congressional debate on the Sherman Antitrust Act, Henry M. Teller, a Republican senator from Colorado, dismissed the argument that lower consumer prices justified the ruthless exercise of monopoly power. "I do not believe," Teller argued, "that the great object in life is to make everything cheap."

Conclusion

1. Osha Gray Davidson (1990) points out that the disparities of wealth promulgated in rural areas by industrialized farming are also inimical to democracy. See also Schlosser 2001.

References

Abbott, Susan. 1992. "Holding on and Pushing Away: Comparative Perspectives on an Eastern Kentucky Child-Rearing Practice." *Ethos* 20:33–65.

Abbott-Jamieson, Susan. 2005. "Mediating Perceptions of Parent/Child Co-sleeping in Eastern Kentucky." In *Appalachian Cultural Competency: A Guide for Medical, Mental Health, and Social Service Professionals,* edited by Susan E. Keefe, 121–42. Knoxville: University of Tennessee Press.

Abram, David. 1996. *The Spell of the Sensuous.* New York: Vintage.

Acquaviva, Gary J. 1980. "Teaching Philosophy in Appalachia: An Existential Approach." Paper presented at Appalachian Studies Conference, East Tennessee State University, Johnson City, March 21–23.

Adeh, Elnaz H., Stephen P. Good, Marc Calaf, and Chad W. Higgins. 2019. "Solar PV Power Potential Is Greatest over Croplands." *Scientific Reports,* no. 9, 11442.

Agnew, John A. 1989. "The Devaluation of Place in Social Science." In *The Power of Place: Bringing Together Geographical and Sociological Imaginations,* edited by Agnew and James S. Duncan, 9–29. London: Unwin Hyman.

AgWeb. 2019. "Our Incredible Vanishing Farmland." *Farm Journal* AgWeb, January 21, 2019.

Allen, Barbara. 1990. "The Genealogical Landscape and the Southern Sense of Place." In *Sense of Place*, edited by Allen and Thomas J. Schlereth, 152–63. Lexington: University Press of Kentucky.

American Farmland Trust. Farmland Information Library. http://www.farmlandinfo.org. March 9, 2001.

American Folklife Preservation Act. 1976.

Anderson, C. 1992. "Identifying Groups for Negotiations about Land." In *Cross Cultural Management of Natural and Cultural Heritage,* edited by R. Hill, 74–85. Cairns, Queensland, Australia: Cairns College of Technical and Further Education.

Anderson, E. N. 1996. *Ecologies of the Heart.* New York: Oxford University Press.

———. 2010. *The Pursuit of Ecotopia.* Santa Barbara, CA: Praeger.

———. 2013. Foreword to *Environmental Anthropology Engaging Ecotopia: Bioregionalism, Permaculture, and Ecovillages,* edited by Joshua Lockyer and James R. Veteto, xi–xviii. New York: Berghahn.

Anderson, Howard P., Jr. 2000. Report. October 2.

Anderson, Peter. 2020. "Atlantic Coast Pipeline Battle Is Far from Over." *Appalachian Voices* June 18, 2020.

Andrews, Laura. 2010. "God Is Great, God Is Green? Evangelical Protestants in the Environmental Movement." Paper presented at Society for the Scientific Study of Religion and Religious Research Association Annual Meeting, Baltimore, MD, October 29–31.

Andrews, Richard N. L., Paul Cromwell, Gordon A. Enk, Edward G. Farnworth, James R. Hibbs, and Virginia L. Sharp. 1977. *Substantive Guidance for Environmental Impact Assessment: An Exploratory Study.* Institute of Ecology.

Andrzejewski, Adam. 2018. "Mapping the U.S. Farm Subsidy $1M Club." *Forbes,* August 14, 2018.

Anthony, Ted. 1998. "This Land Is Your Land, This Land Is My Land—Unless." *Roanoke Times,* February 2, 1998.

Antonsich, Marco. 2010. "Meanings of Place and Aspects of the Self: An Interdisciplinary and Empirical Account." *GeoJournal* 75:119–32.

Appalachian Land Ownership Task Force. 1983. *Appalachian Land Ownership Study.*

Appalachian Voices. 2000. "Ecologists Working to Save Biologically Rich Lands." *Appalachian Voices,* Late Summer 2000, 15.

Appalshop. 1979. *Strip Mining: Energy, Environment, and Economics.* Videorecording. Whitesburg, KY: Appalshop Film & Video.

———. 1988. *On Our Own Land.* Videorecording. Whitesburg, KY: Appalshop Film & Video.

AppraisalEconomics.com. 2018. "How Much Is a Wind Turbine Lease Worth?" July 31, 2018.

APST 460. 1993. "Appalachian Studies Seminar." Radford University, Radford, VA, Spring 1993.

Arbogast, John. 1998. "Article Says Trees Make Us Feel Better in Urban Setting." *Roanoke Times,* January 25, 1998.

Asch, Timothy, and Napoleon Chagnon. 1970. *The Feast, a Film.* Washington, DC: National Audiovisual Center.

atlanticcoastpipeline.com. 2020. "Dominion Energy and Duke Energy Cancel the Atlantic Coast Pipeline." ACP Releases. July 5, 2020.

Balée, William, and Clark L. Erickson. 2006. *Time and Complexity in Historical Ecology.* New York: Columbia University Press.

Barbaro, Ronald, and Frank L. Cross, Jr. 1974. *Primer on Environmental Impact Statements.* Westport, CT: Technomic.

Barho, Rebecca Hayes. 2021. "CEQ Tweaks NEPA Regulations." *JD Supra Legal News,* June 29, 2021.

Barlett, Peggy F. 1993. *American Dreams, Rural Realities: Family Farms in Crisis.* Chapel Hill: University of North Carolina Press.

Barrett, Richard A. 2004. *Culture and Conduct: An Excursion in Anthropology.* 2nd ed. Belmont, CA: Wadsworth.

Basso, Keith H. 1988. "'Speaking with Names': Language and Landscape among the Western Apache." *Cultural Anthropology* 3 (2):99–130.

———. 1996. *Wisdom Sits in Places: Landscape and Language among the Western Apache.* Albuquerque: University of New Mexico Press.

Basso, Keith H., and Henry A. Selby. 1976. *Meaning in Anthropology.* Albuquerque: University of New Mexico Press.

Bateson, Gregory. 1972. *Steps to an Ecology of Mind.* New York: Ballantine.

Batteau, Allen. 1979. "The American Culture of Appalachia." Paper presented at American Anthropological Association Annual Meeting, Cincinnati, OH.

———. 1982. "Mosbys and Broomsedge: The Semantics of Class in an Appalachian Kinship System." *American Ethnologist* 9 (3):445–66.

———. 1983. "Rituals of Dependence in Appalachian Kentucky." In *Appalachia and America: Autonomy and Regional Dependence,* edited by Batteau, 142–67. Lexington: University Press of Kentucky.

———. 1990. *The Invention of Appalachia*. Tucson: University of Arizona Press.

Beagle, Ben. 1992. "A Million Bucks a Mile." *Roanoke Times,* October 20, 1992.

Bearinger, David. 1998. *The Need for a Statewide Conversation on the Future of Rural Virginia*. Charlottesville: Virginia Foundation for the Humanities and Public Policy.

Beaver, Patricia D. 1982. "Appalachian Families, Landownership, and Public Policy." In *Holding on to the Land and the Lord: Kinship, Ritual, Land Tenure, and Social Policy in the Rural South,* edited by Robert L. Hall and Carol B. Stack, 146–54. Athens: University of Georgia Press.

———. 1992. *Rural Community in the Appalachian South*. Prospect Heights, IL: Waveland.

Beck, Rachel. 1998. "Forget the Beach: More Travelers Opt to Shop on Vacations." *Roanoke Times,* August 3, 1998.

Bell, Christopher. 2020a. "Federal Judge in Montana Narrows Vacatur of Nationwide Permit 12." *National Law Review* 10 (134): May 13.

———. 2020b. "Federal Judge Prohibits Use of U.S. Army Corps of Engineers' Nationwide Permit 12 for Utility and Pipeline Projects." *E2 Law Blog,* Greenberg Traurig, LLP. April 17.

Bell, Shannon Elizabeth. 2016. *Fighting King Coal: The Challenges to Micromobilization in Central Appalachia*. Cambridge: Massachusetts Institute of Technology.

Bell, Shannon Elizabeth, Jenrose Fitzgerald, and Richard York. 2019. "Protecting the Power to Pollute: Identity Co-Optation, Gender, and the Public Relations Strategies of Fossil Fuel Industries in the United States." *Environmental Sociology* 5 (3):323–38.

Bellah, Robert N. 1970. *Beyond Belief*. New York: Harper and Row.

Bellah, Robert N., Richard Madsen, William M. Sullivan, Ann Swidler, and Steven M. Tipton. 1985. *Habits of the Heart: Individualism and Commitment in American Life*. New York: Harper and Row.

Bengston, Ginny, and Rebecca L. Austin. 2016. *The Proposed Mountain Valley Pipeline —— National Forest Segment Cultural Attachment Report*. Applied Cultural Ecology, LLC. Sun Valley, NV.

Berkes, Fikret. 2008. *Sacred Ecology*. 2nd ed. New York: Routledge.

Berry, Wendell. (1970, 1972) 2012. *A Continuous Harmony: Essays Cultural and Agricultural*. Berkeley, CA: Counterpoint.

———. (1977) 1996. *The Unsettling of America: Culture & Agriculture*. San Francisco: Sierra Club Books.

———. 1981. *The Gift of Good Land: Further Essays Cultural and Agricultural*. San Francisco: North Point.

Bielo, James. 2000. "Religious Experience in an African-American Church: Sunday Service and Beyond." Paper for "Anthropology 480: Practicing Ethnographic Methods." Radford University, Radford, VA.

Billings, Dwight B., and Kathleen M. Blee. 2000. *The Road to Poverty: The Making of Wealth and Hardship in Appalachia*. New York: Cambridge University Press.

Billings, Dwight B., and Ann E. Kingsolver, eds. 2018. *Appalachia in Regional Context: Place Matters*. Lexington: University Press of Kentucky.

Billings, Dwight B., Gurney Norman, and Katherine Ledford. 1999. *Confronting Appalachian Stereotypes: Back Talk from an American Region*. Lexington: University Press of Kentucky.

Bingham, Sam. 1996. *The Last Ranch: A Colorado Community and the Coming Desert*. New York: Harcourt Brace.

Biondo, Brenda. 2000. "Stand by Your Land." *Nature Conservancy,* September/October, 26–33.

Birckhead, Jim. 1996. "Dreaming Down Under: The Cultural Politics of People and 'Country.'" In *Nature and the Human Spirit: Toward an Expanded Land Management Ethic,* edited by B. L. Driver, Daniel Dustin, Tony Baltic, Gary Elsner, and George Peterson, 206–14. State College, PA: Venture.

Bird-David, Nurit. 1993. "Tribal Metaphorization of Human-Nature Relatedness: A Comparative Analysis." In *Environmentalism: The View from Anthropology,* edited by Kay Milton, 112–25. New York: Routledge.

Bishop, Mary. 1996. "Too Late for Cities, Small Towns?" *Roanoke Times,* April 11, 1996.

Black, Peter E. 1981. *Environmental Impact Analysis.* New York: Praeger.

Bleicher, J. (1980) 1990. *Contemporary Hermeneutics: Hermeneutics as Method, Philosophy and Critique.* New York: Routledge.

Block, Edward L. 1999. "Minimum Lot Size Proposal Brings Controversy in —— County." *Roanoke Times,* November 20, 1999.

Bloom, Stephen G. 2000. *Postville: A Clash of Cultures in Heartland America.* New York: Harcourt.

Blue Ridge Land Conservancy. 2018–19. *Saving Land, Blue Ridge Land Conservancy Annual Report.* Winter.

———. 2020. *Land Savers.* Spring.

Bogert, Frans van der. 1980. "The Cultural Context of Philosophic Criticism." Paper presented at Appalachian Studies Conference, East Tennessee State University, Johnson City, March 21–23.

Borgman, Anna. 1995. "Suburbia's Signs of Stressful Times." *Washington Post,* June 18, 1995.

Borofsky, Robert. 2000. "Public Anthropology: Where To? What Next?" *Anthropology News,* May 2020.

Bourdieu, Pierre. 1977. *Outline of a Theory of Practice.* Translated by Richard Nice. Cambridge: Cambridge University Press.

———. 1984. *Distinction: A Social Critique of the Judgement of Taste.* Translated by Richard Nice. Cambridge, MA: Harvard University Press.

Branam, Chris. 2019. "Installing Solar Panels on Agricultural Lands Maximizes Their Efficiency." *Oregon State University Newsroom* (Corvallis, OR), August 7, 2019.

Bregman, Jacob I., and Kenneth M. Mackenthun, eds. 1992. *Environmental Impact Statements.* Ann Arbor, MI: Lewis.

Brendtro, Larry K., Martin Brokenleg, and Steve Van Bockern. 1990. *Reclaiming Youth at Risk: Our Hope for the Future.* Bloomington, IN: National Education Service.

Briggs, Jean. 1970. "Kapluna Daughter." In *Women in the Field,* edited by Peggy Golde. Chicago: Aldine.

Brody, Jane. 2000. "Planners Need to Design Healthier Suburbs." *Roanoke Times,* October 24, 2000.

Bryant, F. Carlene. 1981. *We're All Kin.* Knoxville: University of Tennessee Press.

Burk, Meredith. 1994. "Cultural Attachment to Land Study." Paper for "Anthropology 411: Appalachian Cultures." Radford University, Radford, VA.

Burleson, Jenn. 2001. "Conservation Easements Grow in ——·" *Roanoke Times,* March 2, 2001.

Burns, Shirley Stewart. 2007. *Bringing down the Mountains: The Impact of Mountaintop Removal Surface Coal Mining on Southern West Virginia Communities, 1970–2004.* Morgantown: University of West Virginia Press.

Buttel, Frederick. 1982. "The Political Economy of Part-Time Farming." *Geojournal* 6:293–400.

Buttimer, Anne. 1974. *Values in Geography.* Washington, DC: Association of American Geographers.

———. 1980. "Home, Reach, and the Sense of Place." In *The Human Experience of Space and Place,* edited by Buttimer and David Seamon, 166–87. New York: St. Martin's.

Cagle, Sarah. 1998. "Landowner Preserves 1 Mile of Riverside." *Roanoke Times,* November 14, 1998.

———. 1999. "——— County Farmers Fear Proposed Zoning Changes." *Roanoke Times,* November 21, 1999.

Callicott, J. Baird. 1989. *In Defense of the Land Ethic: Essays in Environmental Philosophy.* Albany: State University of New York Press.

Campbell, Elizabeth, and Luke Eric Lassiter. 2010. "From Collaborative Ethnography to Collaborative Pedagogy: Reflections on the Other Side of Middletown Project and Community-University Research Partnerships." *Anthropology & Education Quarterly* 41 (4):370–85.

Canter, David. 1977. *The Psychology of Place.* London: Architectural Press.

Canter, Larry W., and Loren G. Hill. 1979. *Handbook of Variables for Environmental Impact Assessment.* Ann Arbor, MI: Ann Arbor Science.

Carden, Darlene H., Caryn Ergenbright, Brad Jackson, Kimberly Ledbetter Comerford, Brad Nyholm, Amy Sokoloff, Rebecca Taylor, Danny Wolfe, and Melinda Bollar Wagner. 1994. "Drawing the Line between People and Power." Paper presented at Appalachian Studies Conference, Virginia Tech, Blacksburg, March 11–13.

Carroll, Mike. 2019. *Considerations for Transferring Agricultural Land to Solar Panel Energy Production.* NC Cooperative Extension. New Bern: North Carolina State University and North Carolina A&T State University, November.

Carson, Fiddlin' John. 1924. "The Farmer Is the Man That Feeds Them All." New York: Okeh Recording 40071-A. [Different versions exist.]

Casey, Edward S. 1987. *Remembering: A Phenomenological Study.* Bloomington: Indiana University Press.

———. 1993. *Getting Back into Place: Toward a Renewed Understanding of the Place-World.* Bloomington: Indiana University Press.

———. 1996. "How to Get from Space to Place in a Fairly Short Stretch of Time: Phenomenological Prolegomena." In *Senses of Place,* edited by Steven Feld and Keith H. Basso, 13–52. Santa Fe, NM: School of American Research.

———. 1997. *The Fate of Place: A Philosophical History.* Berkeley: University of California Press.

Castle, Emery N. 1995. *The Changing American Countryside: Rural People and Places.* Lawrence: University Press of Kansas.

CEI 2020. CEI (Competitive Enterprise Institute) Comments on Proposed Updated NEPA Procedural Regulations. March 10.

Centner, Terence J. 2004. *Empty Pastures: Confined Animals and the Transformation of the Rural Landscape.* Urbana: University of Illinois Press.

CEQ (Council on Environmental Quality). 1978. S 1508.14. National Environmental Policy Act—Regulations Implementation of Procedural Provisions.

Chambers, R. 1991. "Shortcut and Participatory Methods for Gaining Social Information for Projects." In *Putting People First: Sociological Variables in Rural Development,* edited by Michael M. Cernea. New York: Oxford University Press.

Chance, Donald. 1999. "America's Land-Use Dilemma: Will We Ever Learn?" *Roanoke Times,* May 30, 1999.

Chapin, F. Stuart, III, and Corrine N. Knapp. 2015. "Sense of Place: A Process for Identifying and Negotiating Potentially Contested Visions of Sustainability." *Environmental Science & Policy* 53:38–46.

Checker, Melissa. 2014. "Anthropological Superheroes and the Consequences of Activist Ethnography." *American Anthropologist* 116 (2):416–20.

Checker, Melissa, Dana-Ain Davis, and Mark Schuller. 2014. "The Conflicts of Crisis: Critical Reflections on Feminist Ethnography and Anthropological Activism." *American Anthropologist* 116 (2):408–20.

Cheremisinoff, Paul N., and Angelo C. Morresi. 1977. *Environmental Assessment & Impact Statement Handbook.* Ann Arbor, MI: Ann Arbor Science.

Chibnik, Michael. 1987. Afterword to *Farm Work and Fieldwork: American Agriculture in Anthropological Perspective,* edited by Chibnik, 281–85. Ithaca, NY: Cornell University Press.

Chittum, Matt. 2000. "Protecting Land Takes Guts, Offers Little Glory." *Roanoke Times,* December 3, 2000.

Clauson-Wicker, Su. 2001. "Suburban Farmers: An Endangered Species." *Roanoke Times,* March 18, 2001.

Clauss-Ehlers, Caroline S. 2004. "Reinventing Resilience: A Model of Culturally-Focused Resilient Adaptation." In *Community Planning to Foster Resilience in Children,* edited by Clauss-Ehlers and Mark D. Weist. New York: Kluwer Academic.

Clauss-Ehlers, Caroline S., and L. L. Lopez-Levi. 2002. "Violence and Community, Terms in Conflict: An Ecological Approach to Resilience." *Journal of Social Distress & the Homeless* 11 (4):265–78.

Cohen, A. P. 1985. *The Symbolic Construction of Community.* New York: Tavistock.

Cohen, Erik. 1976. "Environmental Orientations: A Multidimensional Approach to Social Ecology." *Current Anthropology* 17 (1):49–70.

Coleman, James S. 1988. "Social Capital in the Creation of Human Capital." *American Journal of Sociology* 94:95–119.

Coles, Robert. 1967. *Migrants, Sharecroppers, Mountaineers.* Vol. 2 of *Children of Crisis.* Boston: Little, Brown.

Collins, James C. 2001. *Good to Great: Why Some Companies Make the Leap . . . and Others Don't.* New York: HarperBusiness.

Communities in Schools of ——, Virginia. 2012.

Conservation News. 2000. "Land Trusts," Summer 2000.

Consumer Reports. 2021. "Upgrade Your Outdoor Areas," November 2021.

Corwin, Ruthann, Patrick H. Heffernan, Robert A. Johnston, Michael Remy, James A. Roberts, and D. B. Tyler. 1975. *Environmental Impact Assessment.* San Francisco: Freeman, Cooper.

Couto, Richard. A. 1994. "Appalachia." In *Sowing Seeds in the Mountains: Community-based Coalitions for Cancer Prevention,* edited by Couto, Nancy Simpson, and Gale Harris. National Cancer Institute.

Cox, Erin, and Gregory S. Schneider. 2020. "Energy Companies Abandon Long-Delayed Atlantic Coast Pipeline." *Washington Post,* July 5, 2020.

Cox, Ricky. 2012. "Migration Patterns in History." In *Supplement to Arrivals and Departures: In and Out Migration, Virginia,* edited by Cox, Melinda Bollar Wagner, Jessica Baciu, Brittony Fitzgerald, Morgan Hawkins, Patricia Jacobs, and Kathy Murphy. Center for Social & Cultural Research, Radford University. May 1.

———. 2017. "Social Implications—Too Much of a Good Thing: Unintended Consequences of Tourism in the Southern Appalachians." Paper presented at Appalachian Studies Conference, Virginia Tech, Blacksburg, March 9–12.

Cramer, John. 2006. "Residents Report Copters Dousing Them in Herbicide." *Roanoke Times,* July 24, 2006.

Crawford, Charles, and Dennis L. Krebs, eds. 1998. *Handbook of Evolutionary Psychology: Ideas, Issues, and Applications.* Mahwah, NJ: Lawrence Erlbaum.

Creed, Gerald W., and Barbara Ching. 1997. "Recognizing Rusticity: Identity and the Power of Place." In *Knowing Your Place: Rural Identity and Cultural Hierarchy,* edited by Ching and Creed, 1–38. New York: Routledge.

Cronon, William. 1996. "The Trouble with Wilderness: Or, Getting Back to the Wrong Nature." *Environmental History* 1:7–28.

Cunningham, Rodger. 1987. *Apples on the Flood: Minority Discourse and Appalachia.* Knoxville: University of Tennessee Press.

Davidson, Osha Gray. 1990. *Broken Heartland: The Rise of America's Rural Ghetto.* New York: Free Press.

Davis, Donald Edward. 2000. *Where There Are Mountains: An Environmental History of the Southern Appalachians.* Athens: University of Georgia Press.

Decker, Peter R. 1998. *Old Fences, New Neighbors.* Tucson: University of Arizona Press.

Delicate, Jane P. 1994. "Cultural Attachment to Land Study" Paper for "Anthropology 411: Appalachian Cultures." Radford University, Radford, VA.

Dellinger, Paul. 1998. "Timber Bank Gets $500,000." *Roanoke Times,* August 13, 1998.

———. 2006. "End of the Line." *Roanoke Times,* May 8, 2006.

Dettmer, Elke. 1994. "Moving toward Responsible Tourism: A Role for Folklore." In *Putting Folklore to Use,* edited by Michael Owen Jones, 187–200. Lexington: University Press of Kentucky.

Diamond, Seth J., and Robert H. Giles. 1987. "A Vegetational History of Virginia's Ridge and Valley Province." *Archaeological Society of Virginia, Quarterly Bulletin* 42 (2):177–87.

Dirks, Nicholas B., Geoff Eley, and Sherry B. Ortner. 1994. Introduction to *Culture/Power/History: A Reader in Contemporary Social Theory.* Princeton, NJ: Princeton University Press.

Dove, Michael R., and Carol Carpenter. 2008. "Introduction: Major Historical Currents in Environmental Anthropology." In *Environmental Anthropology: A Historical Reader,* edited by Dove and Carpenter, 1–85. Malden, MA: Blackwell.

Downing, Theodore E. 1996. "Mitigating Social Impoverishment When People Are Involuntarily Displaced." In *Understanding Impoverishment: The Consequences of Development-induced Displacement,* edited by Christopher McDowell, 33–48. Oxford: Berghahn.

Downs, Roger M., and David Stea. 1977. *Maps in Minds: Reflections on Cognitive Mapping.* New York: Harper and Row.

Driver, B. L., Daniel Dustin, Tony Baltic, Gary Elsner, and George Peterson, eds. 1996. *Nature and the Human Spirit: Toward an Expanded Land Management Ethic.* State College, PA: Venture.

Dudley, Kathryn Marie. 2000. *Debt and Dispossession: Farm Loss in America's Heartland.* Chicago: University of Chicago Press.

Dukes, E. Franklin. 2011. "The Promise of Community-based Collaboration: Agenda for an Authentic Future." In *Community-based Collaboration: Bridging Socio-ecological Research and Practice,* edited by Dukes, Karen E. Frederick, and Juliana E. Birkhof, 189–215. Charlottesville: University of Virginia Press.

Dukes, E. Franklin, Karen E. Frederick, and Juliana E. Birkhof, eds. 2011. *Community-Based Collaboration: Bridging Socio-ecological Research and Practice.* Charlottesville: University of Virginia Press.

Dumont, Louis. 1985. "A Modified View of Our Origins: The Christian Beginnings of Modern Individualism." In *The Category of the Person,* edited by Michael Carrithers, Steven Collins, and Steven Lukes, 93–122. New York: Cambridge University Press.

———. 1986. *Essays on Individualism.* Chicago: University of Chicago Press.

Dunaway, Wilma A. 1996. *The First American Frontier: Transition to Capitalism in Southern Appalachia, 1700–1860.* Chapel Hill: University of North Carolina Press.

Dyer, Joyce. 1998. *Bloodroot: Reflections on Place by Appalachian Women Writers.* Lexington: University Press of Kentucky.

Editorial Board 2019. "Editorial: Should Pipeline Tree-Sitters Get 20 Years in Prison?" *Roanoke Times,* June 11, 2019.

Egloff, Keith, and Deborah Woodward. 1994. *First People: The Early Indians of Virginia.* Charlottesville: University Press of Virginia.

Eisenhower, Dwight D. 1961. "Military-Industrial Complex Speech." American Civil Rights Review's Document Archive.

Eller, Ronald D. 1979. "Land and Family: An Historical View of Preindustrial Appalachia." *Appalachian Journal,* Winter, 83–109.

———. 2008. *Uneven Ground: Appalachia since 1945.* Lexington: University Press of Kentucky.

Ellingson, Stephen, Vernon Woodley, and Anthony Paik. 2010. "Explaining the Structure of Religious Environmentalism." Paper presented at Society for the Scientific Study of Religion and Religious Research Association Annual Meeting, Baltimore, MD, October 29–31.

Ellis, Neville R., and Glenn A. Albrecht. 2017. "Climate Change Threats to Family Farmers' Sense of Place and Mental Wellbeing: A Case Study from the Western Australian Wheatbelt." *Social Science & Medicine* 175:161–68.

Ergood, Bruce. 1983. "Toward a Definition of Appalachia." In *Appalachia: Social Context Past and Present,* edited by Ergood and Bruce E. Kuhre, 31–40. Dubuque, IA: Kendall/Hunt.

Erickson, Clark L., and William Balée. 2006. "The Historical Ecology of a Complex Landscape in Bolivia." In *Time and Complexity in Historical Ecology,* edited by Balée and Erickson, 187–234. New York: Columbia University Press.

Erikson, Kai. 1976. *Everything in Its Path: Destruction of Community in the Buffalo Creek Flood.* New York: Simon and Schuster.

Ethos. 1998. "Language, Space, and Culture." *Ethos* 26 (1) (March): 3–111.

European Commission. 2019. *The Common Agricultural Policy at a Glance.*

Evans-Pritchard, Edward Evan. 1940. *The Nuer: A Description of the Modes of Livelihood and Political Institutions of a Nilotic People.* New York: Oxford University Press.

Eyles, John, and Allison Williams, eds. 2008. *Sense of Place, Health and Quality of Life.* Aldershot, UK: Ashgate.

Ezzell, Tim. 2016. "'No One's Ever Talked to Us Before': Participatory Approaches and Economic Development in Rural Appalachian Communities." In *Appalachia Revisited: New Perspectives on Place, Tradition, and Progress,* edited by William Schumann and Rebecca Adkins Fletcher, 213–28. Lexington: University Press of Kentucky.

Fabian, Stephen Michael. 1992. *Space-Time of the Bororo of Brazil.* Gainesville: University of Florida Press.

Fabrick, Nathan. 2020. 5 Questions You Should Be Asking before Leasing Your Property for a Solar Project. National Land Realty, LLC.

Farmer, Val. 2000. "The Psychology of Place-Bound People Examined." *Illinois Agrinews*, July 21, 2000.

Feld, Steven, and Keith H. Basso, eds. 1996. *Senses of Place*. Santa Fe, NM: School of American Research.

Feiler, Bruce. 2013a. *The Secrets of Happy Families: Improve Your Mornings, Rethink Family Dinner, Fight Smarter, Go Out and Play, and Much More*. New York: HarperCollins.

———. 2013b. "The Stories That Bind Us." *New York Times*, March 15, 2013.

Fels, John E. 1995. *Visual Sensitivity Mapping of Blue Ridge Parkway Adjacent Lands: Asheville, North Carolina and Roanoke, Virginia*. North Carolina State University: Design Research Laboratory.

Ferguson, James, and Akhil Gupta, eds. 1992. "Space, Identity, and the Politics of Difference." *Cultural Anthropology* 7 (1) (February): 1–129.

Fernandez, James W. 1974. "The Mission of Metaphor in Expressive Culture." *Current Anthropology* 15:119–45.

Fialka, John. 2019. "Farms Can Harvest Energy along with Food." *E&E News*, November 4, 2019.

Field, Liza. 2000. "The Price of a Motherland." *Roanoke Times*, June 18, 2000.

FindLaw 2016. "Your Neighbors' Right to Farm." https://www.findlaw.com. June 20.

Fiscal Analytics. 2017. Fiscal Analytics, Ltd.

Fisher, Stephen L., ed. 1993. *Fighting Back in Appalachia: Traditions of Resistance and Change*. Philadelphia: Temple University Press.

———. 1997. Comment made at authors' meeting for *A Handbook to Appalachia*, Radford University, Radford, VA.

Fisher, Stephen, and Barbara Ellen Smith, eds. 2012. *Transforming Places: Lessons from Appalachia*. Urbana: University of Illinois Press.

Fitchen, Janet M. 1991. *Endangered Spaces, Enduring Places: Change, Identity, and Survival in Rural America*. Boulder, CO: Westview.

———. 1995. "Why Rural Poverty Is Growing Worse: Similar Causes in Diverse Settings." In *The Changing American Countryside: Rural People and Places*, edited by Emery N. Castle, 247–68. Lawrence: University Press of Kansas.

Fitzgerald, Jenrose, Lisa Markowitz, and Dwight B. Billings. 2012. "Not Your Grandmother's Agrarianism: The Community Farm Alliance's Agrifood Activism." In *Transforming Places: Lessons from Appalachia*, edited by Stephen L. Fisher and Barbara Ellen Smith. 210–25. Urbana: University of Illinois Press.

Fitzsimmons, Connie. 2019. "Heed Own Warning." Letter to editor. *Roanoke Times*, December 11, 2019.

Fletcher, George P. 1993. *Loyalty*. New York: Oxford University Press.

———. 2001. Interview by Susan Stamberg, Morning Edition, National Public Radio, March 6.

Fletcher, Rebecca Adkins. 2016. "(Re)Introduction: The Global Neighborhoods of Appalachian Studies." In *Appalachia Revisited: New Perspectives on Place, Tradition, and Progress*, edited by William Schumann and Fletcher, 275–90. Lexington: University Press of Kentucky.

Fjord, Lakshmi. 2021a. "Union Hill Rural Historic District, Buckingham County, Virginia: Fighting the Cost Benefits of Environmental Injustice through Ethnographic Methods." Paper presented at Appalachian Studies Conference, Virtual, March 11–14.

———. 2021b. "'It's Time to Tell the Truth': How the Freedmen Descendant Community of Union Hill, Virginia Fought and Won the Environmental Justice Battle against Dominion Energy." Paper presented at Society for Applied Anthropology, Virtual, March 22–27.

Foster, Stephen William. 1988. *The Past Is Another Country: Representation, Historical Consciousness, and Resistance in the Blue Ridge.* Berkeley: University of California Press.

Foucault, Michel. 1988. *Politics, Philosophy, Culture: Interviews and Other Writings, 1977–1984.* New York: Routledge.

Fox, Julia. 1999. "Mountaintop Removal in West Virginia: An Environmental Sacrifice Zone." *Organization and Environment* 12:163–83.

Frank, Andre Gundar. 1967. *Capitalism and Underdevelopment in Latin America: Historical Studies of Chile and Brazil.* New York: Monthly Review Press.

Fries, Robert. 1997. "Proud to Be Here: One Native of Appalachia Who's Staying Put." *Roanoke Times,* March 23, 1997.

Furze, Brian, Terry De Lacy, and Jim Birckhead. 1996. *Culture, Conservation, and Biodiversity: The Social Dimension of Linking Local Level Development and Conservation through Protected Areas.* New York: John Wiley and Sons.

Garreau, Joel. 1991. *The Edge City: Life on the New Frontier.* New York: Doubleday.

Gaventa, John. 1980. *Power and Powerlessness: Quiescence and Rebellion in an Appalachian Valley.* Urbana: University of Illinois Press.

———. 2018. "The Power of Place and the Place of Power." In *Appalachia in Regional Context: Place Matters,* edited by Dwight B. Billings and Ann E. Kingsolver, 91–110. Lexington: University Press of Kentucky.

Geertz, Clifford. 1973. *The Interpretation of Cultures.* New York: Basic.

———. 1983. *Local Knowledge: Further Essays in Interpretive Anthropology.* New York: Basic.

Giardina, Denise. 1987. *Storming Heaven: A Novel.* New York: Ivy.

Ginsberg, Steven. 2000. "Washington's Boyhood Farm Saved." *Washington Post,* January 23, 2000.

Gleick, James. 1999. *Faster: The Acceleration of Just about Everything.* New York: Pantheon.

Glod, Maria. 2001. "Birdwatching Seen as Path to Relaxation and Nature." *Roanoke Times,* March 4, 2001.

Godinez, Victor. 2000. "Computer Characters Come to Life." *Roanoke Times,* August 27, 2000.

Godkin, Michael A. 1980. "Identity and Place: Clinical Applications Based on Notions of Rootedness and Uprootedness." In *The Human Experience of Space and Place,* edited by Anne Buttimer and David Seamon, 73–85. New York: St. Martin's.

Gold, John R., and Jacquelin Burgess, eds. 1982. *Valued Environments.* London: G. Allen and Unwin.

Goldschmidt, Walter. 1946. *Small Business and the Community.* Committee Print of the U.S. Senate Small Business Committee.

———. 1947. *As You Sow: Three Studies in the Social Consequences of Agribusiness.* Montclair, NJ: Allanheld, Osmun.

———. 2001. "Jim Braun and Public Anthropology." *Anthropology News,* March 5.

Goodell, Jeff. 2006. *Big Coal: The Dirty Secret behind America's Energy Future.* New York: Houghton Mifflin.

Gottmann, Jean. 1961. *Megalopolis: The Urbanized Northeastern Seaboard of the United States.* New York: Twentieth Century Fund.

Gow, Peter. 1995. "Land, People, and Paper in Western Amazonia." In *The Anthropology of Landscape: Perspectives on Place and Space,* edited by Eric Hirsch and Michael O'Hanlon, 43–62. New York: Clarendon.

Graham, Lamar. 1998. "Where Have All the Small Towns Gone?" *Parade Magazine,* December 13, 1998.

Grandoni, Dino, and Darryl Fears. 2021. "Biden Wants to Rebuild Quickly, but Infrastructure Bill May Bulldoze Underprivileged Voices." *Washington Post,* August 12, 2021.

Grant, Daniel J. 2001. "Farmland Loss Continues at Faster Pace." *Illinois Agrinews,* February 9.

Gray, John. 1999. "Open Spaces and Dwelling Places: Being at Home on Hill Farms in the Scottish Borders." *American Ethnologist* 26 (2):440–46.

Greeley, Andrew M., and William C. McCready. 1974. "Some Notes on the Sociological Study of Mysticism." In *On the Margin of the Visible,* edited by Edward A. Tiryakian, 303–22. New York: Wiley.

Green, Justin. 2010. "Re-structuring the Religion-Environment Connection: Changes in Environmental Schemas and Denominational Resources." Paper presented at Society for the Scientific Study of Religion and Religious Research Association Annual Meeting, Baltimore, MD, October 29–31.

Greenbaum, Thomas L. 1993. *The Handbook for Focus Group Research.* Rev. and expanded ed. New York: Maxwell Macmillan International.

Greene, Brian. 2021. "Biden Administration Is Off to a Fast Start: Day One Actions on Energy, Environmental, and Climate Issues." *Kirkland & Ellis Energy Blog,* January 21.

Greenfield, Susan. 2015. *Mind Change: How Digital Technologies Are Leaving Their Mark on Our Brains.* New York: Random House.

Greil, Arthur L., and Thomas Robbins. 1994. "Introduction: Exploring the Boundaries of the Sacred." In *Between Sacred and Secular: Research and Theory on Quasi-religion,* vol. 4 of *Religion and the Social Order,* edited by Greil and Robbins, 1–26. Greenwich, CT: JAI.

Grossman, Ron, and Charles Leroux. 1996. "A Lonely Road." *Chicago Tribune,* December 29, 1996.

Guebert, Alan. 2000. "A Tax Break for the Rich Courtesy of 'Family Farmers.'" *Illinois Agrinews,* June 23, 2000.

Gupta, Akhil, and James Ferguson, eds. 1997. *Culture, Power, Place: Explorations in Critical Anthropology.* Durham, NC: Duke University Press.

Gusfield, J. R. 1967. "Tradition and Modernity: Misplaced Polarities in the Study of Social Change." *American Journal of Sociology* 72:336–51.

Ha, Kim, Shadi Atallah, Tamara Benjamin, Lenny Farlee, Lori Hoagland, and Keith Woeste. 2017. "Costs and Returns of Producing Wild-Simulated Ginseng in Established Tree Plantations." *Purdue Extension,* March.

Haag, Matthew. 2020. "New Yorkers Are Fleeing to the Suburbs." *New York Times,* August 30, 2020.

Habitus 2000: "A Sense of Place. 2000. School of Architecture, Construction and Planning, Curtin University of Technology, Perth, Western Australia, September 5–9." Paper presented at American Anthropological Association Annual Meeting, Washington, DC, November 19.

Hager-Smith, Leslie. 2000. "This Farm's Crop Is Thriving on Asphalt." *Roanoke Times,* July 18, 2000.

Haley, Brian, and Larry Wilcoxen. 1997. "The Making of Chumash Tradition." *Current Anthropology* 38 (5):767.

Hall, Dan. 1997. "Acres of Heritage." *Chicago Tribune,* December 28, 1997.

Hall, Edward T. 1959. *The Silent Language.* Garden City, NY: Doubleday.

———. 1976. *Beyond Culture.* Garden City, NY: Doubleday.

Halmo, David B., Richard W. Stoffle, and Michael J. Evans. 1993. "Paitu Nana Suagaindu Pahonupi (Three Sacred Valleys): Cultural Significance of Gosiute, Paiute, and Ute Plants." *Human Organization* 52 (2):142–50.

Hammack, Laurence. 2022a. "With Construction at a Standstill, Mountain Valley Pipeline Looks for Solutions." *Roanoke Times,* March 20, 2022.

———. 2022b. "Appeals Court Won't Revisit Decision to Reject Mountain Valley Pipeline Permit." *Roanoke Times,* April 1, 2022.

Handler, Richard. 1994. "Romancing the Low: Anthropology vis-a-vis Cultural Studies vis-a-vis Popular Culture." *POLAR: Political and Legal Anthropology Review* 17 (2):1–6.

Harder, Nick. 2000. "It Takes Some Work to Be a Good Neighbor." *Roanoke Times,* November 5, 2000.

Harmon, Amy. 1998. "Study Uncovers Sad, Lonely World in Cyberspace." *Roanoke Times,* August 30, 1998.

Harrington, Lisa M. Butler. 2018. "Alternative and Virtual Rurality: Agriculture and the Countryside as Embodied in American Imagination." *Geographical Review* 108 (2):250–73.

Harris, T. M., D. Weiner, T. A. Warner, and R. Levin. 1995. "Pursuing Social Goals through Participatory GIS: Redressing South Africa's Historical Political Ecology." In *Ground Truth: The Social Implications of Geographic Information Systems,* edited by J. Pickles, 196–222. New York: Guilford.

Harvey, David. 2001. *Spaces of Capital: Towards a Critical Geography.* New York: Routledge.

Hazlitt, Henry. 1946. *Economics in One Lesson.* New York: Harper.

Healy, Robert, and James Short. 1979. "Rural Land: Market Trends and Planning Implications." *Journal of the American Planning Association* 45 (3):305–17.

Hicks, George L. 1976. *Appalachian Valley.* New York: Holt, Rinehart, and Winston.

Hillery, G. A., Jr. 1955. "Definitions of Community: Areas of Agreement." *Rural Sociology* 20 (2):111–23.

Hinton, John. 2019. "Winston-Salem Man Charged with Felony after He Chained Himself Last Week to Equipment at Pipeline Project in West Virginia." *Winston-Salem Journal,* April 30, 2019.

Hirsch, Eric. 1995. "Landscape: Between Place and Space." In *The Anthropology of Landscape: Perspectives on Place and Space,* edited by Hirsch and Michael O'Hanlon, 1–30. New York: Clarendon.

Hirsch, Eric, and Michael O'Hanlon, eds. 1995. *The Anthropology of Landscape: Perspectives on Space and Place.* Oxford: Clarendon.

Hiss, Tony. 1990. *The Experience of Place.* New York: Knopf.

Hocker, Philip M., and Joseph H. Maroon. 2010. *Virginia's State Tax Credit for Land Conservation.* The Conservation Fund.

Hoey, Brian A. 2014. *Opting for Elsewhere: Lifestyle Migration in the American Middle Class.* Nashville, TN: Vanderbilt University Press.

Horning, Audrey J. 2000. "Shenandoah's Secret History." *Archaeology,* January/February, 44–51.

Hostetler, John A., and Gertrude Enders Huntington. 1967. *The Hutterites in North America.* New York: Holt, Rinehart, and Winston.

Hough, Michael. 1990. *Out of Place: Restoring Identity to the Regional Landscape.* New Haven, CT: Yale University Press.

Houghton, Dean. 2021. "Plowing a Straight Furrow." *The Furrow,* January, 11–14, 2021.

House, Silas, and Jason Howard. 2009. *Something's Rising: Appalachians Fighting Mountaintop Removal.* Lexington: University Press of Kentucky.

Howarth, William. 1995. "Land and Word: American Pastoral." In *The Changing American Countryside: Rural People and Places,* edited by Emery N. Castle, 13–36. Lawrence: University Press of Kansas.

Howell, Benita J. 1990. "Appalachian Tourism and Cultural Conservation." In *Cultural Heritage Conservation in the American South,* edited by Howell, 125–40. Athens: University of Georgia Press.

———. 1997. "Conceptualizing Attachment to Place in Theory and Practice." Paper presented at American Anthropological Association Annual Meeting, Washington, DC, November 20.

———. 1999. "Contesting Bureaucratic Impact Assessment: The Need for Community-Based Research." Paper presented at Appalachian Studies Conference, Abingdon, VA, March 19–21.

———. 2002. "Appalachian Culture and Environmental Planning: Expanding the Role of the Cultural Sciences." In *Culture, Environment, and Conservation in the Appalachian South,* edited by Howell, 1–16. Urbana: University of Illinois Press.

Hsu, Francis L. K. 1972. "American Core Values and National Character." In *Psychological Anthropology,* edited by Hsu. Cambridge, MA: Schenkman.

Hufford, Mary T. 1987. "Telling the Landscape: Folklife Expressions and Sense of Place." In *Pinelands Folklife,* edited by Rita Zorn Moonsammy, David Steven Cohen, and Lorraine E. Williams. New Brunswick, NJ: Rutgers University Press.

———, ed. 1994. *Conserving Culture: A New Discourse on Heritage.* Urbana: University of Illinois Press.

———. 1998a. "Tending the Commons: Ramp Suppers, Biodiversity, and the Integrity of 'The Mountains.'" *Folklife Center News* 20 (4) (Fall): 3–11.

———. 1998b. "Weathering the Storm: Cultural Survival in an Appalachian Valley." In *An Appalachian Tragedy: Air Pollution and Tree Death in the Eastern Forests of North America,* edited by Harvard Ayers, Jenny Hager, and Charles E. Little, 146–59. San Francisco: Sierra Club Books.

———. 2002. "Reclaiming the Commons: Narratives of Progress, Preservation, and Ginseng." In *Culture, Environment, and Conservation in the Appalachian South,* edited by Benita J. Howell, 100–120. Urbana: University of Illinois Press.

Hull, R. Bruce. 1995. Personal Communication. Forestry Department, Virginia Tech, Blacksburg, VA, February 9.

Humphrey, Richard. 1980. "Academic Philosophy and Appalachian Culture." Paper presented at Appalachian Studies Conference, East Tennessee State University, Johnson City, March 21–23.

Hunter, James Davison. 1991. *Culture Wars: The Struggle to Define America.* New York: Basic.

Hutchinson, John, V. 2000a. "Conservation Easements-Effective Tools for Open Space Conservation." *Virginia Forest Landowner Update* 14 (1):1, 5.

———. 2000b. "Tax Benefits of Conservation Easements." *Virginia Forest Landowner Update* 14 (3):1, 5.

Hyland, Stanley E., and Linda A. Bennett. 2013. "Responding to Community Needs through Linking Academic and Practicing Anthropology: An Engaged Scholarly Framework." *Annals of Anthropological Practice* 37 (1):34–56.

IDS. 2011. *Power Pack: Understanding Power for Social Change.* Power, Participation and Social Change Team, Institute of Development Studies, University of Sussex, Brighton, UK.

Jackson, Laura E. 2003. "The Relationship of Urban Design to Human Health and Condition." *Landscape and Urban Planning* 64 (4):191–200.

Jackson, Peter, and Susan J. Smith. 1984. *Exploring Social Geography.* London: Allen and Unwin.

Jackson, Richard J., and Christopher S. Kochtitzky. 2010. *Creating a Healthy Environment: The Impact of the Built Environment on Public Health.* Centers for Disease Control and Prevention. ResearchGate.

Jacobs, Jane. 1963. *The Death and Life of Great American Cities.* New York: Random House.

Jain, Ravinder K., and Bruce L. Hutchings, eds. 1978. *Environmental Impact Analysis: Emerging Issues in Planning.* Chicago: University of Illinois Press.

Jain, Ravinder, L. V. Urban, G.S. Stacey, and H. E. Balbach. 1993. *Environmental Assessment.* New York: McGraw-Hill.

Jakle, John A., and Keith A. Scule. 1999. *Fast Food: Roadside Restaurants in the Automobile Age.* Baltimore, MD: Johns Hopkins University Press.

James, William. (1902) 1982. *The Varieties of Religious Experience.* New York: Mentor.

Johnson, Frank. 1985. "The Western Concept of Self." In *Culture and Self,* edited by Anthony J. Marsella, George DeVos, and Francis L. K. Hsu, 91–138. New York: Tavistock.

Johnson, Gary, Will Orr, and Laura Rotegard. 1997. *A Process for Scenic Quality Analysis along the Blue Ridge Parkway.* Asheville, NC: Blue Ridge Parkway.

Johnson, Leslie Main. 2000. "'A Place That's Good': Gitksan Landscape Perception and Ethnoecology." *Human Ecology* 28 (2):301–25.

Johnston, Barbara Rose. 1998/1999. "Building a Public Interest Anthropology." *Common Ground,* Winter 1998/Spring 1999, 24–27.

———. 2010. "Social Responsibility and the Anthropological Citizen." *Current Anthropology* 51 (2):235–47.

Johnston, David Cay. 2001. "Talk of Lost Farms Reflects Muddle of Estate Tax Debate." *New York Times,* April 8, 2001.

Jorgensen, Joseph G. 1971. "Indians and the Metropolis." In *The American Indian in Urban Society,* edited by Jack O. Waddell and O. Michael Watson, 66–113. Boston: Little, Brown.

Kahn, Miriam. 2000. "Tahiti Intertwined: Ancestral Land, Tourist Postcard, and Nuclear Test Site." *American Anthropologist* 102:7–26.

Keefe, Susan E. 2009. "Introduction: What Participatory Development Means for Appalachian Communities." In *Participatory Development in Appalachia: Cultural Identity, Community, and Sustainability,* edited by Keefe, 1–44. Knoxville: University of Tennessee Press.

Keen, Russ. 2000. "There Is Life after Farming." *Roanoke Times,* August 26, 2000.

Keesing, R. 1982. *Kwaio Religion: The Living and the Dead in a Solomon Island Society.* New York: Columbia University Press.

Kimmerer, Robin Wall. 2013. *Braiding Sweetgrass: Indigenous Wisdom, Scientific Knowledge, and the Teachings of Plants.* Minneapolis, MN: Milkweed Editions.

Kingsolver, Ann E. 2018. "'Placing' Futures and Making Sense of Globalization on the Edge of Appalachia." In *Appalachia in Regional Context: Place Matters,* edited by Dwight B. Billings and Kingsolver, 17–48. Lexington: University Press of Kentucky.

Kirmayer, Laurence J., Megha Sehdev, Rob Whitley, Stephane F. Dandeneau, and Colette Isaac. 2009. "Community Resilience: Models, Metaphors and Measures." *Journal of Aboriginal Health* 5 (1):62–117.

Klapp, Orrin E. 1969. *Collective Search for Identity.* New York: Holt, Rinehart and Winston.

Klatka, Thomas S. 1991. *An Archaeological Reconnaissance Survey of —— County, Virginia.* Survey Report Series No. 2. Roanoke, VA: Roanoke Regional Preservation Office.

Knight-Ridder/Tribune. 1995. "Court OKs Limits on Land Use." *Roanoke Times,* June 30, 1995.

Kolodny, Annette. 1975. *The Lay of the Land: Metaphor as Experience and History in American Life and Letters.* Chapel Hill: University of North Carolina Press.

Koons, Kenneth E., and Warren R. Hofstra. 2000. *After the Backcountry: Rural Life in the Great Valley of Virginia, 1800–1900.* Knoxville: University of Tennessee Press.

Kottak, Conrad P. 1997. "The New Ecological Anthropology: A Programmatic Statement." Paper presented at American Anthropological Association Annual Meeting, Washington, DC, November 21.

Kozaitis, Kathryn A. 2013. "Anthropological Praxis in Higher Education." *Annals of Anthropological Practice* 37 (1):133–55.

Kuletz, Valerie L. 1998. *The Tainted Desert: Environmental and Social Ruin in the American West.* New York: Routledge.

Kvale, Steinar. 1996. *InterViews: An Introduction to Qualitative Research Interviewing.* Thousand Oaks, CA: Sage.

Lamb, Melissa E. 1999. "'Making a Living or Making a Life' in Off the Grid Appalachia." Paper presented at Society for the Scientific Study of Religion Annual Meeting, Boston, Massachusetts, November 5–7.

Land Policy Task Force. 2013. "Common Sense Meets Home Ground." (Regional Newspaper), February 21, 2013.

Land Trust Alliance. 2020. *Income Tax Incentives for Land Conservation.*

LandmarkDividend.com. 2020. "Wind Turbine Lease Rates—How Valuable Is Your Wind Farm Lease?"

Langdon, Philip. 1994. *A Better Place to Live: Reshaping the American Suburb.* Amherst: University of Massachusetts Press.

Laris, Michael. 2001. "Loudon Blueprint Reins in Growth." *Washington Post,* May 2, 2001.

Lassiter, Luke Eric. 2005a. "Collaborative Ethnography and Public Anthropology." *Current Anthropology* 46 (1):83–106.

———. 2005b. *The Chicago Guide to Collaborative Ethnography.* Chicago: University of Chicago Press.

———. 2010. "What Will We Have Ethnography Do?" *Qualitative Inquiry* 16 (9):757–67.

Lassiter, Luke Eric, Hurley Goodall, Elizabeth Campbell, and Michelle Natasya Johnson. 2004. *The Other Side of Middletown: Exploring Muncie's African American Community.* New York: AltaMira.

Lassiter, Luke Eric, Brian Hoey, and Elizabeth Campbell. 2020. *I'm Afraid of That Water: A Collaborative Ethnography of a West Virginia Water Crisis.* Morgantown: West Virginia University Press.

Lee, Dorothy. 1959. *Freedom and Culture.* Englewood Cliffs, NJ: Prentice-Hall.

———. 1986. *Valuing the Self: What We Can Learn from Other Cultures.* Prospect Heights, IL: Waveland.

Lee, Richard B. 1984. *The Dobe !Kung.* New York: Holt, Rinehart and Winston.

———. 1993. *The Dobe Ju/'hoansi.* New York: Harcourt Brace.

Lefebvrfe, Henri. 1970. *La revolution urbaine.* Paris: Gallimard.

Lengen, Charis, and Thomas Kistemann. 2012. "Sense of Place and Place Identity: Review of Neuroscientific Evidence." *Health & Place* 18:1162–71.

Leopold, Aldo. 1949. *The Sand County Almanac and Sketches Here and There.* Oxford: Oxford University Press.

Lerch, Stephen H. 2020. Personal Communication, July 30.

Levine, Samantha. 1999. "Future of Virginia Agriculture in Doubt as Farmers Grow Older." *Roanoke Times,* February 6, 1999.

Lewis, Helen. 1970. "Fatalism or the Coal Industry." *Mountain Life and Work* 46 (December 1970): 4–15.

Lewis, Helen, Linda Johnson, and Don Askins, eds. 1978. *Colonialism in Modern America: The Appalachian Case.* Boone, NC: Appalachian Consortium Press.

Lewis, Pierce. 1995. "The Urban Invasion of Rural America: The Emergence of the Galactic City." In *The Changing American Countryside: Rural People and Places,* edited by Emery N. Castle, 39–62. Lawrence: University Press of Kansas.

Ley, D., and M. Samuels. 1978. *Humanistic Geography.* Chicago: Maaroufa.

Lichter, Daniel T., and David L. Brown. 2011. "Rural America in an Urban Society: Changing Spatial and Social Boundaries." *Annual Review of Sociology* 37:565–92.

Liebow, Edward B. 1998/1999. "The Heart of the Problem: The Local Burden of National Policies." In "Stewards of the Human Landscape," special double issue of *Common Ground: Archaeology and Ethnography in the Public Interest,* Winter 1998/Spring 1999.

Link, Doris. 1999. "Defending the Community: University Community Cooperation in Environmental Study/Environmental Action." Paper presented at Appalachian Studies Conference, Abingdon, VA, March 19–21.

Linkous, Sam L. 1995. "Home: A Sense of Place." Paper for "Anthropology 493: Practicum in Anthropology." Radford University, Radford, VA.

Lion, Kenworth E., Jr. 2000. Exceptions to the Report of the Hearing Examiner, November 6.

Little, Charles E. 1994. "'Lucy's Woods': A Wrenching Trip. Beckley, WV." Beckley Newspapers.

Litvak, Anya. 2022. "Mountain Valley Pipeline, A Litmus Test for Big Projects, Is Delayed Again." *Pittsburgh Post-Gazette,* May 4, 2022.

Lobao, Linda, and Katherine Meyer. 2001. "The Great Agricultural Transition: Crisis, Change, and Social Consequences of Twentieth Century US Farming." *Annual Review of Sociology* 27:103–24.

Loeb, Penny. 2007. *Moving Mountains: How One Woman and Her Community Won Justice from Big Coal.* Lexington: University Press of Kentucky.

Long, Kate. 1994. *Pieces from the Heart.* Audio recording. Charleston, WV: Kate Long.

Long, Michael E. 1983. "Good Times and Bad in Appalachia." *National Geographic,* 163 (6) (June): 792–819.

Loomis, Ormond H. 1983. *Cultural Conservation: The Protection of Cultural Heritage in the United States.* Washington, DC: Library of Congress.

Lopez, Barry. 1986. *Arctic Dreams.* New York: Scribner's.

Lopez, Tommy. 2019. "MVP Tree-Sitters Allowed to Stay in Pipeline's Path, Judge Rules." WSLS 10 News, Roanoke, VA, August 2, 2019.

Louv, Richard. 2005. *Last Child in the Woods.* Chapel Hill, NC: Algonquin.

Low, Setha. 1994. "Cultural Conservation of Place." In *Conserving Culture,* edited by Mary Hufford, 66–77. Urbana: University of Illinois Press.

Low, Setha, and Sally Engle Merry. 2010. "Engaged Anthropology: Diversity and Dilemmas." *Current Anthropology* 51 (2):203–26.

Lowenthal, D. 1961. "Geography, Experience, and Imagination: Toward a Geographic Epistemology." *Annals of the Association of American Geographers* 51:241–60.

———, ed. 1967. *Environmental Perception and Behavior.* Chicago: Dept. of Geography, University of Chicago.

Luckmann, Thomas. 1967. *The Invisible Religion: The Problem of Religion in Modern Society.* New York: Macmillan.

MacGillivray, Brian H., and Alex Franklin. 2015. "Place as a Boundary Device for the Sustainability Sciences: Concepts of Place, Their Value in Characterising Sustainability Problems, and Their Role in Fostering Integrative Research and Action." *Environmental Science & Policy* 53:1–7.

MacKaye, Benton. (1924) 1962. *The New Exploration: A Philosophy of Regional Planning.* Urbana: University of Illinois Press.

Macrotrends. 2020. Corn Prices—59 Year Historical Chart. https://www.macrotrends.net.

Macy, Beth. 2000. "Critters." *Roanoke Times,* December 27, 2000.

Mannon, Roger. 2000. "Farmers Lend Helping Hands to Put up Silage." (Regional Newspaper), October 5, 2000.

Manzo, Joseph, and Michael Nagy. 1979. "Images of the United States: The View from Southern West Virginia." Paper presented at Appalachian Studies Conference, Jackson's Mill, WV, March 16–18.

Marion, Jeff Daniel. 1976. "In a Southerly Direction." In *Out in the Country, Back Home: Poems,* by Jeff Daniel Marion. Winston-Salem, NC: Jackpine.

Marsella, Anthony J. 1985. "Culture, Self, and Mental Disorder." In *Culture and Self,* edited by Marsella, George DeVos, and Francis L. K. Hsu, 281–308. New York: Tavistock.

Marx, Leo. 2000. *The Machine in the Garden: Technology and the Pastoral Ideal in America.* New York: Oxford University Press.

Masterson, Vanessa A., Richard C. Stedman, Johan Enqvist, Maria Tengö, Matteo Giusti, Darin Wahl, and Uno Svedin. 2017. "The Contribution of Sense of Place to Social-Ecological Systems Research: A Review and Research Agenda." *Ecology and Society* 22 (1):49.

Mauss, Marcel. (1925) 1954. *The Gift: The Form and Reason for Exchange in Archaic Societies.* Translated by W. D. Halls. New York: Norton.

McCarthy, Terry. 2001. "High Noon in the West." *Time,* July 16, 2001, 18–21.

McCracken, J., J. Pretty, and G. Conway. 1988. *An Introduction to Rapid Rural Appraisal for Agricultural Development.* London: International Institute for Environment and Development.

McLuhan, Marshall. 1962. *The Gutenberg Galaxy: The Making of Typographic Man.* Toronto: University of Toronto Press.

———. 1977. Lecture at Radford College, Radford, VA.

McNatt, Linda. 1999. "Future of Virginia's Family Farms Looks Bleak." *Roanoke Times,* April 3, 1999.

Merleau-Ponty, Maurice. (1962) 1994. *Phenomenology of Perception.* Translated by Colin Smith. New York: Humanities Press.

Meyrowitz, Joshua. 1985. *No Sense of Place: The Impact of Electronic Media on Social Behavior.* New York: Oxford University Press.

Milbourne, Paul. 1997. *Revealing Rural 'Others': Representation, Power and Identity in the British Countryside.* London: Pinter.

Miles, Emma Bell. 1905. *The Spirit of the Mountains.* New York: James Pott.

Milton, Kay. 1996. *Environmentalism and Cultural Theory: Exploring the Role of Anthropology in Environmental Discourse.* London: Routledge.

———. 2002. *Loving Nature: Towards an Ecology of Emotion.* London: Routledge.

Minick, Jim. 2000. "Being Faithful to Your Food: One Farmer's View on Stewardship." Paper presented at Appalachian Studies Conference, Knoxville, TN, March 24–26.

Mintz, Martha. 2020. "Invested in Carbon." *The Furrow*, September/October 15–16, 2020.

Mooney, Patrick H. 1988. *My Own Boss? Class, Rationality, and the Family Farm.* Boulder, CO: Westview.

Morgan, David L., ed. 1993. *Successful Focus Groups: Advancing the State of the Art.* Newbury Park, CA: Sage.

Morgenstern, Eve. 2014. *Cheshire, Ohio: A Question of Power* [documentary]. Oley, PA: Bullfrog Films.

Morphy, Howard. 1993. "Colonialism, History and the Construction of Place: The Politics of Landscape in Northern Australia." In *Landscape: Politics and Perspectives*, edited by Barbara Bender, 205–43. Oxford: Berg.

———. 1995. "Landscape and the Reproduction of the Ancestral Past." In *The Anthropology of Landscape: Perspectives on Place and Space*, edited by Eric Hirsch and Michael O'Hanlon, 184–209. New York: Clarendon.

Morse, Cheryl E., and Jill Mudgett. 2018. "Happy to Be Home: Place-Based Attachments, Family Ties, and Mobility among Rural Stayers." *Professional Geographer* 70 (2):261–69.

Moskowitz, Nona. 2015. "Engagement, Alienation, and Anthropology's New Moral Dilemmas." *Anthropology and Humanism* 40 (1):35–57.

Mullendore, Nathan D., Jessica D. Ulrich-Schad, and Linda Stalker Prokopy. 2015. "U.S. Farmers' Sense of Place and Its Relation to Conservation Behavior." *Landscape and Urban Planning* 140:67–75.

Munn, Nancy. 1970. "Transformation of Subjects into Objects in Pitjantjatjara and Walbiri Myth." In *Australian Aborigine Anthropology*, edited by R. Berndt. Nedlands: University of Western Australia Press.

Nabhan, Gary Paul. 2018. *Food from the Radical Center: Healing Our Land and Communities* Washington, DC: Island.

Nash, Roderick. 1967. *Wilderness and the American Mind.* New Haven, CT: Yale University Press.

———. 1989. *The Rights of Nature: A History of Environmental Ethics.* Madison: University of Wisconsin Press.

Nash, Steve. 1999. *Blue Ridge 2020: An Owner's Manual.* Chapel Hill: University of North Carolina Press.

National Agricultural Law Center. 2020. States' Right to Farm Statutes. January 23.

National Environmental Policy Act. 1969.

National Historic Preservation Act. 1966, 1980.

National Natural Landmarks Program. 1999. *Information Bulletin*, no. 1, update 2, July.

National Park Service. 1997. Total Resource Management Guideline Release No. 5.

———. 2018. National Natural Landmarks. https://www.nps.gov.

National Public Radio. 1998. *Morning Edition*, March 18.

———. 1999. *Morning Edition*, June 15.

———. 2000. *Morning Edition*, November 22.

National Register Bulletin Number 38. n.d. *Guidelines for Evaluating and Documenting Traditional Cultural Properties*, by Patricia L. Parker and Thomas F. King. US Department of the Interior, National Park Service, Interagency Resources Division.

National Trust for Historic Preservation. 1999. *Preservation Books Catalog.* Washington, DC: National Trust for Historic Preservation.

———. 2020. "We Are Saving Places." Washington, DC: National Trust for Historic Preservation. https://savingplaces.org.

NC Warn. 2020. "Atlantic Coast Pipeline: Fighting to Block the Expansion of Fracked Gas in North Carolina." https://www.ncwarn.org. June 26.

Neihardt, John G. 1961. *Black Elk Speaks.* Lincoln: University of Nebraska Press.

Nelson, Hal T., Brian Swanson, and Nicholas L. Cain. 2018. "Close and Connected: The Effects of Proximity and Social Ties on Citizen Opposition to Electricity Transmission Lines." *Environment and Behavior* 50 (5):567–96.

New Jersey Law Journal. 2001. "Landowner's Acquiring Title after Effective Date of Wetland Regulations Does Not Bar Takings Claims U.S. Supreme Court." *New Jersey Law Journal,* July 9, 2001.

Newfont, Kathryn. 2012. *Blue Ridge Commons: Environmental Activism and Forest History in Western North Carolina.* Athens: University of Georgia Press.

Newport, Frank. 2018. Gallup Poll, December 7.

Nixon, Ron. 1995. "A New Take on Takings." *Southern Exposure,* Summer 1995, 42–46.

———. 1999. "Mining Alters Life for Mountain Residents." *Roanoke Times,* April 18, 1999.

Norton, Bryan G., and Bruce Hannon. 1997. "Environmental Values: A Place-Based Theory." *Environmental Ethics* 19 (3):227–46.

Nuttall, Mark. 1991. "Memoryscape: A Sense of Locality in Northwest Greenland." *North Atlantic Studies* 1 (2):39–50.

Obenshain, Elizabeth. 1996. "Thanks for a Gift Given to Us All." *Roanoke Times,* November 24, 1996.

Odum, Eugene P. 1969. "The Strategy of Ecosystem Development." *Science* 164 (April).

Oldham, Jennifer. 2020. "Cows over Condos." *Washington Post,* April 11, 2020.

Olson, Alan M., Christopher Parr, and Debra Parr. 1991. *Video Icons and Values.* Albany: State University of New York Press.

Olson, Sigurd F. 1958. *Listening Point.* New York: Knopf.

Ong, Walter J. 1967. *The Presence of the Word: Some Prolegomena for Cultural and Religious History.* New Haven, CT: Yale University Press.

Orbach, Michael K. 2000. "Anthropology and Marine Environmental Policy." Paper presented at American Anthropological Association Annual Meeting, San Francisco, November 19.

Orloff, Neil. 1978. *The Environmental Impact Statement Process: A Guide to Citizen Action.* Washington, DC: Information Resources Press.

Ortner, Sherry B. 1973. "On Key Symbols." *American Anthropologist* 75 (5):1338–46.

Palsson, Gisli. 1996. "Human-Environmental Relations: Orientalism, Paternalism and Communalism." In *Nature and Society: Anthropological Perspectives,* edited by Phillipe Descola and Palsson, 63–81. New York: Routledge.

Panelli, Ruth, and Gail Tipa. 2007. "Placing Well-being: A Maori Case Study of Cultural and Environmental Specificity." *EcoHealth* 4:445–60.

Parkin, Meredith. 2021. "How the Latest Executive Orders and NEPA Regulations Affect Your Projects." *Environmental Science Associates News and Ideas,* May 24.

Parlow, Anita. 1978. "The Land Development Rag." In *Colonialism in Modern America: The Appalachian Case,* edited by Helen Matthews Lewis, Linda Johnson, and Donald Askins, 177–98. Boone, NC: Appalachian Consortium Press.

Parsons, Talcott. 1949. *The Structure of Social Action.* Glencoe, IL: Free Press.

———. 1951. *The Social System.* New York: Free Press.

Partners for Family Farms. 2001. *Sustaining Farmlife and Farmland.* Lexington, KY: Partners for Family Farms.

Paulson, Jerry. 2001. "Protecting Farmland on the Edge: What Policies and Programs Work?" American Farmland Trust. http://www.farmlandinfo.org. March 9.

Perdue, Erika. 1994. "Cultural Attachment to Land Study." Paper for "Anthropology 411: Appalachian Cultures," Radford University, Radford, VA.

Pinker, Susan. 2014. *The Village Effect: How Face-to-Face Contact Can Make Us Healthier, Happier, and Smarter.* New York: Random House.

Plaut, Thomas. 1979. "The Meaning of Land and the Political Process." Paper presented at Appalachian Studies Conference, Jackson's Mill, WV, March 16–18.

———. 1983. "Conflict, Confrontation, and Social Change in the Regional Setting." In *Appalachia and America: Autonomy and Regional Dependence,* edited by Allen Batteau, 267–84. Lexington: University Press of Kentucky.

Poe, Melissa R., Jamie Donatuto, and Terre Satterfield. 2016. "'Sense of Place': Human Wellbeing Considerations for Ecological Restoration in Puget Sound." *Coastal Management* 44 (5):409–26.

Poole, David M. 1988. "Franklin Farmers Itching for Say on Zoning 'Manifesto.'" *Roanoke Times,* May 22, 1988.

Pooley, Eric. 1997. "The Great Escape: Americans Are Fleeing Suburbia for Small Towns: Do Their New Lives Equal Their Dreams?" *Time* 150 (24).

Porteous, J. Douglas. 1990. *Landscapes of the Mind: Worlds of Sense and Metaphor.* Toronto: University of Toronto Press.

Powercube.net. 2020. Power, Participation and Social Change Team, Institute of Development Studies, University of Sussex, Brighton, UK.

Powers, Joe. 2010. County Cost of Community Services Study, Comprehensive Plan, County Planning Commission.

Presbyterian Pastor. 2013. Interview by Melissa Grim, Radford University, Radford, VA, February 2.

President's Commission on Americans Outdoors (US). 1987. *Americans Outdoors: The Legacy, the Challenge, with Case Studies: The Report of the President's Commission.* Washington, DC: Island.

President's Council on Environmental Quality Regulations for Implementing Procedural Provisions of the National Environmental Policy Act. 1978, 1986.

Pritt, Charlotte. 1995. "Drawing the Lines in West Virginia." *Southern Exposure,* Summer 1995, 19–24.

Puckett, Anita. 2000. *Seldom Ask, Never Tell: Labor and Discourse in Appalachia.* New York: Oxford University Press.

Pudup, Mary Beth, Dwight B. Billings, and Altina L. Waller. 1995. *Appalachia in the Making: The Mountain South in the Nineteenth Century.* Chapel Hill: University of North Carolina Press.

Putnam, Robert D. 2000. *Bowling Alone: The Collapse and Revival of American Community.* New York: Simon and Schuster.

Raitz, Karl B., and Richard Ulack. 1984. "Regional Definitions." In *Appalachia: A Regional Geography,* edited by Raitz and Ulack with Thomas R. Leinbach, 9–35. Boulder, CO: Westview.

Rappaport, Roy A. 1976. "Liturgies and Lies." *International Yearbook of Sociology and Religion* 10:75–104.

———. 1994. "Disorders of Our Own: A Conclusion." In *Diagnosing America: Anthropology and Public Engagement,* edited by Shepard Forman, 235–94. Ann Arbor: University of Michigan Press.

Rapport, Nigel. 1996. "Community." In *Encyclopedia of Social and Cultural Anthropology*, edited by Alan Barnard and Jonathan Spencer. London: Routledge.

Rau, John G., and David C. Wooten, eds. 1980. *Environmental Impact Analysis Handbook*. New York: McGraw-Hill.

Redfield, Robert. 1930. *Tepoztlan: A Mexican Village*. Chicago: University of Chicago Press.

———. 1960 (1955). *The Little Community: Peasant Society and Culture*. Chicago: University of Chicago Press.

Reece, Eric. 2006. *Lost Mountain: A Year in the Vanishing Wilderness: Radical Strip Mining and the Devastation of Appalachia*. New York: Penguin.

Reid, Herbert, and Betsy Taylor. 2010. *Recovering the Commons: Democracy, Place, and Global Justice*. Urbana: University of Illinois Press.

Relph, Edward C. 1976. *Place and Placelessness*. London: Pion.

———. 2008. "Sense of Place and Emerging Social and Environmental Challenges." In *Sense of Place, Health and Quality of Life*, edited by J. Eyles and A. Williams, 31–44. Farnham, UK: Ashgate.

Rescia, Alejandro J., Anna Pons, Irene Lomba, Cristina Esteban, and John W. Dover. 2008. "Reformulating the Social-ecological System in a Cultural Rural Mountain Landscape in the Pico de Europa Region (Northern Spain)." *Landscape and Urban Planning* 88:23–33.

Rhodes, Richard. 1989. *Farm: A Year in the Life of an American Farmer*. New York: Simon and Schuster.

Richman, Elana, Nate Lotze, and Andrew M. Loza. 2017. "National Poll Results: How Americans View Conservation." https://ConservationTools.org, Pennsylvania Land Trust Association.

Robinson, Marguerite S. 1968. "'The House of the Mighty Hero' or 'The House of Enough Paddy'? Some Implications of a Sinhalese Myth." In *Dialectic in Practical Religion*, edited by Edmund R. Leach. Cambridge: Cambridge University Press.

Rome, Adam. 2001. *The Bulldozer in the Countryside: Suburban Sprawl and the Rise of American Environmentalism*. Cambridge: Cambridge University Press.

Root, Tik. 2021. "The Professor Who Assigns Value to Nature—Then Persuades World Leaders to Save It." *Washington Post*, July 30, 2021.

Rose, Courtice. 1980. "Human Geography as Text Interpretation." In *The Human Experience of Space and Place*, edited by Anne Buttimer and David Seamon, 123–34. New York: St. Martin's.

Ryden, Kent C. 1993. *Mapping the Invisible Landscape: Folklore, Writing, and the Sense of Place*. Iowa City: University of Iowa Press.

Sahlins, Marshall. 1972. *Stone Age Economics*. Chicago: Aldine.

Sahlins, Marshall, and Elman R. Service. 1960. *Evolution and Culture*. Ann Arbor: University of Michigan Press.

Salamon, Sonya. 1992. *Prairie Patrimony*. Chapel Hill: University of North Carolina Press.

———. 1995. "The Rural People of the Midwest." In *The Changing American Countryside: Rural People and Places*, edited by Emery N. Castle, 352–66. Lawrence: University Press of Kansas.

———. 2003. *Newcomers to Old Towns: Suburbanization of the Heartland*. Chicago: University of Chicago Press.

Sallet, Lori. 2018. 2018 Farm Bill. American Farmland Trust. December 11.

Salstrom, Paul. 1994. *Appalachia's Path to Dependency: Rethinking a Region's Economic History, 1730–1940*. Lexington: University Press of Kentucky.

Sangaramoorthy, Thurka, Amelia M. Jamison, Meleah D. Boyle, Devon C. Payne-Sturges, Amir Sapkota, Donald K. Milton, and Sacoby M. Wilson. 2016. "Place-Based Perceptions of the Impacts of Fracking along the Marcellus Shale." *Social Science & Medicine* 151:27–37.

Santos-Granero, Fernando. 1998. "Writing History into the Landscape: Space, Myth, and Ritual in Contemporary Amazonia." *American Ethnologist* 25 (2):128–48.

Sapir, E. 1921. *Language.* New York: Harcourt Brace.

———. 1929. "The Status of Linguistics as a Science." *Language* 5:207–14.

Satterwhite, Emily. 2019. "Letter: Climate Defenders Fighting for a Better World." *Roanoke Times,* October 12, 2019.

Sauer, Carl Ortwin. 1963. *Land and Life: A Selection from the Writings of Carl Ortwin Sauer.* Berkeley: University of California Press.

Schlosser, Eric. 2001. *Fast Food Nation: The Dark Side of the All-American Meal.* Boston: Houghton Mifflin.

Schnabel, Megan. 2001. "Ginseng—Root of Renaissance." *Roanoke Times,* February 4, 2001.

Schoenbaum, Thomas J. 1979. *The New River Controversy.* Winston-Salem: Thomas F. Blair.

Schumann, William, and Rebecca Adkins Fletcher, eds. 2016. *Appalachia Revisited: New Perspectives on Place, Tradition, and Progress.* Lexington: University Press of Kentucky.

Schutz, Alfred. 1973. *The Problem of Social Reality.* Boston: Kluwer.

Scott, Rebecca R. 2010. *Removing Mountains: Extracting Nature and Identity in the Appalachian Coalfields.* Minneapolis: University of Minnesota Press.

Senators 2020. "Senators to CEQ: Trump Administration's NEPA Proposal Is Hallmark of Entrenched Climate Denial." *States News Service,* February 27, 2020.

Searles, H. F. 1960. *The Nonhuman Environment.* New York: International University Press.

Shapiro, Henry D. 1978. *Appalachia on Our Mind.* Chapel Hill: University of North Carolina Press.

Shapiro, Tricia. 2010. *Mountain Justice: Homegrown Resistance to Mountaintop Removal, for the Future of Us All.* Oakland, CA: AK.

Shepard, E. 1995. "GIS and Society: Towards a Research Agenda." *Cartography and GIS* 22:5–16.

Sherfy, Marcella, and W. Ray Luce. 1989. "Guidelines for Evaluating and Nominating Properties That Have Achieved Significance within the Last Fifty Years." *National Register Bulletin* 22. US Department of the Interior, National Park Service.

Shi, David E. 1985. *The Simple Life: Plain Living and High Thinking in American Culture.* New York: Oxford University Press.

Simonson, Harold P. 1989. *Beyond the Frontier: Writers, Eastern Regionalism, and a Sense of Place.* Fort Worth: Texas Christian University Press.

Sinclair, Melissa S. 2000a. "Builders Promise to Minimize Impact." *Roanoke Times,* August 4, 2000.

———. 2000b. "Pipeline Pits Progress vs. Personal Property." *Roanoke Times,* August 4, 2000.

Siros, Steven M., Alexander J. Bandza, Matthew Lawson, and Jonathan Vruwink. 2020. "Pipeline Projects—The Evolving Role of Greenhouse Gas Emissions Analyses under NEPA." *Energy Law Journal,* May 4, 2020.

Smardon, Richard C., and James P. Karp. 1993. *The Legal Landscape: Guidelines for Regulating Environmental and Aesthetic Quality.* New York: Van Nostrand Reinhold.

Smith, Barbara Ellen. 2018. "Transforming Places: Toward a Global Politics of Appalachia." In *Appalachia in Regional Context: Place Matters,* edited by Dwight B. Billings and Ann E. Kingsolver, 49–70. Lexington: University Press of Kentucky.

Snead, Deborah D. 1991. *County Situation Analysis.* Compiled by the County Unit of the Virginia Cooperative Extension Service: Carter Fleming, Unit Director/Extension Agent and Deborah D. Snead, Extension Agent.

———. 1994. *Impact Statement: U.S. Forest Service, Virginia.* Deborah D. Snead, Chairman, Task Force on U.S. Forest Service District Impact, Virginia.

Soja, Edward. 1989. *Postmodern Geographies: The Reassertion of Space in Critical Social Theory.* London: Verso.

Spain, Daphne. 1993. "Been-heres versus Come-heres: Negotiating Conflicting Community Identities." *Journal of the American Planning Association* 59:156–71.

Sparks, Bertel. 1971. "Changing Concepts of Private Property." *The Freeman,* October, 1971, 583–98.

Spradley, James P. 1979. *The Ethnographic Interview.* New York: Holt, Rinehart and Winston.

———. 1980. *Participant Observation.* New York: Holt, Rinehart and Winston.

Spraker, Jacob. 2009. "Evangelistic Earth, The Gospel of Green: The Unlikely Evangelical Christian Movement to Save the Appalachian Environment." Paper for "Sociology 421: Religious Patterns in Culture," Radford University, Radford, VA.

Sprawl Watch. 2001. "Obesity and Sprawl." *Sprawl Watch* 3 (16) (May 2, 2001).

State Corporation Commission. 1995. Interim Order, Application of Appalachian Power Company, December 13.

Stedman, Richard C. 2002. "Toward a Social Psychology of Place: Predicting Behavior from Place-Based Cognitions, Attitude, and Identity." *Environment and Behavior* 34 (5):561–81.

Steele, Fritz. 1981. *The Sense of Place.* Boston: CBI.

Stein, Dennis. n.d. *Leasing for a Wind Farm.* Michigan State University Extension, East Lansing.

Stephenson, John B. 1995. "Shiloh." In *Appalachia Inside Out,* vol. 1: *Conflict and Change,* edited by Robert J. Higgs, Ambrose N. Manning, and Jim Wayne Miller, 331–40. Knoxville: University of Tennessee Press.

Stewart, Kathleen. 1996. *A Space on the Side of the Road: Cultural Poetics in an "Other" America.* Princeton, NJ: Princeton University Press.

Stilgoe, John R. 1988. *Borderland: Origins of the American Suburb, 1820–1939.* New Haven, CT: Yale University Press.

Stokols, Daniel. 1990. "Instrumental and Spiritual Views of People-Environment Relations." *American Psychologist* 45:641–46.

StrategicSolarGroup.com. 2020. *What Is the Average Solar Farm Lease Rate?* Strategic Solar Group, LLC.

Stuart, Jesse. 1953. *The Good Spirit of Laurel Ridge.* New York: McGraw-Hill.

———. 1963. *A Jesse Stuart Reader.* New York: New American Library.

Sturken, Marita. 1997. *Tangled Memories: The Vietnam War, the AIDS Epidemic, and the Politics of Remembering.* Berkeley: University of California Press.

Sustainable Mountain Agriculture Center. 2001. *Saving Yesterday's Seeds for Today and Tomorrow.* Berea, KY: Sustainable Mountain Agriculture Center.

Swanson, Louis E. 1990. "Rethinking Assumptions about Farm and Community." In *American Rural Communities,* edited by A. E. Luloff and Swanson. San Francisco: Westview.

Tabuchi, Hiroko, and Brad Plumer. 2020. "Is This the End of New Pipelines?" *New York Times,* July 8, 2020.

Tai, Steph. 2020. "Scientific Uncertainty and the Council on Environmental Quality's Proposed Changes to Its National Environmental Policy Act Regulations." *Trends, American Bar Association,* May/June.

Tedlock, Barbara. 1991. "From Participant Observation to the Observation of Participation: The Emergence of Narrative Ethnography." *Journal of Anthropological Research* 47 (1) (Spring): 69–94.

Templeton, Jane Farley. 1994. *The Focus Group: A Strategic Guide to Organizing, Conducting and Analyzing the Focus Group Interview.* Chicago: Probus.

The Economist. 2020. "The Call of the Wild," June 20–26, 2020.

Thomas, Elizabeth Marshall. 1958. *The Harmless People.* New York: Knopf.

Thomas, Philip. 2002. "The River, the Road, and the Rural-Urban Divide: A Postcolonial Moral Geography from Southeast Madagascar." *American Ethnologist* 29:366–91.

Thompson, Dick. 2000. "Asphalt Jungle." *Time,* April/May, 50–51.

Thoreau, Henry David. 1861. "Walking." (First found in 1851 lecture "The Wild.")

Thu, Kendall, and Paul Durrenberger. 1998. *Pigs, Profits, and Rural Communities.* Albany: State University of New York Press.

Tilly, C. 1973. "Do Communities Act?" *Sociological Inquiry* 43:209–40.

Tocqueville, Alexis de. (1835–40) 1969. *Democracy in America.* Translated by George Lawrence. Edited by J. P. Mayer. New York: Doubleday.

Toennies, Ferdinand. (1887) 1957. *Community and Society: Gemeinschaft und Gesellschaft.* Translated by Charles P. Loomis. New York: Harper Torchbooks.

Tomsho, Robert. 1998. "On the Lone Prairie, a Rancher Sees Peril in an Air Force Plan." *Wall Street Journal,* September 15, 1998.

Toumey, Christopher. 1996. *Conjuring Science: Scientific Symbols and Cultural Meanings in American Life.* New Brunswick, NJ: Rutgers University Press.

Towers, George. 1997. GIS versus the Community. *Applied Geography* 17 (2):111–25.

Trainor, Theresa. 1998/1999. "New Species at EPA." In "Stewards of the Human Landscape," special double issue, *Common Ground: Archaeology and Ethnography in the Public Interest* (Winter 1998/Spring 1999).

Tsukayama, Hayley. 2018. "Sony Is Relaunching Its Aibo Robot Dog." *Seattle Times,* August 23, 2018.

Tuan, Yi-Fu. 1967. "Attitudes Toward Environment: Themes and Approaches." In *Environmental Perception and Behavior,* edited by David Lowenthal, 4–17. Chicago: Dept. of Geography, University of Chicago.

———. 1974. *Topophilia: A Study of Environmental Perception, Attitudes, and Values.* Englewood Cliffs, NJ: Prentice-Hall.

———. 1977. *Space and Place: The Perspective of Experience.* Minneapolis: University of Minnesota Press.

———. 1978. Sign and Metaphor. *Annals of the Association of American Geographers* 68:362–72.

Turner, Victor. 1969. *The Ritual Process: Structure and Anti-Structure.* Chicago: Aldine.

United Nations Sub-Commission on Human Rights and the Environment. 1994. *Declaration of Principles on Human Rights and the Environment.* Geneva, Switzerland: United Nations Sub-Commission on Human Rights and the Environment.

Union. 2020. Union, WV, Resident. Personal Communication. August 30.

US Department of Health and Human Services. 2013. *Teen Media Use Part 1—Increasing and on the Move.* The Office of Adolescent Health, November.

US Department of the Interior. 2017. *New 5-Year Report Shows 101.6 Million Americans Participated in Hunting, Fishing & Wildlife Activities.* September 7.

US Environmental Protection Agency. 1997. "Community Social and Cultural Profiling Guide: Understanding a Community's Sense of Place" (working draft, June 9). Washington, DC: US Environmental Protection Agency.

US Fish and Wildlife Service. 2018. *Economic Impact: Birds, Bird Watching and the U.S. Economy.* October 18.

US Forest Service. 1996. *Draft Environmental Impact Statement: APCo 765 kV Transmission Line.* United States Department of Agriculture, Forest Service.

US House of Representatives. 1980. H.R.5496—National Historic Preservation Act Amendments of 1980.

US Supreme Court. 2001. Whitman v. American Trucking Associations, Inc., 531 U.S. 457 (2001).

US Travel Association. 2020. "US Travel Answer Sheet." https://www.ustravel.org.

USA Today. 2000. "Rural Areas Losing Their Attraction." *USA Today,* July 12, 2000.

Usack, Lin. 1994. "Cultural Attachment to Land Study." Paper for "Anthropology 411: Appalachian Cultures," Radford University, Radford, VA.

USDA. 1987. United States Department of Agriculture, Forest Service. *National Forest Landscape Management.* Vol. 2, chap. 8: *Recreation.* Agriculture Handbook No. 666.

———. 2020. *Animal Feeding Operations.* United States Department of Agriculture Natural Resources Conservation Service. June 20.

Vahlberg, Vivian. 2010. *Fitting into Their Lives: A Survey of Three Studies about Youth Media Usage.* Newspaper Association of America Foundation, Arlington, VA.

van Baal, Jan. 1971. *Symbols for Communication: An Introduction to the Anthropological Study of Religion.* Assen, the Netherlands: Koninklijke Van Gorcum.

VDACS. 2001. *Virginia Century Farm Program.* Virginia Department of Agriculture and Consumer Services. https://www.vdacs.virginia.gov.

———. 2020. *Farmland Preservation.* Virginia Department of Agriculture and Consumer Services, Conservation and Environmental. https://www.vdacs.virginia.gov.

Virginia Department of Forestry. 2020. https://dof.virginia.gov.

Virginia Outdoors Foundation. 2020. *Annual Report.*

Virginia Performs. 2017. *Land Preservation. Natural Resources.* https://www.virginia.gov.

Wagner, Melinda Bollar. 1982. "Appalachia in America's Future: Alternative Cultural Forms." In *Critical Essays in Appalachian Life and Culture,* edited by Rick Simon, 88–97. Boone, NC: Appalachian Consortium Press.

———. 1983. *Metaphysics in Midwestern America.* Columbus: Ohio State University Press.

———. 1990. *God's Schools: Choice and Compromise in American Society.* New Brunswick, NJ: Rutgers University Press.

———. 1994/1996. "A Cross-Cultural Study of Ethnopersonality: The Scottish and Appalachian Sense of Self." *ALCA-LINES,* the Journal of the Assembly of Literature and Culture of Appalachia (National Council of Teachers of English) 3 (1)/4 (1).

———. 2018. Letter to the Editor "Response to 'Persistent Misconceptions: Rehabilitating Jack Weller, Reevaluating Harry Caudill' by P. Obermiller, T. Wagner, B. Tucker, and S. Fisher. *Appalachian Journal* 44 (1–2) (Fall 2016/Winter 2017): 96–129." *Appalachian Journal* 45 (3–4) (Spring/Summer 2018): 680–82.

———. 2020. "Celebrating the Local." In *Reinventing and Reinvesting in the Local for Our Common Good,* edited by Brian A. Hoey, 19–58. Knoxville: University of Tennessee Press.

Wagner, Melinda Bollar, Donna Lynn Batley, Kai Jackson, Bill O'Brien, and Liz Throckmorton. 1986. "Appalachia: A Tourist Attraction?" In *The Impact of Institutions in Appalachia: Proceedings of the 8th Annual Appalachian Studies Conference,* edited by Jim Lloyd and Anne G. Campbell, 73–87. Boone, NC: Appalachian Consortium Press.

Wagner, Melinda Bollar, Allen Batteau, and Archie Green. 1983. "Images of Appalachia: A Critical Discussion." In *The Appalachian Experience: Proceedings of the 6th Annual Appalachian Studies Conference,* edited by Barry M. Buxton. 3–9. Boone, NC: Appalachian Consortium Press.

Wagner, Melinda Bollar, and Kristen L. Hedrick. 2001. "University/Community Study of Cultural Attachment to Place in Proposed Power line Corridors." *Practicing Anthropology* 23 (2) (Spring): 10–14.

Wagner, Melinda Bollar, Shannon Scott, and Danny Wolfe. 1997. "Drawing the Line between People and Power: Taking the Classroom to the Community." In *Practicing Anthropology in the South,* edited by James M. Wallace, 110–18. Athens: University of Georgia Press.

Wagner, Melinda Bollar, and Jacob Spraker. 2011. "Religion and the Environment: A Class Research Project." Paper presented at Society for the Scientific Study of Religion Annual Meeting, Milwaukee, WI, October 28–30.

Walls, David S. 1978. "Internal Colony or Internal Periphery? A Critique of Current Models and an Alternative Formulation." In *Colonialism in Modern America: The Appalachian Case,* edited by Helen Matthews Lewis, Linda Johnson, and Donald Askins, 319–49. Boone, NC: Appalachian Consortium Press.

Wartmann, Flurina M., and Ross S. Purves. 2018. "Investigating Sense of Place as a Cultural Ecosystem Service in Different Landscapes through the Lens of Language. *Landscape and Urban Planning* 175:169–83.

Washington Post. 1998. "New England States Team up to Protect 300,000 Acres of Forest." *Roanoke Times,* December 10, 1998.

Watson, J. W. 1968. "The Role of Illusion in North American Geography." *Canadian Geographer* 13:10–27.

Weber, Max. 1948. *The Protestant Ethic and the Spirit of Capitalism.* Translated by Talcott Parsons. New York: Scribner. (Originally published in 1920–21 as *Die protestantische Ethik und der Geist des Kapitalismus.*)

———. 1963. *The Sociology of Religion.* Translated by Ephraim Fischoff. Boston: Beacon. (Originally published in 1922 as "Religionssoziologie" in *Wirtschaft und Gesellschaft,* 2 vols.)

Webber, Melvin M. 1961. "Order in Diversity: Community without Propinquity." In *Cities and Space: The Future Use of Urban Land,* edited by Lowdon Wingo. Baltimore, MD: Johns Hopkins University Press.

Weddle, Katie, Lucille Sherman, and Sky Chadde. 2020. "Hundreds of Farmers Are Dying by Suicide." *Flatland,* March 16, 2020.

Weeden, Robert B. 1992. *Messages from Earth.* Fairbanks: University of Alaska Press.

Weiner, J. 1991. *The Empty Place: Poetry, Space and Being among the Foi of Papua New Guinea.* Bloomington: Indiana University Press.

Weller, Jack E. 1965. *Yesterday's People: Life in Contemporary Appalachia.* Lexington: University Press of Kentucky.

Wenkart, A. 1961. "Regaining Identity through Relatedness." *American Journal of Psychoanalysis* 21:227–33.

Werblow, Steve. 2020. "Made in the Shade" *The Furrow,* Summer 2020, 33.

Whisnant, David E. 1992. "Cultural Capital, Cultural Revisionism and Recalcitrant Cultural Formation: Reflections on Appalachia and Nicaragua." Keynote speech, Appalachian Studies Conference, Asheville, NC, March 20–22.

———. 1999. Comment at Appalachian Studies Conference, Abingdon, VA, March 19–21.

The White House Briefing Room. 2021. Presidential Actions. Executive Order Protecting Public Health and Environment and Restoring Science to Tackle Climate Crisis. January 20.

Whiteford, Linda, and Elizabeth Strom. 2013. "Building Community Engagement and Public Scholarship into the University." *Annals of Anthropological Practice* 37 (1):72–89.

Whorf, B. 1956. *Language, Thought and Reality.* Cambridge, MA: MIT Press.

Wikse, John. 1977. *About Possession: The Self as Private Property.* University Park: Pennsylvania State University Press.

Wilkinson, Kenneth P. 1990. "Crime and Community." In *American Rural Communities,* edited by A. E. Luloff and Louis E. Swanson, 151–68. Boulder, CO: Westview.

Williams, Cratis. 1980. "Appalachian Language and Culture." Lecture. Southwest Virginia Community College, Cedar Bluff, VA.

Williams, Daniel R., Michael, E. Patterson, Joseph W. Roggenbuck, and Alan E. Watson. 1992. "Beyond the Commodity Metaphor: Examining Emotional and Symbolic Attachment to Place." *Leisure Sciences* 14:29–46.

Williams, John Alexander. 2002. *Appalachia: A History.* Chapel Hill: University of North Carolina Press.

Williams, Michael Ann. 1995. *Great Smoky Mountains Folklife.* Jackson: University Press of Mississippi.

Williamson, W. Paul, and Howard R. Pollio. 1999. "The Phenomenology of Religious Serpent Handling: A Rationale and Thematic Study of Extemporaneous Sermons." *Journal for the Scientific Study of Religion* 38 (2):203–18.

Wilson, Alexander. 1992. *The Culture of Landscape: North American Landscape from Disney to Exxon Valdez.* Cambridge, MA: Blackwell.

Wilson, Bobby M. 1980. "Social Space and Symbolic Interaction." In *The Human Experience of Space and Place,* edited by Anne Buttimer and David Seamon, 135–47. New York: St. Martin's.

Winchester, Simon. 2021. *Land: How the Hunger for Ownership Shaped the Modern World.* New York: HarperCollins.

Wingfield, Kevin. 1994. "Cultural Attachment to Land Study." Paper for "Anthropology 411: Appalachian Cultures," Radford University, Radford, VA.

Winthrop, Robert. 1999. "Dilemmas of Tradition." *Practicing Anthropology* 29 (3) (Summer).

Wisconsin Department of Tourism. 2001. *Wisconsin 2001 Spring/Summer Event and Recreation Guide.* Madison: Wisconsin Department of Tourism.

Witt, Joseph D. 2016. *Religion and Resistance in Appalachia: Faith and the Fight against Mountaintop Removal Coal Mining.* Lexington: University Press of Kentucky.

Wood, Alan. 2018. "Taking Mitigation to the Bank." *American Forest Management News,* October 23, 2018, 1–8.

Wood, Paul. 2001. "Area's 'Suburbs' Growing." *News-Gazette,* March 15, 2001.

Woodside, Jane Harris. 1995. "Protecting Appalachia's National Parks: An Interview with NCPA's Don Barger." *Now and Then* 12 (1):5.

Wright, J. K. 1947. "Terrae Incognitae: The Place of Imagination in Geography." *Annals of the Association of American Geographers* 68:1–15.

Wylde, Kaitlyn. 2020. "Why You're Seeing Cottagecore Videos Everywhere Right Now." *Bustle,* May 5, 2020.

Yahn, Jacqueline. 2016. "Frackonomics." In *Appalachia Revisited: New Perspectives on Place, Tradition, and Progress,* edited by William Schumann and Rebecca Adkins Fletcher, 139–54. Lexington: University Press of Kentucky.

Yale Climate Connections. 2019. "Why a Virginia Tech Professor Locked Herself to Pipeline Construction Equipment." Yale Center for Environmental Communication. December 3.

Yancey, Dwayne. 2022. "Why Has Immigration Generally Bypassed This Part of Virginia?" *Cardinal News,* April 12, 2022.

Young, Elspeth. 1992. "Hunter-Gatherer Concepts of Land and Its Ownership in Remote Australia and North America." In *Inventing Places: Studies in Cultural Geography,* edited by Kay Anderson and Fay Gale, 255–72. Melbourne, Australia: Longman Cheshire.

Zablocki, B. 1971. *The Joyful Community.* Baltimore, MD: Penguin.

Zimmerman, Mark J. 2001. "Decision of Note: Supreme Court Clarifies Takings Clause." *Environmental Compliance and Litigation Strategy,* July 2001.

Index

Place Matters: New Directions in Appalachian Studies

Series Editor: Dwight B. Billings

This series explores the history, social life, and cultures of Appalachia from multidisciplinary, comparative, and global perspectives. Topics include geography, the environment, public policy, political economy, critical regional studies, diversity, social inequality, social movements and activism, migration and immigration, efforts to confront regional stereotypes, literature and the arts, and the ongoing social construction and reimagination of Appalachia. Key goals of the series are to place Appalachian dynamics in the context of global change and to demonstrate that place-based and regional studies still matter.

Appalachia in Regional Context: Place Matters
Edited by Dwight B. Billings and Ann E. Kingsolver

Engaging Appalachia: A Guidebook for Building Capacity and Sustainability
Edited by Rebecca Adkins Fletcher, Rebecca-Eli Long, and William Schumann

Literacy in the Mountains: Community, Newspapers, and Writing in Appalachia
Samantha NeCamp

Appalachia Revisited: New Perspectives on Place, Tradition, and Progress
Edited by William Schumann and Rebecca Adkins Fletcher

The Arthurdale Community School: Education and Reform in Depression Era Appalachia
Sam F. Stack Jr.

Sacred Mountains: A Christian Ethical Approach to Mountaintop Removal
Andrew R. H. Thompson

Power and Place: Preservation, Progress, and the Culture War over Land
Melinda Bollar Wagner

Rereading Appalachia: Literacy, Place, and Cultural Resistance
Edited by Sara Webb-Sunderhaus and Kim Donehower

Religion and Resistance in Appalachia: Faith and the Fight against Mountaintop Removal Coal Mining
Joseph D. Witt